SRI
SARADA DEVI
THE HOLY MOTHER

SRI SARADA DEVI

THE HOLY MOTHER

Swami Tapasyananda

Sri Ramakrishna Math

Mylapore, Madras 600 004

Published by
The President
Sri Ramakrishna Math
Mylapore, Chennai-4

© Sri Ramakrishna Math, Chennai
All rights reserved

XI-5M 3C-3-2008
ISBN 81-7120-997-1

Printed in India at
Sri Ramakrishna Math Printing Press
Mylapore, Chennai-4

Preface
to the
SIXTH EDITION

THE BOOK entitled *Sri Sarada Devi the Holy Mother* is published in this, its sixth edition, without the 'Conversations', which formed a considerable part of the book in its earlier editions. This has been done because all these 'Conversations', besides many others too, have been recently published as a book, *'The Gospel of the Holy Mother.'*

In the *Life* new matter extending over forty typed pages has been incorporated. These are mostly facts which were not known when the book was first published in 1940. We are indebted to Swami Gambhirananda's book, *Holy Mother Sri Sarada Devi* (the Holy Mother Centenary Memorial Edition), for these additional facts.

Madras *Publisher*
June, 1986

Preface
to the
First Edition

ALTHOUGH IT IS now nearly two decades since the passing away of Sri Sarada Devi, the Holy Mother, no comprehensive work on her life and teachings has appeared in English. The present work, comprising her biography and conversations seeks to remedy this want and present in one volume everything about the Holy Mother—her life as well as her teachings.

The first part of the book, entitled The Life of the Holy Mother, is a new writing and not a translation, although it incorporates in itself all relevant biographical material from existing literature in Bengali, besides information gathered from such of the Holy Mother's disciples as had lived closely with her and could therefore speak with authority on the various aspects of her life and character. Yogin-Ma and Golap-Ma, the best authorities on her early life are now no more, and all that could be done for gathering material about this part of her life was to depend on existing literature and on the testimony of those who had heard about it from these two close companions of the Holy Mother. Concerning the latter part of her life, however, there are yet many living authorities to give first-hand information. Most of them are monks of the Ramakrishna Order, while the others are those few lady disciples of the Holy Mother who had the privilege of staying with her and serving her in her last days.

Judged by purely objective standards, the Holy Mother's life may look very simple and uneventful, and one may doubt whether it provides a fitting theme at all for the historian to work upon. A contemporary of many a great spiritual luminary of the past, with the figures of the big potentates and military leaders of the time looming large in his eyes, might also have felt in the same way if called upon to record the lives of those personalities whom the world has in later times come to recognize as the salt of humanity. But greatness of the highest type is to be measured not in terms of the political, economic or military values of a life for the moment, but in terms of the character potential it embodies. When considered in this light, the Holy Mother, who was wife, nun, mother and teacher in one, is an arresting figure in the history of mankind, and it is our conviction that through her simple life and character a unique ideal has been revealed to mankind—an ideal which, in spite of its artless simplicity, is dynamic enough to transform the lives of men and women who approach it in the right attitude of mind.

In recounting the events of her life, our aim has been to give an interpretative study of it, bringing into prominence this ideal of Divine Motherhood expressing itself through human character. In other words we have tried to view the life of the Holy Mother as the expression of a great spiritual principle.

It is hoped that the general public would feel interested in this volume, both from a religious and a cultural point of view, and find impressively depicted in the life of this great daughter of Mother India, many of those cherished values that have been created and conserved by the womanhood of this country in the course of its agelong history.

Madras
October, 1940

Publisher

CONTENTS

Preface to the Sixth Edition	v
Preface to the First Edition	vi
1. Ancestry	11
2. Birth and Education	15
3. Marriage	19
4. Visit to Dakshineswar	30
5. The Fiery Ordeal	38
6. The Ascent to Motherhood	45
7. At the Feet of the Master	51
8. In the Service of the Master	60
9. In the Passing of Events	88
10. The Master's Demise and After	100
11. Pilgrimage to Brindavan	108
12. Life at Kamarpukur and After	116
13. In the Setting of Domestic Life	128
14. Her Spiritual Ministry	155
15. Glimpses of her Personality	197
16. More Pilgrimages	245

17. Her Later Life	257
18. Her Message	288
19. The Maha Samadhi	301
20. The Holy Mother as a Revelation of the Motherhood of God	315
Appendices	
1. Chronology	329
2. The Horoscope of the Holy Mother	331
3. Bibliography	332
4. Index & Glossary	335

1. ANCESTRY

ABOUT SIXTY MILES to the west of Calcutta, on the south-eastern border of the Bankura District, is situated the little hamlet of Jayrambati, the native village of the Holy Mother. The rivulet Amodar, a perennial stream of transparent waters, meanders its way along the northern boundary of the village. Today, thanks to railroad and motor traffic, a night's journey is enough to reach Jayrambati from Calcutta. But at the time to which our narrative refers, it was much more inaccessible, since one had to travel for more than two days either on foot or in a palanquin, passing through fields and wildernesses infested by robbers.

Compared with some of the adjoining villages, Jayrambati, with not more than a hundred little mud houses in it, must be considered small. Its soil, however, was fairly rich, and an industrious peasantry raised in it a variety of crops, consisting chiefly of paddy, potatoes and vegetables of various kinds. While self-sufficient in the matter of staple foodstuffs, the village had no bazaar or fairs, and its inhabitants had, therefore, to depend on bigger villages of the neighbourhood like Kotalpur,

Koyapet and Kamarpukur—all within six miles of it—for the purchase of several necessaries of life like cloth, and for the marketing of the surplus products of their fields. In spite of its backwardness, life in it was fairly happy before the ravages of malaria carried misery into its homes in the latter half of the nineteenth century. The monotony of the villagers' life was frequently relieved by the public celebrations of the great Hindu festivals like Durga Puja, Kali Puja, Dol Purnima and the rest, and by the special worship of various deities, be it of Sitala or of Dharma, of Santinath, the Siva image of the neighbouring village of Sihor or of Simhavahini, the Mother deity of Jayrambati itself.

In a population consisting mainly of agriculturists and artisans, the village had only two Brahmin families, the Banerjis and the Mukherjis. The Holy Mother was a daughter of the Mukherji family. Her father Ramachandra Mukherji had three younger brothers—Trailokya Nath, a scholar well-versed in Sanskrit, who met with premature death, and Isvar Chandra, and Nilmadhav who remained lifelong celibate. All the brothers lived as a joint family.

Ramachandra was a poor man, but he was virtuous, upright, and an example of the Brahmanical ideal. 'My father,' said the Holy Mother in later days, 'was a very good man. He was a great devotee of Rama. He had unswerving devotion to the ideal of a Brahmin's life. He could not accept gifts indiscriminately. He loved to smoke, and as he smoked—he was so simple and humble—he would address in a friendly way every passer-by that crossed his door and say cordially, "Come in, brother. Have a smoke."

We come across a remarkable instance of Ramachandra's generosity and goodness when Bengal was in the grip of a terrible famine in 1864. Ramachandra was himself a poor man, making a meagre living from the cultivation of a few acres of paddy fields, the performance of priestly duties, and the making of sacred threads. He had none the less a good stock of paddy from the surplus of the previous year's produce, and without any consideration for his own worldly circumstances, he spent it all in feeding the famine-stricken.

Recounting her impression of this event, which took place in her tenth year, the Holy Mother said to her disciple in later days: 'At one time a terrible famine devastated Jayrambati. People without number would come to our house for food. We had a store of rice from the previous year's produce. My father made Khichuri, cooking that rice and pulse together. The Khichuri used to be kept in a number of pots. All the members of the family would take only that Khichuri. The starving people would also eat the same. He would, however, say, 'A little plain rice of good variety shall be cooked for my daughter (Sarada, the Holy Mother herself). She will eat that.' Sometimes the starving people would come in such large numbers that the food would not be sufficient for them. Then new Khichuri would be cooked, and when the hot stuff was poured in large earthen pots, I would fan and make it cool. Hungry people would be waiting for it. One day a low class girl came there. She had shaggy hair and blood-shot eyes like those of a lunatic. She saw the rice bran soaking in a tub for the cattle and started eating it. We said to her, "There is Khichuri inside the house, go and eat it," but she was too impatient to wait. Is it a joke to bear the agony of an empty stomach?'

Ramachandra had for his partner in life a woman fully worthy of him. His wife Syamasundari Devi—the daughter of Hari Prasad Mazumdar of Sihor—, besides being a strongly-built and industrious woman and an able housewife, was also imbued with the same high ideals as her husband. 'She was,' according to the Holy Mother, 'very simple, guileless and compassionate.' She was devoted to the Deity, and it was her nature always to feel delighted in feeding people and working for their good. In later days when her daughter's circle of devotees increased, she used to love and welcome them with great affection. 'My mother,' said the Holy Mother, 'used to be so pleased when any one of the devotees came to our place. She would look after them with great attention. She looked upon this family of devotees as her own flesh and blood.' ❑

2. BIRTH AND EDUCATION

SRI SARADA DEVI,[1] the Holy Mother, was born the eldest child of her devoted parents on the 22nd of December, 1853. Born and brought up in the rural atmosphere of Jayrambati, her early training was just like that of any poor village girl of India belonging to the higher castes. Even as a little girl, she helped her mother in cooking, and often when the latter could not attend to it for unavoidable reasons, she used to take her place in the kitchen. Referring to these experiences of her early days, the Holy Mother used to say, 'I cooked and my father helped me to take down the big rice pot from the oven.' As to the other types of work she was accustomed to do, she said, 'In my childhood I sometimes used to go into neck-deep water and cut grass for the cows. I carried tiffin to the labourers in the field. During one season the paddy was destroyed by pests, and I had to collect the grain from one field after another.'

As a girl she was too serious and self-composed to give herself up to childish games like others of her age. Aghormani, a companion and playmate of her girlhood, used to say of her, 'Mother was very simple in her habits. She would never quarrel with anybody while playing. When others fell out, she would mediate and establish cordial relations. In play she used to personate herself either as the mistress or governess of the house. Among her playthings there were some dolls, but she was more interested in the clay images of Kali and Lakshmi which she devoutly worshipped with flowers and Bilva leaves. Once on the occasion of the Jagaddhatri Puja, she was meditating on the Goddess with such deep concentration and sense of identification with Her, that the sight of it struck awe in the mind of Ramhriday Ghoshal of Haldepukur.'

Much of her time was taken up with looking after her own younger brothers. Sometimes she went with them to the village school, but since a literary education was not considered quite a necessary accomplishment for a village girl in those days, no one seems to have taken any trouble to teach her or ensure her regular attendance at school. She had, however, a keen desire to study, and in later days learned to read by her own efforts. Referring to this, she said, 'Lakshmi[2] and I used to read the Bengali primer a little at Kamarpukur. My nephew Hriday[3] snatched the book away from me. He said, 'Women should not learn to read and write. Are you preparing yourself in this way to read novels and dramas later on?' But Lakshmi did not give up the book. She belonged to the family; therefore she held on to her book. I too secretly had a copy bought for one anna. Lakshmi used to attend the village school. On returning home she would teach me. But I really improved my capacity to read only long after at Dakshineswar. The Master (ie Sri Ramakrishna) was staying then at Syampukur for treatment. I was all alone. A girl

ॐ Holy Mother, 1898 ☙

Holy Mother's Parental Home at Jayarambati

Birth and Education

belonging to the family of Bhava Mukherji used to come to the temple-garden to bathe in the Ganges. Now and then she would spend a long time with me. She used to give me lessons and afterwards examine me. And in return, I would give her a large quantity of greens, vegetables and other articles of food that were sent to me from the temple-gardens.'

Though she could read quite well, she never mastered the art of writing. In later days a disciple wanted to have an autograph from her, and she agreed in a way. But the effort to write her own name was in vain, she scrawled and scrawled, and being unable to produce anything readable, gave up the attempt.

This does not mean that the rural surroundings of her early days did not provide her with any facilities for education. In India, culture has never been identified with literacy. The Indian mind has devised methods of its own for the training of the head and the heart and for an unconscious assimilation of the nations's highest ideals, without unduly emphasizing the pedagogue's art. The religious life of the family, the atmosphere of self-abnegation and service in which girls grow up, the temple festivals, the recitals of epics, village dramas, devotional narratives,—these and several other factors of like nature provide even women who live a comparatively isolated life with facilities for developing a unified character undistracted by the conflicting thoughts and ideals that flow into the minds of the literate that commercial publishing houses produce.

The Holy Mother had plenty of opportunity to receive the training that such an environment provided. As we have seen, Jayrambati and its neighbourhood were not without religious festivals. Yatra performances (a form of devotional drama) were frequent in those times, and she had occasion to attend many of them. In her instructions to disciples the Holy Mother used to quote verses and aphorisms that had been imprinted on her memory by attending such performances in her early days. What was more, the care and contact of her poor but cultured and devoted parents were an educational facility of no mean importance. That the Holy Mother was powerfully impressed by them is plain from the great regard and appreciation with which she always spoke of them in later days.

And above all, she had, in her early girlhood, the rare good fortune of coming in contact with a great soul in the most intimate relationship of a woman's life—a contact which in time helped her to understand and realize the purpose of education in the highest sense. ❑

---

1. It is customary in Bengal to give two names to a baby—one from astrological considerations and the other for calling in daily life. It is said that the astrological name given to the Holy Mother was Thakurmani, and the common name, Kshemankari. At the request of her aunt who had lost a daughter named Sarada, her common name was changed into Sarada, so that the bereaved mother could feel her child's presence in her niece.

2. A niece of Sri Ramakrishna.

3. A nephew of Sri Ramakrishna and a constant companion and attendant of his for a long time.

3. MARRIAGE

It is generally said that every girl in India is born for marriage. At least this idea was universal some two generations back, although in this latter half of the 20th century, the growing number of professional women remaining single and of orders of Sanyasinis, is making this belief rather antiquated. It was however universally widespread in the days of the Holy Mother's infancy. A daughter, though loved and cherished, was often felt a liability and a burden, and parents did not finally feel relieved until she had been given away in marriage. The feeling of the Indian mind on this point in ancient days has been beautifully expressed by Kalidasa, the great Sanskrit poet and dramatist, in a verse he puts in the mouth of Rishi Kanva, the foster-father of Sakuntala, when his daughter leaves for her husband's home: 'Verily, a daughter is the property of another man. Today, having sent her to her husband, my conscience has become quite clear, as on res-toring a deposit after a long time'[1] (Sakuntalam, 4, 151).

It cannot be denied that this way of thinking has often led parents to hurry their daughters into the matrimonial bond even at a premature age. It is perhaps the very same mentality, buttressed by quasi-religious theories, that has crystallized into such practices as early marriage and child marriage, enforced by social compulsion. That this was not so in the early history of Hindu society is clear from the fact that just like boys, girls also used to be educated in 'forest universities,' some of which at least were run on co-educational lines. In fact, the theory of compulsory pre-puberty marriage for girls of the higher castes came into popularity only along with a change in the conception of women's education. In early Aryan society—and it is also recognized by the orthodox Smritis—girls, like boys, were invested with the sacred thread at the proper age and subsequently initiated into Vedic study and Aryan religious life.[2] How long their education continued, one cannot say, but modern scholars believe that marriage did not come in the way of it in so far as the Vedic hymns chanted and the marriage rituals and practices followed indicate that both the contracting parties were adults.

A time, however, came in later days when the investiture of girls with the sacred thread came to be abandoned. This change of ritual procedure, though apparently simple, was fraught with immense consequences in the educational and matrimonial life of women. The investiture with the sacred thread was, for the Aryan mind, the symbol of the commencement of Brahmacharya, or the period of education. And also, only a person invested with it was entitled to Vedic study and Vedic religious practices. The abandonment of it in the case of woman, therefore, meant her exclusion from the ancient Aryan system of education, the chief characteristics of which were the study of the Vedas and residence in the teacher's house during one's educational career.

It may, however, be asked whether the Hindu lawgivers of later days totally overlooked the educational needs of girls and wanted to reduce them to the position of ignorant domestic slaves. This was far from their intention. What they contemplated was that for woman marriage, which was in effect only a betrothal, would take the place of the ceremony of investiture with the sacred thread (*Manu*, 2.67), and that instead of going to a Guru for study, she would have her education at the hands of her own husband. As investiture with the sacred thread took place in early boyhood, so too the marriage of girls was to take place before they reached the age of puberty. The idea behind it was this. A boy could absorb the ideals of his teacher and have his character moulded by his influence, only if he was put under him at an impressionable age, that is, in his early boyhood. So also it was argued that a girl could become one in mind with her husband, and participate wholeheartedly in his ideals and aspirations only if she was brought under the influence of his personality at a tender age, before her individuality was formed and hardened in its distinctiveness by experiences and contacts of pre-marital life. The husband generally was an adult who had completed his long period of Brahmacharya, or education combined with moral and spiritual training, and the first obligation that marriage placed on him was the education of his wife, that of being the father of her progeny coming only next.

This is the ideal underlying the custom of marrying girls in their childhood. But ideals do not always tally with realities, and the system of child marriage, too, has not been an exception to this. The attainments that the system at its best pre-supposes in the bridegroom are beyond what we may expect in ordinary social life. A bridegroom, according to it, must practically be a sage who has overcome his animal propensities, and is capable of viewing his wife more as a soul in formation than as a member of the opposite sex. Such men are few and far between, and in consequence the vast majority of marriages contracted under the system seldom produce those ideal conditions pre-supposed by it. Of course, when the joint family was a living institution, and the young had the advantage of intelligent guidance from their parents and elders, the evils of the system were much mitigated. In spite of all that, in the vast majority of cases, it has stood in the way of women's education, and has driven girls to the ordeal of motherhood at too premature an age.

But the ideal has its possibilities. Given suitable conditions, it is capable of producing results that compel one's recognition. This is what one finds in the life of the Holy Mother. Here is an example of a girl of five being married to a youth of twenty-three. But the youth was a sage and a great teacher, and the girl a fit recipient of noble teachings. As a consequence we find in their lives a new ideal of conjugal life being evolved—an ideal in which the carnal side of human nature is completely eliminated and the husband plays the part of a spiritual teacher, transferring the richest experiences of his life to the wife, who in her turn becomes a lifelong disciple, finding the highest fulfilment of her life in serving her husband, in absorbing his teachings, and in continuing his life-work after him.

The study of the Holy Mother's life is the study of the gradual unfoldment of this great purpose. The circumstances that led to the singular marriage of the Holy Mother, which facilitated these developments, are given below.

While little Sarada was growing up at Jayrambati assisting her mother in her domestic duties, the great soul whose partner in life she was to become, was passing through a remarkable period of spiritual development in another part of the country. Born in 1836 as the third son of Khudiram Chatterji of Kamarpukur in the district of Hoogly, Sri Ramakrishna had become the priest of Kali at the temple of Dakshineswar in the year 1855. From his very boyhood he was highly devotional and mystical in temperament. Subsequent to his appointment as priest, his duties in the temple kindled his devotion until it became an irresistible passion for the realization of the Divine. He lost interest in worldly life, and began to spend all his time in a state of absorption and in the practice of austerities. In course of time it became impossible for him even to attend to his duties in the temple, and in the end he had to be relieved from his priestly work, so that he might be left entirely to the pursuit of his divine quest. And he spent his time in constant prayer and contemplation, forgetting even food and sleep and almost unaware of the passing of day and night.

Naturally, people who knew not what longing for God was, interpreted the strange behaviour of Sri Ramakrishna as evidence of madness. This distorted information gradually reached the ears of his mother Chandra and his brother Rameswar in their village home at Kamarpukur. So in the year 1858 they had him brought to the village, but they were grieved to find that he had developed an indifference to the world, a mood of apathy for external happenings, and a restless hankering for some unseen reality, which expressed itself occasionally in piteous cries of 'Mother! Mother!' The neighbours began to whisper that he was possessed by an alien spirit. So methods of exorcism were tried, but the spirits invoked denied that he had any physical or mental malady. Probably Sri Ramakrishna had some vivid experiences of the Divine during this period, and as a consequence his relatives soon noticed an abatement of his disquieting symptoms. Even without any remedy, occult or medical, he became quieter and his boyish gaiety and old habit of neighbourliness returned. But his indifference to worldly life and his strange habits, such as meditation in the solitude of the cremation ground, persisted. As these habits were natural with him from boyhood, they were not interpreted as being of any serious consequence.

This, no doubt, brought a sense of relief to Chandra and Rameswar, but they did not feel secure until something was done to render the recovery permanent. After consultations, they decided upon a final

Marriage 25

and drastic remedy. They would arrange for Sri Ramakrishna's marriage.[3] For it was thought that a loving wife and the responsibility of a family would be the best means to turn his mind to worldly life and its prospects.

So Sri Ramakrishna's mother and brother set out at once to find out a suitable bride, but this was by no means an easy task. Their family was poor, and the amounts demanded as bridal money by most of the parents with marriageable girls were much beyond the means of Rameswar Chatterji. They had begun this matrimonial quest without Sri Ramakrishna's knowledge; for they expected rebellious protests from him if he were informed. But strange to say, when the news reached his ears in course of time, he expressed ready acquiescence. And what was more, on seeing his mother and brother sad at the frustration of all their efforts to find a suitable bride, he said to them one day in an inspired mood, 'Vain is your search in this place and that. Go to Jayrambati and there, in the house of Ramachandra Mukherji, you will find her who is marked out for me.'[4]

Though little relying on it, they took up the suggestion and made enquiries at Ramachandra's house. Ramachandra was found willing to give his daughter Sarada in marriage, but the bridegroom's party at first felt some hesitation, as the girl was only a little child of five, and Sri Ramakrishna was past twenty- three then. Any way, since no better match could be arranged, they had to accept the offer, and before long the marriage of little Sarada with Sri Ramakrishna took place in May, 1859[1] at the bride's paternal house in Jayrambati. The bride was then brought to Kamarpukur, four miles to the west of Jayrambati. Rameswar Chatterji paid a bridal money of Rs.300 to Ramachandra on the occasion.

The marriage was perforce simple, as the family resources of both the parties did not admit of any elaboration of ceremonials or gifts. Chandra Devi, however, had borrowed a number of jewels from her rich neighbours, the Lahas, so that the bride might not be without some ornaments at the time of marriage rites. Now after the bride's coming to Kamarpukur, it was time to return the jewels to their owners. Chandra Devi was in a delicate situation. How could she tear away the jewels from the person of her little daughter-in-law who had already found a warm corner in her heart? Sri Ramakrishna, however, understood her difficulty and came to her rescue. While the little girl was sleeping, he cleverly removed all the jewels and sent them to the Laha family. When she woke up, she no doubt made enquiries of the missing jewels, perhaps tearfully; for she loved those bright and sparkling ornaments. And poor Chandra Devi could do no more than clasp her in a warm embrace and console her with the promise that her son would make her much better jewels afterwards.[6] To add to the tragedy of the situation, the incident came to the notice of an uncle of the girl who was then present in the house. He was very much enraged at this, and took the girl back to her paternal home that very day. But Sri Ramakrishna made light of the affair, saying that whatever they might think about the incident, they could not nullify the marriage!

Marriage

Sri Ramakrishna stayed in his village for about one year and seven months after his marriage. During this period, in December, 1860, his wife attained her seventh year. According to the family custom he went on this occasion to spend a few days at his father-in-law's house.[7] In later days the Holy Mother had a hazy remembrance of this visit. She remembered how, of her own accord, she touched her husband's feet in salutation and fanned him. Everyone present laughed on seeing this. Afterwards Hriday, the Master's nephew, who accompanied him on this occasion, sought her and worshipped her[8] with lotus flowers to her great embarrassment.

Shortly after, Sri Ramakrishna returned to Kamarpukur with his wife, and after spending some days there returned to Calcutta. The Holy Mother also returned to her parental home. ❑

---

1. अर्थो हि कन्या परकीय एव तामद्य सम्प्रेष्य परिग्रहीतुः ।
जातोऽस्मि सखो विशदान्तरात्मा चिरस्य निक्षेपमिवार्पयित्वा ॥

2. The condition that existed in Aryan society in early days is well reflected in the following verse from the Smriti of Yama.

पुराकल्पे कुमारीणां मौञ्जीबन्धनमिष्यते ।
अध्यापनञ्च वेदानां सावित्रीवचनं तथा ॥

'In former ages girls were invested with the sacred thread (Upanayana). They could teach the Vedas and repeat the Savitri Mantra.'

This verse, however, could not be found in the present editions of Yama's Smriti that we consulted. But it is quoted by Madhavacharya, an author of great standing in orthodox circles, in his commentary on Parasara Samhita (Cf. p. 83 Bombay Sanskrit Series Edition). Madhava's purpose in quoting it is only to discourage Upanayana at present by pointing out that such concessions were applicable only to the distant ages of the past (Kalpas) according to Puranic computations. But to a mind endowed with a historical sense it is a positive proof of the full educational and religious equality allowed to women. It is also known from ancient literature that women performed Vedic sacrificial rites like men, (See *Ramayana* 2, where Kausalya performs Svasti Yaga alone and *Ibid.*, 2, 88, 18-19 and 5, 15, 48 where Sita twice discloses her discharging religious duties in the morning and evening like men). Even Jaimini quotes Badarayana to show that women could perform Vedic sacrifices. Now the recognition of this automatically presupposes investiture with the sacred thread and Vedic education.

According to Altekar (*Vide* his *Women in Hindu Civilization*) women enjoyed these religious privileges more or less till the beginning of the Christian era. But changes were gradually coming in. At 500 B.C., as we may gather from Harita, a few women (Brahmavadinis) made an intensive study of the Vedas after Upanayana while the majority of girls (Sadyo-vadhus) underwent the formality of the ceremony shortly before marriage. The Brahmavadinis did not marry but followed the ascetic life. Many centuries later Manu (*Manusmriti*, 2, 66) favoured women's Upanayana without the reciting of Vedic Mantras. Still later writers like Yajnavalkya (200 A.D.) advocated the more straightforward course of prohibiting the ceremony altogether. It is interesting to note in this connection that among the Parsis (Zoroastrians), a branch of the ancient Vedic Aryans, the ceremony is still performed for girls.

3. The pre-puberty marriage prevalent among the Hindus was a mere betrothal but religiously and legally valid. Law, however, has now abolished these practices and the age of marriage for girls has legally been raised to sixteen.

4. There is another tradition regarding the marriage. Once, when the Holy Mother was only two years old, she was taken by her mother to Sihor to witness a temple festival. Sri Ramakrishna also was present there. In social gatherings, village women sometimes play with little girls, asking them which of the assembled boys they would like to marry. On this occasion, when they put this question to little Sarada, it seems she pointed to Sri Ramakrishna.

5. About the time of her marriage, the Holy Mother used to say, 'I was married at the time when dates ripen. I do not remember the exact month. Within ten days of my marriage, when I went to Kamarpukur, I plucked date fruits there. Dharma Das Laha (a neighbour and the landlord of Kamarpukur) came, and on seeing me, asked, 'Is this the newly married girl?' For I was so small that the father of Surju took me to Kamarpukur in his arms.'

Marriage

6. As a matter of fact Sri Ramakrishna had ornaments made for the Holy Mother in later days, and she used to wear some of them till the end. See chap. 8.

7. Referring to this visit of the Master, the Holy Mother used to say: 'The Master came to Jayrambati when I was seven years old. You know there is the custom called "going back to the father-in-law's house in couple." That time he said to me. "If anyone asks you at what age you were married, tell him it was at five and not at seven." ' He said this, thinking that, being a mere child of five at the time of marriage, she might not remember that occasion and confuse this second ceremony with the marriage.

8. According to scriptures that inculcate Mother-worship, a virgin of tender age may be looked upon as a symbol of the Divine Mother, and worship may be offered to her in that spirit. It is generally done as an item in certain forms of elaborate ceremonial worship but sometimes independently also.

4. VISIT TO DAKSHINESWAR

YEARS PASSED. Sri Ramakrishna was away at Dakshineswar performing austerities and experiencing the bliss of God-consciousness. Did he remember the girl whom he had wedded as an infant of five? Probably not. For when one was not aware of one's own body, how could one remember one's worldly relationships?

Meanwhile little Sarada had grown up into a young woman. She was now eighteen, fully mature in body and in mind. Sweet memories of her husband were, no doubt, lingering in her mind. When she was thirteen she had spent a month and a half with him at Kamarpukur. A few months after, when she was fourteen, she could again live for about seven months in his company during his visit to his village home in 1867. She had found him very tender and kind at that time. He was, no doubt, above the ordinary run of men in his love of God and purity of mind, but in other respects she had found him perfectly normal and human. She had noticed an utter selflessness in the care and cordiality he had bestowed on her then, and her mind had been much impressed by the instructions he had given her about God and devotional life and about the way of discharging one's duties and responsibilities in the world. To the Hindu wife, who is taught to look upon her husband as a veritable God, as her sole refuge here and hereafter, there is nothing more gratifying than the consciousness of having secured his respect and attention. To the Holy Mother, therefore, this occasion of her first real contact with her husband was an unforgettable experience. Recalling the inner feelings she experienced in those days, she used to tell her women disciples, 'I then felt as if a pitcher of bliss was kept in my heart. It was a constant experience with me then. It is very difficult to convey an idea of this experience to others.'[1]

Several years had now passed since that brief spell of bliss. The contact with her divine husband had enriched her consciousness with a sense of peace and introspectiveness, with a spirit of unselfish service and a feeling of unruffled satisfaction in all conditions of life. But the young wife in her could not help feeling an urge to be by his side and be of service to him. At the same time the voice of another sentiment seemed to whisper to her, as if to silence this impatience. It seemed to say: 'He who was so very kind to you at the very first meeting will never forget you. In good time, he will, of his own accord, call you to his side. Wait in patience for that blessed occasion.'

Thus silencing her impatience and giving no expression of any kind to her innermost longings, she kept herself busily engaged day and night in the various duties of her father's household. And she would have waited indefinitely in patience and submissiveness, had it not been for the very unpleasant shock that village gossip often gave her mind. Neighbours whispered that her husband had gone mad, and that he was going about naked, shouting the name of Hari. Not only that. As she expressed it to her disciples in later times, 'In my early days at Jayrambati I was always busy with some work or other, and would never visit my neighbours; for people would blurt out at the very sight of me, "Dear me, Syama's daughter has been married to a lunatic!" I avoided meeting anybody in order to escape such criticism.'

At first she was tempted to ignore this kind of talk as idle gossip. But at the same time her mind was not free from anxious questionings. What should she do if the worst were true? Had he really changed from the pure, pious and loving soul that she found him to be some four years back? In that case, would it be proper for her to be staying at her father's house? Was it not her duty then to be by his side and be of service to him? Days were spent in anxious thoughts of this kind, quite unknown even to her nearest kith and kin. Finally, she came to the conclusion that under the circumstances, it was better for her to go once to Dakshineswar and see things for herself. She could then decide as to where her duty lay.

Very soon an opportunity presented itself. Some women distantly related to her were going to Calcutta to have a bath in the Ganges on the auspicious occasion of Sri Chaitanya's birth anniversary. She told them that she too would accompany them for that purpose. They communicated the information to her

ೲ Sri Ramakrishna ಌ

৩০ **Nahabat** ෪

father Ramachandra. Ramachandra was not slow in understanding his daughter's real object in visiting Calcutta. So he offered to escort her himself.

An auspicious day was then selected, and the party soon started on their long journey towards the end of March,[2] 1872. They had to travel a distance of about sixty miles on foot; for in those days there was no railway or steamer service to Calcutta, and the only other alternative means of travel, namely, the palanquin, was beyond the financial capacity of people like them. The first two days of the journey were very pleasant. Corn-fields and lotus ponds greeted their eyes everywhere, while the shade of antique-looking banyan trees offered them protection from the heat of the noonday sun. They were not, however, destined to complete their journey in the same joyous fashion. For on the third day the Holy Mother, who was not accustomed to such long walks, fell ill of high fever, probably owing to the fatigue of the journey. Ramachandra was constrained to break the journey and take shelter in a wayside rest house until his daughter was again fit to travel.

The Holy Mother felt very anxious over this unexpected trouble on the way. She was, however, much relieved in body and mind by a wonderful vision she had at night. Of this she spoke to her devotees in later days to the following effect: 'I was lying unconscious owing to fever, without any sense of decorum even. Just then I saw a woman, pitch dark in complexion, sitting by my side. Though she was dark, I have never seen another so beautiful as she. She stroked my aching head with her soft cool hands, and I felt the heat in my body subsiding. 'Where are you from?' I asked her. And she replied, 'From Dakshineswar.' At this I was speechless with wonder and exclaimed, 'From Dakshineswar! I too am going to Dakshineswar to see my husband. But this fever has unfortunately detained me on the way.' To this she replied, 'Don't worry. You will soon be all right and see your husband at Dakshineswar. It is for your sake that I have kept him there.' I said to her, 'Indeed! Is it so? But who are you to me?' 'I am your sister,' she replied. I was much astonished to hear this. After this conversation I fell asleep.'[3]

Next morning Ramachandra found that his daughter was free from fever. He, therefore, thought it better to proceed than stay indefinitely in that inconvenient rest house on the wayside. Fortunately, as they proceeded, they came across a palanquin which they engaged. That night, too, the Holy Mother had a relapse of the fever. It was, however, a mild attack, and she did not mention it to anybody. So they proceeded, and covered the distance little by little, reaching Dakshineswar at 9 o'clock in the night.

And what was the type of welcome that awaited her at Dakshineswar? Let her speak in her own simple way. 'I went straight to the Master's room,' she said, 'while the others went to the Nahabat (ie orchestra block or concert house) where my mother-in-law was living. The Master said to me, "Ah! You are here! All right." And he asked someone to spread a mat on the floor. Then he added, "Alas! Would that my Mathur[4] were alive now! By his death my right hand, as it were, is broken." Mathur had died a few months before. Akshay (the son of the Master's elder brother) also was dead. Should I have had to live in that inconvenient place (ie the Nahabat) had Mathur been alive? He would have built a mansion for me. Anyway, after seeing the Master I wanted to go to the Nahabat. But the Master said, "No, no. Stay here. It would be rather difficult for the doctor to see you in the Nahabat." I spent the night in the room. A woman companion slept with me. Hriday gave us two or three baskets of puffed rice; for all had finished their supper when we arrived. Next day a doctor visited me. Within a few days I felt all right, and went to live in the room in the Nahabat. My mother-in-law was then staying in the Nahabat. Before that she had been living in a room in the building used by the owners of the temple garden. Akshay had died in that house. Therefore she left it. She said, "I shall not live there any longer. I shall live in the Nahabat and turn my face towards the Ganges. I do not need the building any more."'

The Holy Mother was cured of her fever, but the physical relief she felt was nothing compared with her mental appeasement on account of her first experiences at Dakshineswar. The worst fears she had in mind were now laid at rest. Experience proved those disquieting rumours to be nothing but the idle gossip of worldlings whose hearts and heads were blind to the spiritual glory of Sri Ramakrishna. He had not forgotten her, nor was there any indication of his sanity being in peril. The care and solicitude he showed at the time of her illness, and the personal attention he bestowed on her treatment and nursing, went to strengthen the previous impressions. She had now no more doubts regarding her duty for the rest of her life. She decided to stay at Dakshineswar and be of service to the Master and his revered mother.

Ramachandra, too, rejoiced to see his daughter so cordially received by her husband and to find her happy in his company. So, after a few days' stay at Dakshineswar, he returned home alone, free from the anxious thoughts about his daughter's future, which must have been tormenting his mind till then. ❑

---

1. Narrating the lighter incidents of her life during her stay at Kamarpukur on this occasion, the Holy Mother would say; 'When I was still quite young, the Master once came to Kamarpukur with stomach trouble. During the early hours of the morning he would wake up from sleep and tell us about the dishes I should prepare for his midday meal. I would follow his directions. One day I found that I had not a particular spice with which he wanted the vegetables flavoured. My sister-in-law (Sri Ramakrishna's elder brother's wife) asked me to cook without that spice. The Master heard those words and said, "How is it? If you have not the spice, get it from the market. It is not proper to cook the curry without the spices necessary for it. I sacrificed the rich dishes of Dakshineswar temple and came here for the flavour of that spice, and you want to deprive me of that! That won't do." My sister-in-law felt ashamed and sent for the spice.

'The Brahmani (ie Yogesvari, the Sannyasini who instructed Sri Ramakrishna in Tantric practices) was then with us. The Master addressed her as mother, and I therefore looked upon her as my mother-in-law. I was rather afraid of her. She was very fond of red-pepper. She used to cook her own dishes—all hot stuff. Often she offered me these preparations. I would silently eat them and wipe out the tears from my eyes. When she asked me how I liked them, I said in fear, "Very nice!" My sister-in-law, however, would remark, "Oh! they are very hot." I noticed that the Brahmani was displeased at such remarks. She would say, "Why do you say so? My 'daughter' approves of these dishes. Nothing can please you. I will not give you my curries any more.' "

Visit to Dakshineswar

And the Holy Mother would laugh as she narrated these incidents.

It was during this period that the Brahmani picked up a quarrel with Hriday and left the Master's company.

2. According to some, the occasion was *Dol-purnima* which fell on 25th March. According to others it was *Chaitra samkranti*, which came a month later.

3. This is the first authenticated mystical phenomenon that we come across in her life. There are, however, traditions regarding certain occult facts about the period of her life already covered. The following is a brief statement of these traditions.

(a) The first is regarding her birth. Her mother Syamasundari Devi had once gone to Sihor to attend a religious festival. There, while she sat under a tree near the temple, she experienced as if a quantity of air entered into her body and made her feel heavy. Just then a beautiful girl of five or six, dressed in a red silk sari, descended from the tree, and throwing her tender arms round her neck, said, 'Mother, I am coming to your house.' That girl seemed to enter into the body of Syamasundari Devi who fell into a trance.

(b) The Holy Mother is reported to have told a disciple; 'You see, my child, I used to notice during my childhood that a girl, just like me, would always roam about with me and help me in all my work. She would also laugh and play with me. That continued until my tenth or eleventh year.'

(c) While she was thirteen, she once went to Kamarpukur. Being very young and new to the house, she used to feel afraid to go to the outer tank for her bath. One day, coming out of the backdoor of the house, she was thinking of her difficulty, when she found all of a sudden eight women near her. As she proceeded to the street leading to the tank, they escorted her, four of them walking in front and the other four behind. They bathed with her in the tank of the Haldars, and came back with her to the house. This happened for several days. She could not make out who these women were.

4. Son-in-law of Rani Rasmani, the foundress of the Dakshineswar temple, who became the proprietor of it after her time. He was both the patron and devotee of Sri Ramakrishna, and used to spend money unstintedly for his service.

5. THE FIERY ORDEAL

IT IS IN the stress of circumstances that a truly great man reveals the strength of his character. Imagine the reaction of a lifelong ascetic when he is suddenly confronted with his young wife, who has come with the definite purpose of meeting him and, possibly, of asserting her claim over him. If he were a stern ascetic, he would shun her; if not, he would gradually succumb to her influence. Sri Ramakrishna did neither. His reactions had a uniqueness of their own. It has already been mentioned that he received her cordially, but what followed was even more remarkable. He decided to avail himself of his wife's presence at Dakshineswar to do two things—first, to fulfil his foremost duty to her as a husband, namely, to educate her in the high ideals of life for which he stood, and secondly, to subject his own mind to a crucial test in point of same-sightedness and freedom from lower instincts. Of these, the first was a long and subtle process of spiritual education, which will be described elsewhere. As for the second, Sri Ramakrishna, on meeting his wife, remembered the precious advice he had been given by his master,

Totapuri, when he knew that his disciple was married. A wife, he said, presented no danger to one, if one were really established in Brahman. He whose mental purity was based upon a strong sense of distinction between the sexes, was no doubt a good aspirant, but the realization of Brahman was still far away from him. For a true seer of Brahman would see no difference between man and woman, and his purity of behaviour would be based, not on a sense of moral conflict, but on this supersensuous perception of unity. So Sri Ramakrishna felt that the presence of his wife at Dakshineswar was for him an opportunity to test his own attainment in this respect. He was a radical by temperament, and when an idea entered his mind, he felt he must carry it out at once. So unlike an ordinary ascetic he allowed his wife to be by his side and serve him to her heart's content. Not only that, for about six months of her stay at Dakshineswar, he permitted her even to sleep with him in the same room.

This was, indeed, a fiery ordeal for any youthful ascetic, but not for Sri Ramakrishna. His discriminating mind could not be caught in any worldly snare. The nature of this test and the reactions of his mind to it are best described in the eloquent words of Swami Saradananda, the disciple and biographer of Sri Ramakrishna. He writes: 'One day, seeing the Holy Mother sleeping by his side, the Master discriminated within himself: "O mind, this is what the world calls the body of a woman. Men wistfully run after it. But one who goes after it remains enmeshed in body-consciousness, and cannot attain God. Now, O my mind, be not insincere—

say not one thing outside and have another idea in the heart. Tell me, do you want this woman's body, or do you want the Lord? If the first, here it is in front of you, and you are free to have it." Discriminating in this way, he was about to touch the Holy Mother, when his mind recoiled so violently that he was absorbed in Samadhi for the whole night! Next morning the name of the Lord had to be uttered long in his ears before his mind came to the sense plane.'

This will give one an idea of the kind of conjugal life that the Holy Mother had with her saintly husband. To complete the picture of it, another incident quite characteristic of Sri Ramakrishna may be mentioned here. One day his youthful wife was massaging his feet. She put him a straight question. 'How do you look upon me?' she asked. And Sri Ramakrishna replied, 'The Mother who is the Deity in the temple, the mother who gave birth to me and now resides in the Nahabat—even she is now massaging my feet. I look upon you in that light—as the embodiment of Motherhood.' These are, indeed, puzzling words for the sense-bound mind of man, but they were only a commonplace in the mouth of Sri Ramakrishna, the true worshipper of the Universal Mother.

There have been people who have expressed sympathy for the Holy Mother on account of what they consider the barrenness of her married life. For did not the very greatness of her husband stand in the way of her experiencing the substance of matrimonial life, and what is more, the greatest privilege of a woman, namely, motherhood? Indeed, her own mother,

The Fiery Ordeal

Syamasundari remarked in the hearing of Sri Ramakrishna, 'My Sarada has been married to a lunatic. She will never know the happiness of being addressed as "mother".' At this Sri Ramakrishna remarked, 'Well, mother, you need not worry about that. Your daughter will have so many children that she will be tired of being addressed day and night as "Mother".'

But the remarkable fact about this phase of the Holy Mother's life is that, unlike her sympathisers, she herself never felt aggrieved on this account. In later times it was with a feeling of exaltation that she would refer to those blessed days she had spent with the Master. She used to say: 'The divine state in which the Master used to be absorbed, passes all description. In ecstatic moods he would smile or weep, or at times remain perfectly still in deep Samadhi. This would sometimes continue throughout the night. In that divine presence my whole body would tremble with awe, and I would anxiously await the dawn. For I knew nothing of ecstasy in those days. One night his Samadhi continued for a very long time. Greatly frightened, I sent for Hriday. He came and began to repeat the name of the Lord in the Master's ears. When he had done this for a little while, external consciousness reappeared. After this incident, the Master came to know of my difficulty, and taught me the appropriate divine names that should be uttered in the ear in particular states of Samadhi. Thenceforth my fear was much lessened, as he would invariably come to earthly consciousness on the utterance of the particular divine names. But even after this, I sometimes kept awake whole nights, as there was no knowing when he would fall into Samadhi. By degrees he came to know of my difficulty. He learnt that, even after the lapse of a considerable length of time, I could not adjust myself to his Samadhi temperament. So he asked me to sleep separately at the Nahabat.'

Indeed, the attitude of pity which some feel for the Holy Mother for what they consider her enforced virginhood in married life, is based upon a total ignorance of her exalted spiritual state. If she chose, it was perhaps open to her to have drawn Sri Ramakrishna to the ordinary level of life. But she was constituted otherwise. 'Do you want to drag me down into Maya?' Sri Ramakrishna asked her once in the early days of his association with her at Dakshineswar. 'Why should I do that?' came the prompt reply, 'I have come only to help you in the path of religious life.'[1]

A noble answer, indeed! Only a woman of immaculate purity of mind could have given it. There was no artifice in it, no hypocritical intention to please anybody. It was the spontaneous expression of her nature, of the lofty ideal of life that had unconsciously become hers as much as her husband's.

In fact the world at large has not yet recognized the important part played by the Holy Mother in fulfilling this aspect of Sri Ramakrishna's life. Often there is a tendency to attribute this unique feature of their married life entirely to the saintly character of Sri Ramakrishna. But it is forgotten that at least an equal share of the credit for this is due to the Holy Mother. For such an ideal could be translated into life only because she was his match in point of purity and cooperated with him wholeheartedly in the fulfilment of the ideal.

Sri Ramakrishna himself was the first to appreciate her exalted spiritual state and to recognize the immense value of her contribution to his religious life. 'Had she not been so pure,' he said to his disciples in later times, 'who knows whether I might not have lost my self-control from her inducements? After marriage I prayed to the Divine Mother, "O Mother, remove even the least taint of carnality from the mind of my wife." When I lived with her, I understood that the Mother had really granted my prayer.'

This admission of Sri Ramakrishna, especially in the light of his conduct towards the Holy Mother soon after her arrival at Dakshineswar, is full of import. It gives us a glimpse of the spiritual evolution of the Holy Mother during the days when the Master was performing austerities at Dakshineswar. Does the above prayer of the Master signify an affirmation of mind by which he made her in spirit the participant of his memorable religious practices? Did it establish an unconscious spiritual link between the two individuals, so that in spite of distance and years of separation, the one could draw the sap of holiness that the other was accumulating in the solitude of the Dakshineswar temple-garden? The spiritual fitness that the Master recognized in the Holy Mother on her unexpected appearance at Dakshineswar justifies such an inference. Besides, the Master's own words reveal the subtle unseen relation that existed between him and his chief disciples. 'The devotees are like Kalmi greens,' he said, 'if one end of it is pulled, the whole group of shoots connected with it must come out.'

The same fact is further confirmed by the remarkable form of worship that Sri Ramakrishna performed as the culmination of his spiritual practices. In that rite he placed the Holy Mother on the pedestal of the Deity and worshipped her as the great Mother of the universe. It looks as if her association with him in this final act of his austerities is the conclusion of a long process of soul-culture beginning with the prayer at the time of his marriage, which, strangely enough, coincides approximately with the commencement of his austerities.

The next chapter will describe in more detail this great act of worship that Sri Ramakrishna performed with the Holy Mother as the symbol of the Deity. ❑

---

1. The Holy Mother spoke of this to Yogin-Ma.

6. THE ASCENT TO MOTHERHOOD

IT WAS THE 5th of June, 1872,[1] the day for the special worship of Phalaharini-Kali, or the Deity as Mother Kali destroying the effects of the past deeds of beings. The Kali temple of Dakshineswar was *en fete* with ceremonial decorations. By night, when the worship of the Divine Mother was to take place, a good crowd had gathered in the temple, and everywhere there was singing and excitement characteristic of temple festivities.

The doors of the Master's room remained closed. The noisy crowd had not invaded its precincts; for people were busy with many things outside, and besides, the Master had not yet become very widely known. Within the room, too, preparations were being made for the Master to perform the worship of the Divine Mother that day. A boy named Dinu, a distant nephew of his, brought the Bilva leaves, while Hriday made the necessary arrangements for the rite. The Master had asked the Holy Mother beforehand to be present in the room at the time of worship. At 9 p.m. she arrived. The others had by that time finished the arrangements and left the room, leaving the Master and the Holy Mother alone within.

Now the worship began. The Master sat near the western door of his room facing the east. After he had finished the purification of materials and other preliminary ceremonies, he beckoned to the Holy Mother to take her place on the seat set apart for the Deity. It was a low stool with ritualistic drawings on it, kept towards the right of the worshipper, and she sat on it facing the west. She was already in a mood of spiritual fervour, and obeyed the Master's directions as one under hypnosis. The Master now sprinkled her several times with holy water, and then addressed the following prayer of invocation; 'O Divine Mother, Thou eternal Virgin, the mistress of all powers and the abode of all beauty, deign to unlock for me the gate of perfection. Sanctifying the body and mind of this woman, do Thou manifest Thyself through her and do what is auspicious.'

Then he identified the Holy Mother with the Deity through the ceremony of Nyasa, which consists in touching the different parts of the body with appropriate Mantras and identifying them in mind with the different parts of the Deity. After that, he offered her worship with sixteen items, as one does before the divine image. In the course of it he applied red paint to the sides of her soles, put the vermilion mark on her forehead, dressed her with a new cloth, and placed a little of sweets and betel-leaf in her mouth. Knowing that she was naturally of a very bashful disposition, a disciple once asked her whether she did not feel any

The Ascent to Motherhood 47

hesitation or shyness when the Master did all this to her. She replied, 'No. I saw him, no doubt, doing all this, but I had no inclination to utter a word even.'

In fact, all through the worship the Holy Mother was in a state of semi-absorption, and at the close of it, in deep Samadhi. The Master, too, was in an ecstatic mood while doing the worship, and by the time it came to an end, he also was absorbed in Samadhi. Thus in that transcendental union of the spirit, the worshipper and the worshipped realized their identity of being as Existence-Knowledge-Bliss Absolute.

A long time passed in that state of spiritual absorption. It was only when the second watch of the night had fairly advanced that the Master regained a little of physical consciousness. Then he resigned himself completely to the Divine Mother, and in a supreme act of consecration, offered to the Deity manifest before him, the fruits of his austerities, his rosary, himself and everything that was his. He then uttered the following Mantra: 'O Goddess, I prostrate myself before Thee again and again—before Thee, eternal consort of Siva, the three-eyed, the golden-hued, the indwelling Spirit in all, the giver of refuge, the accomplisher of every end, and the most auspicious among all auspicious objects.'

The worship[2] was now over. Towards the close of it Hriday came into the room. After regaining normal consciousness, the Holy Mother saluted the Master mentally, and walked away to her room in the Nahabat.

The significance of this great rite on the lives of these two souls can hardly be over-estimated. For Sri Ramakrishna it signified the final triumph of the spirit over the body, the destruction of all that is animal in man, the recognition of Divinity even where the ordinary man is least disposed to see it. It marked the successful conclusion of his spiritual strivings, and his establishment of the status of a divine man.

In the life of the Holy Mother, too, it had a significance of equal importance. It symbolized her participation in Sri Ramakrishna's life in a twofold sense. It has already been stated how the Master, at the very time of his marriage, gave a powerful stimulus to his wife's spiritual growth by the prayer he addressed to the Divine Mother. That had brought about a gradual transformation in her, obliterating from her mind even the last vestiges of the lower nature, so that when she again reappeared in the concluding act of the drama of his spiritual endeavours, he found in her a fitting partner in life, well-matched with him in every respect. And so by the performance of that great rite, in which he surrendered all his spiritual practices and their fruits before the Deity whom he identified with the Holy Mother, he virtually made her a participant of all his austerities and spiritual attainments. It is sometimes asked why the Mother did not perform various forms of devotional practices like the Master. The answer to this apparently puzzling question is to be found in the Shodasi Puja, by virtue of which the Holy Mother became a full sharer in the spiritual glory of the Master. Indeed, as we shall see, she did practise a good deal of austerities afterwards, but they were not so for mental purification or for spiritual attainment; they were mainly intended as an example to others or for the

The Ascent to Motherhood 49

benefit of her disciples. To use an analogy of the Master, she resembles in this respect the type of plant that bears fruits first, and then the flowers. As the spiritual counterpart of the great world-teacher Sri Ramakrishna, she had no need to re-enact the same scenes of the one common drama which they were together staging before mankind. She had other parts to play by way of fulfilling and supplementing the Master's work.

In another sense also the Shodasi Puja is a landmark in her life. It made her a vital part of Sri Ramakrishna's mission. In that rite the Master invoked in her the presence of the Divine Mother—the same Supreme Energy that was manifesting Itself through his own personality. Henceforth, just as in the case of the Master, her body and mind became the venue of expression for that Energy. Her future actions were all, therefore, devoid of any personal object, but meant to fulfil the great mission that was being worked out through the Master. She and the Master could henceforth be described as two bodies actuated by the same spirit—the Divine Mother. As we shall see, for the rest of her life she helped the Master in his work through personal service. After his passing away, his mantle fell on her, and through a long period of spiritual ministry she fulfilled what he had left unfinished. ❑

---

1. Regarding the exact date of this event there are two versions. The Holy Mother arrived at Dakshineswar for the first time in March, 1872. According to the version of Swami Saradananda in his biography of Sri Ramakrishna, the worship took place about one year after this, ie on the

Phalaharini-Kali Puja of 1873, the date of it being 25th May. In the Bengali book entitled *Mayer Katha*, Vol.2, the Holy Mother is reported to have said that it took place about a month and a half after her arrival at Dakshineswar. In that case it would be on the occasion of the Phalaharini Kali Puja of June, 1872.

Sj. Ramachandra Datta in his Bengali life of Sri Ramakrishna has mentioned that this worship took place at Jayrambati. Contradicting this, the Holy Mother says in *Mayer Katha*, Vol.2: 'Ram Babu has written in his book that this worship was performed at Jayrambati. Ah me! People in that part of the country are so gossipy. They always used to cut jokes, saying, "Who is it that has married the poor girl? A crazy man!" Worshipping a woman there! That would have finished both of us!'

2. The form of worship Sri Ramakrishna performed is technically called Shodasi Puja. The term requires a little explanation. It does not mean, as is sometimes interpreted, 'the worship of a girl of sixteen.' For the matter of that, the Holy Mother was eighteen or more at the time of this worship. It really means the worship of the Divine Mother as Shodasi—the third of the ten Mahavidyas known as Kali, Tara, Shodasi, Bhuvanesvari, Bhairavi, Chhinnamasta, Dhumavati, Bagala, Matangi and Kamala. The Divine Mother is called Shodasi in this aspect probably because she is conceived as a wonderfully beautiful girl always aged sixteen. In this worship one can use as the emblem of worship either a picture, a pitcher, an earthen image, a Yantra (ie a ritualistic drawing), or a young woman.

7. AT THE FEET OF THE MASTER

THE LIFE OF the Holy Mother at Dakshineswar was by no means eventful, if by events we understand striking happenings in the external world. It was a life of quiet unobtrusive service, coupled with the realization of spiritual truths in the silence of the soul. Of these two phases of her life, the first will be treated at length in the next chapter. Here we shall confine our attention to her spiritual practices under the guidance of the Master.

While for the purpose of exposition one may separate these aspects of her life, they form an integral whole from the point of view of her discipleship and spiritual development. For, among her spiritual practices, the first and foremost was the service of the Master, who was to her, as she said in later days, 'God Eternal and Absolute as her husband and in the general spiritual sense.' Every Hindu woman who has received the right spiritual training looks upon her husband as a symbol of the Divinity and believes that unselfish service to him in the right attitude of mind is her principal means of spiritual progress. Her faith in this respect receives encouragement and support from the Mahabharata story which depicts how a woman, by performing her duty to her husband and family, attained a spiritual eminence which an ascetic could not with all his austerities in a solitary forest. While every woman may put this attitude into practice in regard to her husband, the efficacy of it, however, is much greater, if the object of her adoration is a personality of high spiritual development. For, in that case, close contact and loving thought, which service invariably requires, give her an opportunity to participate in the spiritual consciousness of a highly evolved being and thereby to raise herself to the same spiritual level as his.

The Holy Mother's service of Sri Ramakrishna possessed this higher efficacy; for he, the object of her love and adoration, was a perfect man, nay, an incarnation of the Divinity. By the intensity of his life and thought he has generated a wave of spiritual energy, a stress or proclivity in the higher levels of consciousness. By putting oneself within the orbit of its influence through devout contemplation on his personality, one's mind gradually gets established in the same level of consciousness without all the drudgery and fluctuations of fortune attendant on mere individual struggle. It is in this sense that every incarnation is said to establish a new way of spiritual striving and to continue to be a potent force in the lives of men even long after his earthly career. To the Holy Mother was given the opportunity of communing with such a divine man through personal service, and thus not only of being herself drawn to that current of spiritual consciousness centering on him, but also showing the way to this attainment to future generations.

Service requires the aid of devotion and meditation in order to be converted into a spiritual energy; for without it one cannot engender the attitude of mind capable of transforming work, which is merely mechanical, into an energy of a higher quality. So in the training that Sri Ramakrishna gave to the Holy Mother, the practice of devotion and meditation formed an important part. What she was required to do was to absorb that burning renunciation and insatiable hankering for God that formed the characteristic features of his life. The kind of teaching that Sri Ramakrishna imparted to her can be understood from the following words he addressed to her one day: 'The moon is addressed as uncle by all children. So also God is the "uncle," the common property, of all. Everyone has a right to call on Him. Whoever thus calls on Him becomes blessed by realizing Him. If you, therefore, turn your attention to Him, you too can attain Him.' It is said, this instruction was given to her a few days before the Shodasi Puja, and it had a powerful effect on her mind.

Another day the Holy Mother went to the Master's room with a woman devotee to serve his night meal. Her face was veiled; for her shyness was so great that in those days she never appeared even before the Master without the veil. That day the Master began to speak to her of God and the spiritual life in a highly inspired mood. As he proceeded, he lost all sense of time and talked away the whole night, unmindful of the hour. The Holy Mother, too, was caught up in the magic of his words, and stood listening to him, oblivious of everything else. When dawn broke, she found herself standing before him with the veil entirely thrown back from the face, lost in the fervour of his words. Daylight recalled her to herself, and she quickly drew the veil and ran to the Nahabat.

Besides such general instructions and exhortations, the Master also initiated her into the practice of Japa and meditation, which form the basis of higher spiritual discipline. While at Kamarpukur, the Holy Mother had been given Shakti Mantra (the holy word for worship of the Deity as Divine Mother) by a Sannyasin named Purnananda. She was again initiated by the Master, who wrote the Bija (the mystic syllable forming the core of a Mantra) on her tongue. It is known that she used to spend long hours in Japa and meditation even in the midst of the very heavy work in the service of the Master and devotees. She told her niece Nalini: 'What a lot of work I did when I was of your age! And yet I could find time to repeat my Mantra *a hundred thousand times* every day.'

Beyond a few glimpses of this kind, we have little record of the Master's spiritual instructions to her and the way in which he imparted them.[1] The Holy Mother seldom spoke of this subject to others. But we know for certain that the Master's teachings had a tremendous effect on her pure mind. To a disciple she gave a glimpse of her inner life in the following words: 'During my days at Dakshineswar, I used to get up at 3 o'clock in the morning and sit in meditation. Often I used to be totally absorbed in it. Once, on a moonlit night, I was performing Japa, sitting near the steps of the Nahabat. Everything was quiet. I did not even know when the Master passed that way. On other days I would hear the sound of his slippers, but on this, I did not. I was totally absorbed in meditation. In those days I looked different. I used to put on ornaments and had a cloth with red borders. On this day the cloth had slipped off from my back owing to the breeze, but I was unconscious of it. It seems 'son Yogen'[2] went that way to give the water-jug to the Master and saw me in that condition. Ah! the ecstasy of those days! On moonlit nights I would look at the moon and pray with folded hands, "May my heart be as pure as the rays of yonder moon!" or "O Lord, there is a stain even in the moon, but let there not be the least trace of stain in my mind!" If one is steady in meditation, one will clearly see the Lord in one's heart and hear His voice. The moment an idea flashes in the mind of such a one, it will be fulfilled then and there. You will be bathed in peace. Ah! What a mind I had at that time! Brinde, the maid servant, one day dropped a metal plate in front of me, with a bang. The sound penetrated into my heart.[3] In the fullness of one's spiritual realization, one will find that He who resides in one's heart, resides in the heart of others as well—the oppressed, the persecuted, the untouchable and outcast. This realization makes one truly humble.'

There is ample evidence to make one believe that she attained to exalted states of spiritual consciousness during this period of her life. But she was by nature so modest and unassuming that she would seldom speak to others of such facts of her life as might glorify her in their eyes. Sometimes certain happenings leaked out when any of her companions happened to be by her side. One such instance we come across in the account left by Yogin-Ma of an exalted spiritual mood she witnessed personally in the Holy Mother. We give below her own words, a little abridged:

'When the Mother first came to Dakshineswar, she had not experienced Samadhi. Though she practised meditation and Japa every day with utmost devotion, we did not hear of her going into Samadhi at that time. On the other hand she even felt frightened at the sight of the Master's Samadhi in the days when she slept in his room. After I had been acquainted with her for some time, she said to me one day, "Please speak to the Master that through his grace I may experience Samadhi. On account of the constant presence of devotees, I hardly get any opportunity to speak to him about it myself." I thought it was quite right that I should carry out her request.

'Next morning Sri Ramakrishna was seated on his bed alone when I went to his room, and after saluting him in the usual way, communicated the Mother's prayer to him. He listened to it, but did not give any reply. Suddenly he became very serious. When he was in that mood, no one dared to utter a word before him. So I left the room after sitting there silently for a while. Coming to the Nahabat, I found the Mother seated for her daily worship. I opened the door a little and peeped in. Strange to say, she was giggling and the next moment weeping. This went on alternately for some time. Tears were rolling down her cheeks in an unceasing stream. Gradually she became very much absorbed into herself. I knew she was in Samadhi. So I closed the door and came away.

'A long while after, I went again to her room. She said to me, "Are you just returning from the Master's room?" And I replied, "How is it, Mother, that you say you never experience Samadhi and other high spiritual moods?" She was abashed and smiled.

'After that event I sometimes used to spend the night with her at Dakshineswar. Though I wanted to sleep on a separate bed, she would never listen to it. She would drag me to her side. One night somebody was playing the flute outside. That brought on her a high spiritual mood. She was laughing at intervals. With great hesitation I sat in one corner of the bed. I thought that, being a worldly person, I should not touch her at that time. After a long while her mind came to the ordinary state.'

In later days, after the passing away of the Master, she had more frequent experiences of this exalted state. This will be dealt with in detail in the proper place.[4] Suffice it to say here that soon after her contact with the Master, her mind, pure and disciplined as it was, attained to great heights of concentration and illumination. Ecstasies and visions are only the by-products of spiritual realization. They may or may not appear according to temperament. The essence of realization, however, consists in a transformation of the inner life, and not in any external manifestation. The Holy Mother was speaking from experience when she put this idea so beautifully in the following words: 'What else does one obtain by the realization of God? Does one grow a pair of horns? No, our mind becomes pure, and through that pure mind comes enlightenment.'

In conclusion it may be stated here that the training that the Master imparted to her did not exclude secular matters, especially the way of conducting oneself in everyday life. He instructed her that in arranging articles of domestic use, one must think out beforehand where particular things were to be kept. Those that were frequently required must be kept near at hand and the others at a distance. When a thing was temporarily removed from a place, particular care should be taken to see that it was put back exactly in the same place, so that one might not fail to locate it even in darkness. He taught her also the way of rolling wicks, dressing vegetables, making betel rolls, cooking, and doing other items of domestic work. He taught her that while travelling in a boat or carriage, she should always be the first to get in and the last to get out; for then only one could properly check whether all the luggage had been taken in and taken out. The secret of one's success in social relationships, he told her, depended entirely on one's capacity to adjust one's conduct according to time, place, circumstances, and the nature of people one had to deal with and their behaviour. Physically every one was made of flesh and bones, but the mind within was constituted in entirely different ways. So one should be very careful in selecting one's friends and associates. With some, one might mix freely, with others only a nodding acquaintance was advisable, and with still others it is better not to talk at all.

Thus the Master took pains to make the Holy Mother efficient in both spiritual and secular matters and prepared her for the great mission that he was to entrust to her at the close of his life. ❑

---

1. It is also known from her own words that the Master taught her various Mantras pertaining to different aspects of the Deity, with instructions as to how to impart them.

2. The Holy Mother used thus to distinguish Swami Yogananda (Yogen), a Sannyasin disciple of Sri Ramakrishna, from Yogin-Ma, a woman disciple of the Master and a lifelong companion of hers, whom she addressed merely as Yogin or 'daughter Yogin.' See ch.17 for an account of both these persons.

3. The Holy Mother was then meditating in the Nahabat and felt the sound like a clap of thunder, and she burst into tears. According to textbooks on Yoga (the art of concentration), when the mind is just getting into a very tense state of concentration, even a slight sound will appear like a peal of thunder.

4. See chaps. 9 and 11.

8. IN THE SERVICE OF THE MASTER

IN ALL, THE Holy Mother stayed at Dakshineswar for over thirteen years, with occasional intervals of short visits to her parental home in Jayrambati. This was a period of great inner development in her life, a few glimpses of which have been given in the previous chapter. It now remains to give an account of what may be described as the external part of her spiritual practice, namely, her service of the Master, as also the other interesting incidents that took place during her association with him.

For the greater part of this long period, she stayed in the Nahabat, an exceedingly inconvenient place for one to stay in. It was a very small two-storeyed block, in the upper room of which lived Sri Ramakrishna's mother during the last few years of her life. The small room on the ground floor was given to the Holy Mother to live in. To make it a fit residence for a Purdah lady, the verandah about it was covered with screens of plaited bamboo slips reaching above the head. As a consequence sunlight scarcely entered into it. Moreover, since she used to cook for the Master and his aged mother, she was obliged to use this room as a provision store and kitchen also. Thus she sat and slept with vegetable baskets and sacks of rice and pulses about her, while above her head hung in slings the pots containing special articles of food to suit the Master's delicate stomach. 'The room,' the Holy Mother used to say in later days, 'was so low that at first I would knock my head against the upper frame of the door. One day, I got a cut on the head. Then I became accustomed to it. The head bent of itself as soon as I approached the door. Many stout aristocratic women of Calcutta frequently came there. They never entered the room. They would stand at the door and lean forward holding the jambs. And peeping in they would remark, addressing me, "Ah, what a tiny room for our good girl! She is, as it were, in exile, like Sita."'[1]

The Master was not blind to the difficulties of her life at the Nahabat. But he was helpless in the matter of remedying them. For death had already removed from him his ardent devotee Mathuranath, the son-in-law of Rani Rasmani and the proprietor of the temple, who used to look after all his personal needs with scrupulous attention and unstinting liberality. Mathur would have made every arrangement for the Holy Mother's comfortable stay at Dakshineswar, had she gone there in his lifetime. But the new proprietor who succeeded him was not so close to the Master.

Besides, there was no other place in the temple suitable for her residence. For she was very shy by temperament and could never stand the public gaze. Even before the Master, she appeared only veiled in her early days. Her day generally began between 3 and 4 a.m. before any human being was up. At that early hour she would finish her bath in the Ganges[2] and get back to her room unnoticed by anyone. After that she would seldom come out of the room. Even for drying her luxuriant hair, she would wait till 1 p.m. when there would be no one in the neighbourhood of the Nahabat. She would then come out, and sitting on the steps of the Nahabat, bask in the sun and dry her hair. In fact she lived so quietly and unobserved by anybody that to quote her own words, 'The manager of the temple said, "We have heard that she lives here, but we have never seen her." '

This natural modesty and reserve of hers was, no doubt, very much appreciated by the Master. About this the Holy Mother once said: 'The Master used to say, "Dear Hridu (ie his nephew Hriday), I was extremely concerned about her when she first came here. She came from the country and did not know about the ways of city life.[3] I thought people would criticize her movements and we should all be hurt. But she is so wonderful that she has hidden herself completely from view.[4] I never saw her go outside for a wash or the like." When I heard about his remark, I became anxious about myself. I knew that whatever idea flashed in his mind, came to happen. With great earnestness I use to pray to the Mother of the Universe, "O Mother Divine, please be gracious enough to protect my modesty." '

None-the-less the Master was very careful that continuous stay in that dark narrow room should not imperil her health. In fact, after staying there for some time, she got a rheumatic pain in the legs. To quote her own words about its origin: 'I used to stand behind the screen round the verandah of the Nahabat, and hear the Master sing and see him dance in ecstasy through the holes in the screen. It was standing there so long that brought on rheumatism in my legs.' As the Master knew all this, he took particular care to see that she did not injure her health. Of this the Holy Mother used to say: 'He would tell me, "A wild bird, if kept within a cage day and night, gets rheumatic. So you should have a walk at times in the neighbourhood." ' At noon when people generally retired after the midday meal, the Master would go to the Panchavati and see whether there was anybody in the neighbourhood. If there was none, he would tell me, "Just go out. There is no one." He would stand outside his room for a while, and I would go out of the place by the back gate and visit the ladies of the locality near Ramlal's house. After spending the rest of the day in conversation with them, I would come back at dusk when all people generally went to the temple to attend the evening service.'

Realizing the Holy Mother's difficulties from insufficient accommodation, some of the devotees of the Master built a small cottage for her near the temple in 1874. Sambhu Mallick, acquired a plot of land on lease for Rs.250, and began constructing the cottage on it. Captain Visvanath Upadhyaya, the agent of the Nepal Government in Calcutta, was a great devotee of the Master. As he was in charge of the Nepal Government's timber yard in Calcutta, he offered to give all the timber necessary for the cottage. Accordingly, three logs of wood were towed up the Ganges, but unfortunately one of these was carried away by the flood tide at night. Strangely enough, Hriday, Sri Ramakrishna's nephew, was displeased with the Holy Mother for this, as he attributed it to her ill-luck and want of faith. When the Captain heard of the incident, he sent another log, and with it the construction of the house was completed.

The Holy Mother lived in this house for about a year. To help her and keep company with her, a maid-servant was engaged. There the Holy Mother would cook the food for the Master and bring it to the temple to serve it personally to him. The Master, too, to please her as well as to see whether everything was going on well, would visit her house once in the day, and after spending a little time there, invariably come back to the temple by dusk. One day, however, there was a break in this rule. He had gone in the evening to the Mother's house, but owing to heavy rain he could not come back. So he had to spend the night in the house, and while the Holy Mother was serving him food, he jocularly remarked, 'Do not the priests of the Kali temple go home at night? I am also doing likewise, am I not?'

About one year after, Sri Ramakrishna had a severe attack of dysentery, and in order to be by his side to nurse him, she returned to the Nahabat. Afterwards she seems to have never gone back to her cottage. For what reason she did not do so, is not known.

The Holy Mother's chief duty at Dakshineswar was cooking. Sri Ramakrishna had a very delicate stomach which easily got upset by any irregularity in food. The preparation of his food, therefore, had to be done with scrupulous care and attention, and it was found that only the Holy Mother could do it in just the way that suited the requirements of his health. Whenever she was away from Dakshineswar, the Master used to suffer, and he would sometimes send word to her asking her to come back soon. Referring to his utter dependence on her in this respect, he once humorously remarked to somebody, 'Well, what does a "wife," signify in the case of one like me?' And he himself gave the reply jokingly, 'Don't you see? But for her, who would have prepared my food in just the way that suits my health?'

In earlier days, she had to cook only for the Master and his old mother, Chandra Devi. As we have seen, Chandra Devi shifted to the Nahabat in order to be close to the Ganges. The Holy Mother was her companion and attendant. Yogin-Ma reports that even amidst her heavy duties the Holy Mother used to be so vigilant about the service of her mother-in-law that before she called out her name in full, she would rush to her side. When Yogin-Ma remonstrated with her, saying that by running in such haste she might knock her head against the doorway and hurt herself, she would reply, 'It does not matter much even if it happens so. She is my Guru, and she is also my mother. Ah, she is so old, and if I do not go to her in time, she may be put to inconvenience. That is why I run to her in such haste.'

As days went on and devotees began to gather round the Master, the volume of cooking the Holy Mother had to do, increased. For, at times several devotees would stay with the Master, and they had to be fed and taken care of. From some of her recorded conversations we get a glimpse of the heavy work that fell on her. She said to a disciple: 'I used to cook for the Master. He had poor digestion. So he could not eat the food offerings from the Kali temple. I had to cook also for the devotees of the Master. Latu lived with him. Having had a difference with Ram Datta, he had come away. The Master said to me, 'He is a nice boy; he will knead flour for you.' I had to cook day and night. When Ram Datta came, he would shout after getting out of the carriage. 'Today I shall have Chapatis (Indian bread), and gram Dal (a kind of soup).' Then I would at once start cooking. I used to make Chapatis out of three or four seers of flour.[6] When Rakhal lived there, I often made Khichuri for him. The Master one day asked me to cook nicely for Naren. I prepared some Mung (green gram) soup and Chapatis. When the meal was over, the Master asked Naren, 'How did you enjoy the meal?' 'Very well,' he replied, 'but it tasted like sick diet.' At this the Master said to me, 'What sort of stuff have you cooked for him? You must prepare for him thick gram Dal and heavy Chapatis.' Finally I prepared those things and Naren was very pleased. Suren Mitra gave ten rupees a month for the expenses of the devotees. Gopal Senior did the marketing. Dancing, devotional music, ecstasy and Samadhi went on day and night. I made little holes in the bamboo-mat screen, so that I could watch through it.[7] Standing there continually, I got this rheumatism in the end.'

Sometimes her skill as a cook was tried to the utmost. One evening some distinguished gentlemen came to Sri Ramakrishna, and the Holy Mother had to prepare food for them. Her stock of vegetables was exhausted. She had nothing left for curry but a few cast-off leaves of cabbage and some bits of vegetables not deemed good enough for the earlier meal. She was in deep perplexity, but Gopaler-Ma, a woman disciple, assured her she could make a delicious dish out of these remnants. 'Very well,' the Holy Mother replied, 'I will try. If it succeeds, all the merit will go to you. If it fails, the blame too will be yours.' She cooked it quickly and carried it to the room of the Master. Sri Ramakrishna asked in surprise where she had found the materials for so wonderful a curry. But she could not take the praise or blame—it belonged to Gopaler-Ma!

In fact, the Holy Mother's daily programme of life at Dakshineswar was one of unremitting service and ardent practice of devotion. She would, as already stated, get up between 3 and 4 a.m. and after bathing in the Ganges, spend the morning hours in meditation and worship. For the Master used to insist on meditation both in the morning and evening.[8] Then she would attend to cooking. After that, if there were no devotees near the Master, she would go to him and massage his body with oil. While the Master was engaged in his bath, she would prepare betel rolls. Then she would take the Master's food[9] to him, and personally serve it and stand by his side as he partook of it. For she had to engage him in some light conversation, so that his meal might not be disturbed by the sudden onset of Samadhi or any such higher mood. Besides, as in feeding a little child, she often had to have recourse to various tricks in feeding the Master. For, the sight of a large quantity of food on the plate would make him nervous, and he would refuse to take it, fearing it would upset his stomach. So she would hide the real quantity of rice by pressing it down into a small heap. In the same way she would take from the milkman more than the usual half a seer of milk allotted to the Master, and boil it down into the usual quantity.[10] By adopting such methods, she used to feed the Master well, and under her loving care, his health invariably improved. When such improvement became marked, he used to tell her, 'Just see how I am growing fatter by taking the food cooked by you.'

The feeding of the Master over, she would take some tiffin and sit for making betel rolls. During that time as well as afterwards, she would sing devotional songs within herself in a low humming tune, always taking care to see that no one outside heard it. At 1 p.m. she took her midday meal and rested for a while. After that till 3 p.m. she basked in the sun and dried her hair, sitting on the steps of the Nahabat. Then she would trim the lamps for the evening, have an afternoon wash, and make things ready for cooking at night. At dusk she burnt incense before the Deity and sat for meditation. Afterwards she attended to cooking, fed the Master and his mother, took her own food, and retired to bed.[11]

Besides attending to all these regular items of work, she had to receive quite a large number of visitors in later days. For all the women disciples of the Master used to call on her at the Nahabat whenever they visited

Dakshineswar, and if some of them wanted to spend a night or two with her, she had to find accommodation for them.

Though her life at Dakshineswar was thus crowded with work, she felt it in no way a burden. For to be of service to the Master was her highest delight. What pained her sometimes was that she could not get sufficient opportunity to attend on him. For example, her only chance in the course of the day to stay by the Master's side was when she carried his meals to his room. Once she was unwittingly deprived of this privilege by Golap-Ma, a woman disciple of Sri Ramakrishna. Being asked by the Master to serve his food on one occasion, Golap-Ma began to do so every day afterwards, thus usurping that cherished duty of the Holy Mother and depriving her of her only opportunity of seeing the Master at close quarters. She felt very much grieved at heart for this, but kept silent, as she was never in the habit of putting forward her own claims as against those of others. For though Sri Ramakrishna was the nearest and dearest object of her heart, her pure mind was so free from any sense of monopoly over him that she recognized the equal right of everyone else to serve him.[12] It was perhaps with reference to these days of Golap-Ma's interference that the Holy Mother said to a disciple in later times: 'At that time I would see the Master perhaps once in two months. I used to console my mind by saying, "O mind, are you so fortunate that you can see him every day?"' Sri Ramakrishna, however, came to understand her feeling and rectified the mistake.

This sensitiveness of the Master to the feelings and difficulties of the Holy Mother, in spite of the very limited occasions of personal contact between them, is something very remarkable. It is illustrative of how true spiritual love can be thoroughly impersonal and non-physical, and yet be vigilantly operative for the welfare of the object of affection.

Here are a few more illustrations of this fact from this period of the Holy Mother's life. Once Golap-Ma, of whom we spoke before, took to the habit of spending long hours with the Master in the evenings. Sometimes she would be with him till ten o'clock, and the Holy Mother had to watch over her food till then at the Nahabat. That was very inconvenient to her. One day Sri Ramakrishna heard her saying, 'Let the cat or dog spoil her food; I cannot keep guard over it any more.' Next day he told Golap-Ma how she was inconveniencing the Holy Mother by this habit, but she replied innocently, 'No, the Mother loves me dearly. She calls me by my first name, as if I were her own daughter.' Sri Ramakrishna, however, corrected her.

Speaking on this point, Gauri-Ma, another woman disciple of Sri Ramakrishna, said, 'These two beings, residing only at a distance of about fifty yards, would not meet each other for long stretches of time, but in spite of it, there was much warmth between them. Once I saw how, when the Mother had a headache, Sri Ramakrishna was very anxious and frequently asked Ramlal, "O Ramlal, why has she got headache?"'

Once in the course of a conversation about the Master, the Holy Mother said, 'He was a man of perfect renunciation, but still he had his worry about me. One day he asked me, "How much money do you need for your expenses in a month?" I said, "Just five or six rupees will suffice." Next he asked me, "How many Chapatis do you eat in the evening?" I almost died of shame. How could I answer that? But as he asked me again and again, I had to reply, "Five or six." ' On the basis of this, he calculated that she would require a capital of six hundred rupees for her bare maintenance, and deposited that amount with Balaram Babu, a lay disciple. Balaram invested it in his estate, and used to make a remittance of rupees thirty half-yearly to the Holy Mother as the proceeds of this investment.

The Master's solicitude for her was not confined merely to her physical welfare. For, in spite of his being an ascetic, he did everything in his power to bestow on her that subtle satisfaction which a woman feels on her husband showing special consideration for her personal tastes and inclinations. It is interesting to note how he came to divine the Holy Mother's liking for ornaments and thought it his duty to satisfy the same. To quote the Holy Mother's own words on the point, 'He used to say, "Her name is Sarada. She is the incarnation of Saraswati.[13] Therefore she likes to put on some ornaments." Once he said to Hriday, his nephew, "See how much money there is in your box.[14] Have some nice gold ornaments made for her." The Master was then ill; still he spent three hundred rupees on those ornaments.[15] And mind you, he himself could not touch money.' Referring to this, he would sometimes jocularly remark, 'Oh! I have this much of relation with her!'

Concerning the Holy Mother's decor in those early days Yogin-Ma says: 'At that time the Mother lived in the Nahabat like the most revered Sita. She wore a piece of cloth with broad red borders and put vemilion at the parting of her hair. Her thick tresses almost touched her knees. She wore a gold necklace, a big nose-ring, ear-rings and bracelets—those which Mathur Babu had given the Master when he practised spiritual discipline assuming the role of a handmaid of the Divine Mother.

The Holy Mother, no doubt, liked to put on these ornaments with which the Master presented her affectionately. But she loved him and his reputation for saintliness more than these. For, one day officious Golap-Ma said to her, 'Mother, Manomohan's mother says, "The Master is a man of such great renunciation, and yet the Holy Mother wears ear-rings and other gold ornaments. Does it look well?" ' Next morning, when Yogin-Ma, another woman disciple of the Master, visited her, she noticed that the Mother had only a pair of gold bracelets on her wrists. She had taken off all other ornaments because of the previous day's remarks. After much persuasion Yogin-Ma succeeded in making her put on the ear-rings and one or two ordinary ornaments. She never put on all of them any more, because immediately after, the Master fell ill.

In various other ways also did the Master try to please her and make her feel how close she was to his heart. Here are a few instances. Once at Dakshineswar there was a complexion contest, the competing parties being the Master himself and the son-in-law of a devotee. Both were noted for the brightness of their complexion.[16] The Master appointed the Holy Mother to be the umpire and then he and the other competitor walked side by side on the Panchavati ground for her to see and judge. The impartial umpire that she was, she gave her verdict in favour of the other man, whom she pronounced to be a shade fairer than the Master.

Once, while the Holy Mother was with the Master at Kamarpukur, she and one of the ladies of the family were eager to go to see the performance of some strolling players, but the Master would not let them go. When he saw how disappointed they were, he was greatly concerned and tried to console them. He himself acted out a play he had but once seen, giving the words, the songs, the music, and everything. They were so carried away by his performance that they forgot all about the one they had missed.

Another funny incident that took place at Kamarpukur may be narrated in the Mother's own words. 'At Kamarpukur,' she said, 'Lakshmi's mother and I used to cook. She could cook very well. One day the Master and Hriday were taking their meals together. Referring to a preparation made by Lakshmi's mother, the Master said, "O Hridu, the one who has cooked this may be compared to the physician Ramdas." And tasting the curry prepared by me, he said, "Ah, whoever has cooked this is Srinath Sen." Now Ramdas was a renowned physician while Srinath Sen was only a quack. So he meant that Lakshmi's mother was an expert and I only an amateur. At this Hriday said, "What you say is true. But you can get your Srinath Sen at all times. She can render you all kinds of service, even massage your feet. You have only to send for her and she comes. But physician Ramdas takes a big fee for his visit. Besides, you cannot get him at all hours. Further, people at first consult a quack. This quack is your friend at all times." The Master said, "That's true, that's true. She is always available.' "

Amidst all this gay talk and the familiar relationship of everyday life, the Master always maintained an attitude of perfect reverence towards the Holy Mother. He never failed to notice the core of purity and spiritual power that lay behind her veil of modesty and meekness. He looked upon her as a divine being—as a veritable embodiment of Saraswati, the Goddess of learning—born to confer knowledge on mankind. He knew that, being his Sakti, she would have to continue his spiritual ministry, and he commissioned her to do accordingly. 'The people round about live like worms in darkness,' he said to her. 'You should look after them.' In his own lifetime he asked one of his young disciples, Sarada Prasanna, who came to be known as Swami Trigunatita in later days, to take initiation from her, telling him, by means of a Vaishnava couplet,[17] that her spiritual power was no less than his own. When the wife of Kalipada Ghosh approached him for some spiritual aid to divert her husband from evil ways, the Master directed her to the Holy Mother. By the Mother's blessing the conversion did take place, and Kalipada became one of the great lay devotees of the Master. He imparted to her all the great Mantras that he had made dynamic by his austerities and devout contemplation,

In the Service of the Master

leaving instruction with her to initiate people with these. While speaking about her way of initiation, she said in later days, 'I have received all these Mantras from the Master himself. Through these one is sure to achieve perfection.' In his last days at Cossipore, Sri Ramakrishna said to her very feelingly, 'Well, won't you do anything? Am I to do all?' To this the Holy Mother replied, 'I am a woman. What can I do?' But the Master said, 'No, no. You have much to do.' It was due to his vivid perception of her mission in life that he sought so much to bring her into close contact with his select devotees like Latu, Yogen, Rakhal and Narendra, besides the numerous women devotees who flocked to him. Through this close association with devotees the Master developed in her a better realization of her grave responsibilities as his spiritual counterpart and released her latent sense of motherliness toward all beings. She could therefore say, when questioned by a devotee why she survived the Master, 'You must be aware that the Master looked upon all in the world as Mother. He left me behind for demonstrating that Motherhood to the world.'

Being aware of her great spiritual powers, he was very particular to shield her from slights or insults, because he knew that, if her anger was really roused, it would have very serious consequences on those who caused it. Once Hriday showed disrespect to the Holy Mother in the presence of Sri Ramakrishna. She bore it calmly and returned to the Nahabat. Sri Ramakrishna, anxious for Hriday's welfare, said to him, 'Well, you often slight me. But don't you do that with her. You may be saved if the being that resides in this body (ie in him) raises its hood, but if the being that is in her is angry, even Brahma, Vishnu and Mahesvara won't be able to save you.'[18]

In his own conduct the Master was always careful to see that he did not wound her feelings or even go against her wishes, when even she gave positive expression to any, as it sometimes happened on questions of fundamental principles. The following are some instances of this. In those days many devotees brought large quantities of sweets and fruits to Sri Ramakrishna. The Holy Mother who was very generous by nature, would keep a little of it for the Master and practically none for herself, and distribute nearly the whole of it among the devotees and the children of the neighbourhood. One day the Master saw this, and interpreting it as a sign of extravagance, said to her in a complaining tone, 'How can you manage, if you spend in this manner?' In spite of all her submissiveness to the Master, her feelings were a little wounded at these words, because they seemed to question that magnanimity and liberality of nature which were hers as the mother of all. So she was seen to walk away from the place with a grave face. The Master at once understood the situation, and called out rather nervously to his nephew, 'Look here, Ramlal, go and pacify your aunt. If she is angry, I shall be undone.'

To cite another instance, an old woman used to visit the Holy Mother at the Nahabat and spend long hours in conversation with her. The woman had led an unclean life. Sri Ramakrishna knew this, and told the

Mother that it was not quite desirable for her to associate with her. What exactly his idea was in assuming such an attitude is difficult to say; for he knew very well that the Holy Mother was above every possibility of corruption. Probably his idea was that it might set a bad example to his women devotees, and make them unmindful of maintaining the sanctity of the home atmosphere. Whatever that might be, his wish on this point clashed with the Holy Mother's attitude of motherly sympathy for all, whether good or bad. So, as Yogin-Ma noticed, when in spite of the Master's prohibition, that woman continued to visit her now and then, addressing her as 'Mother,' she would, with great maternal affection, make her sit, talk to her kindly, and give her something or other to eat. Sri Ramakrishna noticed all this, but did not comment on it or show any annoyance. By nature he never tolerated any wrong action on the part of his devotees and his acquiescence in the Holy Mother's conduct in this respect means that he understood the depth of her sentiment and approved of it in his heart of hearts.[19]

At one time a woman unknown to any of the devotees used to visit the Master. She was at first taken to be mad, but afterwards it turned out that she was a follower of the path of Madhura Bhava (conjugal relation with the Deity). One day she indiscreetly proposed to the Master that she be allowed to maintain towards him the peculiar mental attitude sanctioned by her sect. This irritated him very much, and he began to abuse her loudly. The Holy Mother was hearing all this from the Nahabat, and she blushed as a mother would do if her daughter were insulted in her presence. She at once sent Golap-Ma to fetch the woman to her, with the remark, 'Just see, even if she had said anything indiscreet, he could have sent her to me instead of abusing her in this manner.' When Golap-Ma brought the woman, the Mother received her very kindly and said to her, 'My daughter, if he feels annoyed at your presence there, you can very well come to me.'

Another instance illustrating the same point took place in connection with the feeding of young devotees. In later days several of them used to spend their nights occasionally with the Master with a view to practising meditation during the night under his guidance. Knowing that overeating would stand in the way of meditation, the Master had strictly regulated the number of Chapatis allowed to each according to his physical capacity. One day he asked Baburam (later Swami Premananda) how many pieces he was taking at night. On being told that he was taking five or six, the Master said it was too much, and asked him why he did so. Baburam answered that he took whatever the Holy Mother gave him. At this the Master went to the Holy Mother, and said complainingly that she would spoil the spiritual prospect of those young men by overfeeding them. But the Holy Mother replied, 'Why do you worry so much because he has eaten two Chapatis more? I shall look after their welfare. You need not find fault with them for eating.' Evidently the mother could not feel content without feeding her children to their satisfaction. The Master understood the point and laughed away the whole affair.

Thus the Master showed the utmost deference to the Holy Mother's wishes on fundamental questions, and while receiving her loving service and moving with her in all frankness and childish joviality, he always maintained an attitude of profound respect towards her as his spiritual counterpart and the fulfiller of his life's mission. This attitude was often implicit, but sometimes it expressed itself in striking little actions. One day the Holy Mother entered the Master's room with his meal. He thought it was his niece Lakshmi and asked her in a careless way to shut the door. In doing so he used the word 'tui' an expression meaning 'thou' but used only for addressing a junior or an inferior person. When the Holy Mother responded, saying that she was doing so, the Master felt very much embarrassed, and said, 'Ah! is it you!? I thought it was Lakshmi. Please forgive me.' The Holy Mother replied that it did not matter at all, and that there was nothing wrong in his addressing her as he did Lakshmi. But the Master was not quite satisfied. Next morning he went to the Nahabat and said to the Holy Mother, 'Well, I couldn't sleep at all last night. I was so worried because I spoke to you rudely.' Referring to this the Holy Mother often said in later times, especially when she was worried or treated disrespectfully by some of her senseless relations, 'I was married to a husband who never addressed me as "tui." Ah! how he treated me! Not even once did he tell me a harsh word or wound my feelings! He did not strike me even with a flower!'

The Holy Mother in turn reciprocated a hundredfold this regard and reverence that the Master showed her. This she did, not only by the loving and reverential service she rendered to him every day, but by the way in which she tuned her thoughts and aspirations to the dominant note of his life. There is no better way in which the wife of a great man can show her love and regard for her husband than by cultivating such a spontaneous and whole-hearted receptivity to his ideals and thus becoming his helpmate in the fulfilment of his life's mission. We have already seen how the Holy Mother proved herself worthy of her great husband in respect of divine love and control over the senses. To complete the picture, we may mention here another striking incident illustrating how deeply she had absorbed the Master's ideal of renunciation. Among the Master's devotees there was a rich Marwari merchant named Lakshminarayana. One day, finding the Master's bedsheet unwashed, he wanted to deposit ten thousand rupees in his name, so that from the interest of it all his personal needs might be met. The living embodiment of renunciation that he was, Sri Ramakrishna could not brook the proposal, and he requested the merchant never to mention such a thing in his presence. As a test perhaps, the Master directed the merchant to the Holy Mother, telling him that he might give the amount to her if she had no objection to accept it. But the Holy Mother rejected the proposal, saying that if she accepted the money it would be as good as his accepting it, because all the amount would then go only to his service. It is said the Master was very much pleased with the reply.

In later days the Holy Mother always spoke of the Master as pre-eminently a teacher of renunciation. One day a disciple said to her, 'Mother, what a unique thing our Master gave to the world! He has established the harmony of all religions.' To this the Mother replied: 'My child, what you say about the harmony of religions is true. But it never seemed to me that he had practised the different religions with any definite motive of preaching the harmony of religions. Day and night he remained overwhelmed with the ecstatic thought of God. He enjoyed the sport of the Divine by practising spiritual disciplines, following the paths of the Vaishnavas, Christians, Mussalmans and the rest. But it seems to me, my child, that the special feature of the Master's life is his renunciation. Has any one ever seen such natural renunciation?' As she said to another, renunciation was his ornament.

Once a niece of hers, when taken to task by her for her worldly attachment, retorted that she (the Holy Mother) had not known the value of a husband. The Holy Mother's reply was very significant. 'Yes' she said with pride, 'my husband was a naked fakir!'

One may conclude the account of the conjugal life of this holy couple by briefly recapitulating its principal features that make it an object-lesson to humanity. In the Holy Mother we find a combination of an ideal wife and disciple. Her highest delight consisted in serving her husband heart and soul without any consideration of personal difficulties. For her it was neither a slavish drudgery nor the conventional fulfilment of an obligation. Self-abnegation, modesty, submissiveness—these no doubt were in ample evidence in her conduct, but they were in her case the very antipodes of slavishness and conventionality in so far as they formed the expression of deepest love and remained consistent with a dignified pursuit of principles.

Her participation in her husband's life was not confined to mere external service of him. She grasped the central principle of his life and made it a part and parcel of her own self. So well did she absorb them that she ever remained a help, never a hindrance, to him in the realization of his life's mission. As such, she won her husband's unqualified love and respect.

And withal the most wonderful thing is that this holy couple set so perfect an example of married love, and yet were free from the least taint of corporeal passion. In fact, it is the great lesson of their lives that in the highest specimens of humanity, love is not dependent on sex or any consideration of physical intimacy. Many a modern thinker on questions of sex-life is disposed to separate the life of love from the function of procreation and invest the former with an independent value in itself, in spite of the association one finds between them in nature. Even a Christian writer like Nicholas Berdyaev argues that to make love dependent on, or subordinate to, procreation is to transfer the principle of cattle breeding to human relation. He may or may not be right in this view. Many who hold the cultivation of holiness as the highest ideal of life might have agreed with this view if such thinkers had admitted the possibility of transcending the instinctive side of sex in a perfect union of souls. But they are particular in insisting that love between the sexes can never be perfect without physical expression. For example, Edward

Carpenter remarks on this subject: 'But equally absurd is any attempt to limit (love)...to the spiritual with a somewhat lofty contempt for the material—in which case it tends...to become too like trying to paint a picture without the use of pigments. All the phases are necessary, or at least desirable—even if...a quite complete and all-round relation is seldom realized.'[20]

The conjugal life of the Holy Mother and Sri Ramakrishna contradicts this view and sets another norm, at least for the noblest of mankind. For those in whom consciousness is yet centred in the body, love without sex may be like painting without pigment. But there are men and women who transcend the body-consciousness and realize the Self behind it. If they happen to paint the life of love as an example for humanity, the pigment they use is not sex but the Self. The Upanishads recognize it when they say: 'It is not for the sake of the husband that the husband is loved, but it is for the sake of the Self that he is loved. It is not for the sake of the wife that the wife is loved, but it is for the sake of the Self that she is loved. It is not for the sake of the sons that the sons are loved, but it is for the sake of the Self that the sons are loved.' (*Brihadaranyaka Upanishad* 1, 4, 5).

A perfect example of this principle is furnished by the life of the Holy Mother and Sri Ramakrishna. In their case both stood for a common ideal of great sublimity, each helped to elicit the best that was in the other, and both found perfect satisfaction in mutual service, without the aid of any corporeal passion to hold them together in love and amity. If one enquires as to what constituted the cementing principle in this perfect union, one arrives at the Self, of which everything else is but a reflection. ❑

1. While recounting these, the Holy Mother would turn to her nieces and say, 'You won't be able to stay in such a room even for a day.' 'True, aunt!' they would ejaculate, 'everything is so different with you.' Today when we think of those days of the Holy Mother's life with a devotional halo superimposed on it, we are not likely to take a realistic view of the situation as it existed then, and therefore fail to make a proper estimate of the privation that the Mother had to suffer and the glorious ideal of devotion she has set thereby. No other devotee of the Master had to stand anything like that, except it be some of the young devotees of the Master like Swami Ramakrishnananda who waited on him day and night at his sick bed in his last days. This aspect of the Mother's life is an example of the highest ideal of Bhakti as Seva (service) wherein the difference between personal enjoyment and suffering gets lost in the sense of elation brought about by the knowledge that it is all undergone for the welfare or pleasure of the object of reverential love.

2. It is said that once, on going to the Ganga at that early hour without any light, she was about to tread on a crocodile lying on the shore. The Master, on hearing of it, advised her never to go without a lantern.

3. She herself narrated a funny story relating to her experiences of city life, illustrating how strange the environment appeared to her. She said: 'I had never seen water taps before. I came to Calcutta one day and entered a room where there was a tap. I opened the tap. Before the water rushed out, there came a hissing sound, like that of a snake, out of the tap. I was terror-stricken and ran from the room. I at once came to the other ladies of the house and cried, "There is a snake in that water pipe. It is hissing." They laughed and said, "There is no snake there. Do not be afraid. The hissing sound comes from the pipe before the water rushes out." Then we laughed and laughed till our sides began to ache.'

4. This does not at all mean that the Master wanted all women to be behind the Purdah and never take part in any activity outside. In fact several of his women disciples—Lakshmi-Didi, Golap-Ma and Gauri-Ma, for instance—were somewhat masculine in their temperament, without any exaggerated sense of feminine shyness. At least one of them, Gauri-Ma, started a public educational institution for women. The Master never asked these women to remain behind the Purdah. His idea was that the bashful and the forward were different types and they must be allowed to

grow in their own way. It is significant in this connection to note the following words of the Holy Mother on Lakshmi-Didi; 'Lakshmi (the niece and disciple of the Master) used to sing and dance before the Master imitating the professional musicians. The Master said to me, "That is her attitude; but you must not imitate her and lose your modesty."'

5. Latu later on became a monastic disciple of Sri Ramakrishna and came to be known as Swami Adbhutananda. One day he was meditating at dusk. The Master went up to him and said, 'That (ie the Deity), on whom you are meditating, is making Chapatis in the Nahabat. Go and help her by kneading the flour.'

6. According to Yogin-Ma, she used to make Chapatis from seven pounds of flour and betel rolls without number. Besides she would boil milk for the Master for a long time, as he liked the thick cream.

7. According to Lakshmi-Didi, the Master purposely kept the northern door of his room open, so that the Holy Mother could see all this from the Nahabat. Seeing the holes in the bamboo-mat screen becoming bigger day by day, the Master would humorously remark to his nephew, Ramlal, 'O Ramlal, your aunt's seclusion (Purdah) is going to be affected!' To this Ramlal would reply, 'You alone are responsible for that. Why do you keep the northern door open in spite of my repeatedly closing it?'

8. Sri Ramakrishna was always a hard taskmaster in matters spiritual. If on any day the Holy Mother and Lakshmi-Didi, who lived with her at the Nahabat, failed to get up at the usual time, he would, as he passed that way in the early morning, pour water into their bed from his water jug, so that they might get up and begin meditation.

9. As long as his mother was alive, the Master would go to the Nahabat and have his food with her. After her passing away, his food used to be served in his room.

10. There is an interesting description she herself gave to a disciple about how she fed the Master with milk. She said, 'When the Master was ill, Dr. Ganga Prasad Sen of Kumartooly was consulted. The physician prescribed some medicine and forbade water. The Master began to ask one and all, "Well, can I live without water?" He asked this question of everyone, even of a five year old child. All replied, "Yes, sir, you can." "Can I?" he asked me. "You can," I replied. He then said, "You are to wipe the water from even washed pomegranate cells. See if you can do it." At that I said to him, "Well, everything will be done by the grace of Mother Kali. We shall try our utmost." The Master made up his mind at last. He stopped drinking water and took the medicine. Every day I used to give him three to four seers of milk to drink—later on even five to six seers. The man who milked the temple cows used to give me milk in large quantities. He would say to me, "If I give all this milk to the temple, the priests will take it home after worship and give it away to anyone and

everyone. But if I leave the milk here, the Master will have it." He used to give me up to five or six seers of milk. He was a good man, full of devotion. I used to give him sweets. I would boil it down to a seer and a half. The Master would ask me, "How much milk is there?" I would say, "A seer or a seer and a quarter." He would remark, "Perhaps more. I see such a thick layer."

'One day Golap (a woman disciple) was there. He asked her, "How much milk is there?" And she told the truth. "Ah! so much milk," he exclaimed, "that is why I get indigestion. Call her, call her." I came in, and he told me of what Golap had said about the milk. I pacified him telling, "Oh! Golap does not know the measurement. How can she know how much the pot contains?'

'Another day he asked Golap about the milk and she said in reply, "One full bowl from here and another from the Kali temple." At this the Master got nervous again. He sent for me, and began to ask about the exact measurement of the bowl as to how many Paos and Chataks it contained. I replied, "I do not know about Paos and Chataks. You will drink milk. Why all these enquiries about measurement? Who knows about all these calculations?" He was not satisfied. He said, "Can I digest all this milk? I shall get indigestion." Really, that day he did get indigestion. He did not take anything that night, except a little sago water.

'Golap said to me afterwards, "Well, Mother, you should have told me about it before. How could I know? His whole evening meal is spoiled." In reply I said to her, "There is no harm in telling so about food. Thus I coax him to eat." In this way he picked up his health and was almost cured of his illness.'

11. In addition to these daily duties, she used to do quite a number of odd jobs. For example, she said one day to a lady disciple; 'The Master used to tell me, "You must always be active. You should never be without work. For, when one is idle, all sorts of bad thoughts crop up in the mind." One day he gave me some hemp and asked me to prepare some string suspenders with it. He said he wanted them to hang the pots of sweets etc. kept for his young disciples. I made the suspenders accordingly, and with the fibre that was left, stuffed a pillow. I used to lie down on a stiff mat under which I spread some hessian, and placed that pillow under my head. Now you see all these beds and mattresses, but at that time I used to have the same sleep as now. I don't see any difference.'

12. Another incident illustrating this trait of the Holy Mother was told by Golap-Ma. One day, as the Holy Mother was bringing the Master's plate of food, she saw a lady standing near the Master's room. She hurriedly came to her and wanted to be allowed to carry the Master's food that day. The Holy Mother gladly handed over the plate to her.

Afterwards, when the lady had left, and the Holy Mother was fanning the Master during his meal, he told her that he found it very difficult to take that food as the woman who carried it was not pure in life. The Holy Mother admitted that she knew about it, and requested the Master to take his food somehow that day. When she was thus appealing to him, he asked her to give word that she would never hand over his food to any body else in future. At this, the Holy Mother laid aside the fan and said with folded hands, 'That I cannot; for if anyone wants something of me, I feel I must grant it. But anyway I shall try my best to carry your food myself.' Sri Ramakrishna at once understood the nobility of her outlook, and said nothing more on the subject. He continued his meal, talking joyously with her on various subjects.

13. Sri Ramakrishna once said to Golap-Ma regarding the Holy Mother; 'She is the incarnation of Saraswati (the wisdom aspect of the Divine Mother). She is born to bestow knowledge on others. She has hidden her physical beauty lest people should look upon her with impure eyes and thus commit sin.'

14. Mathur Babu had made an arrangement by which Sri Ramakrishna used to get a monthly pension of rupees seven from the temple funds. This used to be kept in a box.

15. There is a tradition according to which Sri Ramakrishna had a vision of Sita at the Panchavati. He found that she was wearing bracelets with many tiny facets like those of a diamond. It was in imitation of these that he had the golden bracelets made for the Holy Mother.

16. In those days Sri Ramakrishna had a golden complexion. It was in later days that he became dark.

17. The couplet that the Master sang runs;

अनन्त राधार् माया कहने ना जाय्

कोटि कृष्ण कोटि राम् हय् जाय् रय् ।

'Infinite and inscrutable is the Maya of Radha. Crores of Krishna and crores of Ramas are brought forth, saustained and dissolved (by it).'

18. Hriday did not, however, profit by this instruction. The consequences of it will be seen in Chap.9.

19. Cf. also the example of a woman taking away the plate of food for the Master from the Holy Mother's hand, mentioned a few paragraphs above.

20. Edward Carpenter: *The Drama of Love and Death.*

9. IN THE PASSING OF EVENTS

DURING THE PERIOD of thirteen years that the Holy Mother spent at Dakshineswar, there were several events in her life that had no direct bearing on her relation with Sri Ramakrishna. It is necessary to make a rapid survey of these events in order to complete this period of her life. In the course of these years, she went at least seven times from Dakshineswar to Jayrambati and back. One need not note the dates of these visits except a few which are connected with important incidents in her life.

Her stay at Dakshineswar on the first occasion lasted for about one year and a half. In October, 1873, nearly one and a half years after her first arrival at Dakshineswar, she returned to Jayrambati. Within a few months of this, her aged father Ramachandra Mukherji died on the 26th April, 1874. His death put the family into great financial difficulty. The income from priestly duties with which Ramachandra used to supplement his all-too-inadequate returns of his paddy fields, was no longer available. Not only that; even the yield of the paddy fields diminished for want of efficient supervision. The four sons of Ramachandra, the younger brothers of the Holy Mother, were too young, and even the eldest of them had not yet completed his priestly education. The whole responsibility of the family, therefore, fell upon their widowed mother Syamasundari Devi. She was, however, a very resourceful and energetic woman, and refused to be overwhelmed by these adverse circumstances. To supplement the meagre income of the family, she began to husk paddy for the Banerji family of the neighbourhood, and as for the education of her children, she sent three of them to the houses of her relatives who undertook to teach them.

In those trying days her daughter Sarada (the Holy Mother) was a great source of strength to her. Not only did she encourage her mother by her advice and companionship, but relieved her of much heavy labour by doing herself the hard manual work of husking, by which the family now earned its precarious living.

As time went on, conditions improved a little. The eldest of the brothers, Prasanna Kumar, having completed his education, began to earn something, though small, by priestly work in Calcutta. The two other brothers next to him in age, Kali Kumar and Barada Prasad, became useful in the management of their lands, while the youngest, Abhay Charan, who was the most intelligent among them all, was sent for school education through the help of some kind friends.[1] Eventually he qualified himself as a medical man, but, as we shall see, met with premature death. The Holy Mother took considerable interest in the fortunes of all these brothers; for, her life was inextricably connected with theirs. As the eldest girl of the family, she was their nurse in their infancy and they all grew up under her charge. Even in later life they always looked up to her for help and guidance.

The improvement in the material condition of the Holy Mother's family is also associated with the institution of Jagaddhatri Puja in their home some time after the demise of Ramachandra Mukherji. Once at the village Kali Puja conducted by one Nava Mukherji, that gentleman, owing to some quarrel with the Holy Mother's family, refused to accept the rice that Syamasundari Devi had vowed to the Deity. The poor lady was much aggrieved at it, and spent a whole night weeping. She was at a loss to decide what she should do with the rice set apart for the Deity. She was, however, relieved of her grief and worry when at night she saw in a vision the Deity as Jagaddhatri asking her to offer to Her the rice she had vowed to Kali. From that day the idea of worshipping Jagaddhatri became a passion with her. Although in straitened circumstances, she performed the worship with due *eclat*, meeting the expenses of it from the sale of a quantity of paddy she secured from a neighbouring house. Next year Syamasundari Devi wanted to perform the worship again and asked the Holy Mother to help her in making preparations. But the Holy Mother objected to it, saying that it had been done once and that there was no need to bother themselves again with all the heavy work involved in it.

'That night,' said the Holy Mother in later days, 'I saw in a dream that three of them arrived—Jagaddhatri and Her two companions, Jaya and Vijaya. I remember it distinctly. They said to me, "Shall we go away then?" "Who are you all?" I asked. One of them said, "I am Jagaddhatri." In reply I said, "No, why should you go? Stay here. I did not ask you to go away."'

From that time onwards the Jagaddhatri Puja became an annual function in the Holy Mother's home, and she used to take a leading part in arranging for the celebration. As she said later on: 'Since that time I have been going home as far as possible every year at the time of the Jagaddhatri Puja. I am to help in polishing the utensils and look after other things. Formerly there were not many people in the family. I would go home to cleanse the pots and pans. Later Yogen (Swami Yogananda) got a set of wooden utensils. He said to me, "Mother, you do not have to scour pots and pans any more." He also secured a piece of land to provide for the expenses of the Puja.'[2]

Shortly after her father's death the Holy Mother came back to Dakshineswar about April, 1874. It was on this occasion that Shambhu Mallick built a small cottage for her. She lived in it only for about a year; for, as already said, she had to come back to the Nahabat in order to nurse Sri Ramakrishna during an attack of dysentery. The Master was soon cured, but the Holy Mother in turn suffered from an attack of the same illness. It was dysentery of a very virulent type, and only with the best medical help rendered to her by the devoted Shambhu Mallick could she get a little relief from it. When she was better, she went to Jayrambati in September, 1875. Unfortunately, after her arrival there, she had a severe relapse. Her mother and brothers treated and nursed her to the best of their capacity, but everyone doubted whether she would recover at all. Even the Master felt anxious on hearing of her condition, and remarked sorrowfully to Hriday, 'Is she born only to die? Is she not destined to gain the end of human life?'

In this extremity, the Holy Mother decided on a bold measure. Since all human remedies had failed, she would now try the chance of obtaining some divine aid. In the neighbourhood of her home there was the temple of the Divine Mother in Her aspect as Simhavahini. She decided to go there and perform the rite of Hatya, according to which one was to lie before the Deity giving up food and drink, with the determination to starve to death if no divine remedy was revealed. Her condition was now desperate. In consequence of the dysentery, her whole body was swollen. Her nose and eyes were running, and by constant loss of tears she was practically blind, even a full moon night being, as she said, absolutely dark to her. In that condition, unknown to her mother and brothers, she went into the temple with the help of a friend and laid herself down before the Deity in a mood of supplication. We have it on her own authority that within a short time the Goddess revealed two medicines—one to her mother for the dysentery and the other to herself for the trouble in the eye.[3] Both the medicines were tried. As a result she got back her eyesight that very day while her other ailments disappeared in a short time.[4]

Next year the Holy Mother again fell ill, this time of malaria with enlargement of the spleen. Her mother took her for treatment to a quack in the neighbouring village of Koyapat. This man's peculiar way of treatment consisted in branding the region of the spleen with burning plum wood, keeping a kind of green leaf over the surface to be branded. He also introduced a religious element into his system of spleen therapeutics, as he administered his treatment within the precincts of the Siva temple of Badanganj in the name of the Deity. The Holy Mother was subjected to this operation. We do not know what curative effect it had on her, but it is known that she bore the painful operation calmly and did not require anyone to hold fast her limbs, as it had always to be done in the case of the other patients of this physician.

She went to Dakshineswar for the third time in January, 1877. Chandra Devi, her mother-in-law, who had been residing at Dakshineswar, had passed away in the meantime.

Her fourth visit to Dakshineswar took place in February, 1881. Unfortunately the occasion was marred by the insolent conduct of Hriday towards the Holy Mother and her party. The respect which everyone in the temple showed him, and the consciousness that even Sri Ramakrishna was under his control, had of late brought about a transformaton in Hriday. His greed had increased, and he had begun to bid openly for people's respect by posing as a saint. Proud, haughty and overbearing, he got into the habit of insulting everyone he came in contact with, including even Sri Ramakrishna. In the blindness and folly of this new mood, he lost his old love for the Master, and even seemed to entertain a grudge against him for his rejection of Lakshminarayan's offer of ten thousand rupees. As a consequence he began to oppress and tease him in various ways. Sri Ramakrishna, however, put up with all his overweening behaviour, considering the great services he had rendered him in the past.

It was in the days when Hriday was on the war path that the fourth visit of the Holy Mother to Dakshineswar took place. To narrate the events in her own words: 'I came to Dakshineswar for the fourth time with mother, Lakshmi and several other women. I had vowed an offering to Siva of Tarakeswar during my previous illness. I redeemed that vow on our way to Dakshineswar. We spent the first night in Calcutta. It was spring time. The next day we came to Dakshineswar. At the sight of us, Hriday said, "Why have you come here? What's your business?" He was discourteous to us. Hriday and my mother hailed from the same village; so he showed her scant respect. Displeased at his behaviour, my mother said, "Let us go back. With whom shall I leave my daughter?" The Master, afraid of Hriday, did not say "yes" or "no," though he heard and saw everything."[5] All of us started back for Jayrambati that same day. While leaving the place I said to myself, addressing Mother Kali in the temple, "O Mother, I shall come here again if You deign to bring me back." Shortly after, Hriday was sent away from the Kali temple, because he worshipped the daughter of Trailokya (son of Mathur Babu), placing flowers at her feet.[6] Ramlal, the Master's nephew, became the permanent priest of the Kali Temple. That turned his head! He began to neglect the Master. The Master would be lying down somewhere, in an ecstatic mood, and his food would dry up. There was no one else in the Kali Temple to look after him. So whenever any one came to our part of the country from Dakshineswar, the Master would request me through Lakshman of Kamarpukur, "I am in difficulty here. Ramlal, since becoming a priest, has joined the other priests of the temple. He does not look after me much. Please be sure to come. Take a litter, a palanquin, or any other conveyance. I shall bear the cost whatever it is—be it ten rupees or twenty rupees or more." At last I came to Dakshineswar in February, 1882, after an absence of about a year.'

Subsequently, she had occasion to return to Dakshineswar only twice (in 1884 and 1885) during the Master's lifetime. There are no events worth recording in connection with these visits, except that at the time of the visit in 1884, Sri Ramakrishna had an accident resulting in a dislocation in the left arm.

It was during one of these several visits of the Holy Mother to Dakshineswar that an event, revealing certain striking features of her character, took place.[7] She was then travelling on foot, along with a party consisting of some of her relatives and several others, both men and women. In those days people travelling from Jayrambati to Calcutta had first of all to go up to Arambag, then proceed to Tarakeswar, passing through the wilderness of Telobhelo and Kaikala for about ten miles, and from there go to Baidyabati and cross the Ganges. The wilderness referred to was in those days infested by dacoits, and even today in the middle of it one can see a terrible image of Kali, to whom the dacoits at one time used to make human sacrifices. On this occasion, the Holy Mother's party was crossing the wilderness towards the evening with a view to reaching Tarakeswar before night fall. As there was not much time left for the approach of night, the party was proceeding rather fast, but the Holy Mother, who was already tired, lagged behind. Twice her companions waited for her, but on finding her still lagging behind, they told her that, if they proceeded at that rate, they would not be able to cross the wilderness even by the close of the first quarter of the night, and that consequently all would fall a prey to the dacoits. The Holy Mother did not want that the others should risk their lives for her sake. She asked them, therefore, to proceed without waiting for her, and agreed to meet them at a particular shop at Tarakeswar.

The party soon passed out of sight. The Holy Mother walked as fast as she could but, being very tired, could not proceed much farther than the middle of the wilderness by nightfall. She was now filled with fear and did not know what to do. Just then she saw a tall man of very dark complexion coming towards her, with a long staff resting on his shoulder. At a little distance behind him was another, who seemed to be his companion. Within a short time the man drew near her and called out to her in a harsh voice, 'Who is standing there at this time of the night?'

Though terror-stricken, the Holy Mother now showed great resourcefulness and presence of mind. She replied to him in an appealing tone, 'Dear father, my companions have all gone away leaving me here. I seem also to have lost my way in the darkness. Would you please help me to reach my companions? Your "son-in-law" is staying at Rasmani's temple at Dakshineswar. I am going to meet him. If you accompany me so far, he will be highly pleased with you.'

By this time the second person also came up. The Holy Mother now understood that it was a woman and the wife of the man with the staff. She, therefore, felt very much encouraged and, approaching the woman and holding her by the hand, said, 'Mother, I am your daughter Sarada. I am in great difficulty. Fortunately father and yourself have come here. Otherwise I do not know what I would have done.'

The Holy Mother's gentle words, her simplicity and innocent behaviour, her perfect trust and fearlessness—all made a deep impression on the man and his wife. They felt a parental affection for her and consoled her as they would their own daughter. As she was very much tired, they did not allow her to proceed that night. They took her to a small shop in the village of Telobhelo and gave her some refreshments. The woman then made a bed for her with her own clothes and protected her the whole night like her own daughter.

Next morning they took her to Tarakeswar and made arrangements for her food and accommodation in a shop. Her companions, who had gone in advance of her the previous evening, met her in that shop. She introduced the couple, her new "father" and "mother," to them and told them of the great service they had rendered her. Some time later, after having finished worship in the temple and taken food and rest, she took leave of her benefactors tearfully, and accompanied the party to Baidyabati.

Referring to this incident, the Holy Mother used to say in later days: 'In one night we became so intimate that, when we parted, I began to weep. With great difficulty I came away from them. I requested them again and again to meet me at Dakshineswar, whenever they found it convenient. They accompanied me for a considerable distance. The woman then collected some peas from a wayside field and tying them to my cloth, said with tears in her eyes, "Daughter Sarada, when you take popped rice at night, use these also with it." They also came to Dakshineswar several times with sweets. The Master, hearing the whole story from me, behaved towards them very cordially like a son-in-law. My surmise is that, though these people are now good and gentle, my "dacoit father" must have committed many highway robberies.' ❏

---

1. About the education of this brother the Holy Mother said in later days; 'My youngest brother had passed the matriculation examination. He was very well up in the school, and then he studied medicine. After Naren met him, he said of him, "I never knew that Mother had such an intelligent brother. The others are all like ordinary priests." Yogen defrayed his educational expenses, and then Yogen died. Rakhal paid forty rupees for his books.' This brother was the father of Radhu who, as we shall see, played such an important role in the latter part of the Holy Mother's life.

2. This worship of Jagaddhatri is still continued at Jayrambati. The function is now organised and performed not by any of the members of the Holy Mother's family, but by the branch of the Ramakrishna Math established at the birthplace of the Holy Mother. In the latter days of her life, the Holy Mother purchased three acres of agricultural land for meeting the expenses of the annual worship. According to the stipulation of

Swami Saradananda, this land is in the possession of the families of the Mother's brothers, but they are to contribute a fixed quantity of paddy every year for the worship.

3. As regards the medicine revealed to her she said, 'I heard the Goddess say to me, "Press out the juice of the gourd flower, mix it with salt, and apply it drop by drop to your eye."'

4. Since that time Simhavahini of Jayrambati has become a living Goddess. People have a strong faith that great power is manifested through the Deity in that temple. Before the cure of the Holy Mother very few used to visit the temple, but now many people hailing even from distant parts go there on the special days of the week. Pilgrims carry earth from the foot of the shrine, thus causing a pit of considerable size to be formed. This earth is supposed to possess great curative power. Members of the Holy Mother's family officiate in this temple.

5. The Master's conduct on this occasion is a little puzzling. Perhaps he maintained this attitude, knowing full well that it would lead to endless quarrels and insults if they were asked to stay there against Hriday's will. And, perhaps he also foresaw that Hriday's days at Dakshineswar were fast coming to a close.

6. Trailokya, the proprietor of the temple, belonged to a lower caste. It is believed that if a Brahmin worshipped a girl of lower caste in that way, she would become a widow. Hence the proprietor was angry with Hriday and dismissed him immediately from his position as the priest of Kali, with the order that he should never enter the precincts of the temple. It is to be noted that this misfortune befell Hriday soon after his insulting the Holy Mother. It was in fact a direct consequence of it. Hriday's life afterwards was miserable, compared with his earlier days, and he himself came to repent of his conduct. In this connection may be remembered the Master's words, quoted earlier, that one might insult him (the Master) with impunity, but dire consequences would befall one who insulted the Holy Mother.

7. We cannot conclusively say on which occasion this event took place, except that it could not have been during the first or the fourth visit. It might have taken place in 1877 during her third visit.

10. THE MASTER'S DEMISE AND AFTER

THE HAPPY DAYS of the Holy Mother at Dakshineswar were now drawing to a close. In the summer of 1885 the Master fell ill of cancer in the throat, and by September he was taken to Syampukur, Calcutta, for treatment. After this, the Holy Mother continued to stay at Dakshineswar for some time more. It was during these days when she had comparative leisure that she learnt reading from a girl of Bhava Mukherji's family.

While the Holy Mother was thus staying alone at Dakshineswar, her heart, already grief-stricken at the Master's illness, was tormented by a cruel remark made unwittingly by her dear companion, Golap-Ma. In the course of a conversation with Yogin-Ma, Golap-Ma remarked that the Master left Dakshineswar, probably because he was annoyed with the Holy Mother. This officious conjecture of Golap-Ma reached the Holy Mother's ears. She felt stabbed in her heart, as it were. Unable to bear the grief, she went immediately to Calcutta in a carriage, and with tears in her eyes, asked the Master about the truth of Golap-Ma's statement. The Master consoled her very tenderly, saying that the statement was absolutely untrue, and sent her back to Dakshineswar in a peaceful mood. He then sent for Golap-Ma, scolded her severely for her false and mischievous surmise, and asked her to beg the Holy Mother's forgiveness. Golap-Ma, full of repentance, walked at once to Dakshineswar, and weepingly implored the Holy Mother to pardon her. But the Mother, who never bore enmity to anyone, laughed it out without saying a word. She gently patted Golap-Ma thrice on the back addressing her, and the poor lady felt all her grief assuaged.

After the Master's departure from Dakshineswar, the Holy Mother did not continue to stay there long. The devotees who had undertaken the responsibility of the Master's care and treatment at Calcutta began to feel the pressing need of an expert hand for preparing his diet and feeding him. They could think of no better person than the Holy Mother, but they felt that, with her characteristic bashfulness, it would be impossible for her to stay among so many men at that rented house at Syampukur, which had no women's quarters attached to it. Anyway, with the Master's permission, they carried the suggestion to the Holy Mother, and were surprised to note that she readily agreed, the thought of serving the Master being enough in her case to drive away all considerations of personal convenience. She therefore shifted to the Syampukur house without delay. A small shed on the terrace, the only place in that house where there was some privacy, was allotted to her. There she stayed all through the day and cooked the Master's diet, coming down only to feed him or otherwise attend on him. At such times she would send word through Gopal Senior or Latu—the two disciples with whom alone she talked directly—to clear the room of all people. As there was only one bath room, she would get up at 3 a.m. before anybody was up and, after attending to personal needs, quietly slip into her shed. At night everyone retired to bed by 11 o'clock, and then she would come to a room in the second storey to snatch a few hours of sleep. Thus silently she spent day after day at Syampukur in the service of the Master, fervently hoping that he would be cured.

Sri Ramakrishna was brought to Syampukur in September, 1885. He stayed there only for about three months. The house was in many respects inconvenient, and besides, the doctors suggested a change to some place outside the city. So a garden-house was secured at Cossipore, and the Master was taken there on the 11th December, 1885. The Holy Mother also accompanied him and, as at Syampukur, busied herself in cooking for the Master and in nursing him.

There are only a few incidents to record relating to this period of her life. One day Niranjan and some other young disciples were going to take date juice from a tree in the compound. The Master was then in a very bad condition and could not even move about without help. But to her surprise the Holy Mother noticed him running out of the room that day. She, therefore, went to his room to see what the matter was. It was empty, and within a short time she found the Master returning. When she spoke to him about the same incident next day, he said, 'Oh! It is all your imagination! Your brain must have been heated by too much cooking!' But it appears that, on being further pressed for an explanation, he said that there was a cobra under the date tree from which the boys were going to take the juice, and that in order to protect them, he had, by his higher powers, gone to the place in advance and driven the cobra away. His making light of the incident at first was perhaps to discourage too much importance being paid to such miraculous happenings.

The devotees had made unstinting arrangements for the treatment of the Master at the Cossipore garden. Dr. Mahendra Nath Sarkar, one of the best medical men of Calcutta, was engaged for treatment, and several of the Master's young devotees stayed day and night with him for nursing him. But it became increasingly clear to all that all effort was in vain. Besides what they could infer from the slowly deteriorating condition of the Master, the Holy Mother and the devotees had indications of the coming end from the fulfilment of certain predictions that the Master had made. They had already been warned by the Master some time back that they must be prepared for his approaching end, when they found him spending nights at Calcutta, accepting food indiscriminately and eating preparations left after distribution to others, and receiving the adoration of a large number of people as a manifestation of the Deity. The first of these conditions was fulfilled even before he left Dakshineswar, and the last one, too, was now found to be coming true. This was brought to the notice of the Holy Mother by a striking incident. Some devotees went to Dakshineswar to see the Master, but were disappointed to learn that he had left for Calcutta for treatment. They had brought some sweets to present to the Master, but as he was away, they made an offering of it before his picture and partook of the Prasad. When this incident was reported to the Holy Mother at Cossipore, she recalled the Master's prediction and her mind was filled with forebodings of the coming end.

In spite of the best medical aid and the careful nursing by his young disciples and the Holy Mother, the Master's illness showed no signs of improvement. When all treatment had failed, the Holy Mother decided to invoke divine aid. She went to the temple of Siva at Tarakeswar and lay before the Deity for two days without food and drink, supplicating for some divine remedy for the Master's illness. 'During the night of the second day,' she said, referring to this incident, 'I was startled to hear a sound. It was as if someone was breaking a pile of earthen pots with one blow. I woke from my torpor and the idea flashed in my mind. "Who is husband and who is wife? Who is my relative in this world? Why am I about to kill myself?" All my attachment for the Master disappeared. My mind was filled with utter renunciation. I groped through darkness and sprinkled my face with holy water from the pit at the back of the temple. I also drank a little water as my throat was parched with thirst. I felt refreshed. The next morning I came to the Cossipore garden. No sooner had the Master seen me than he asked, "Well, did you get anything? Well, everything is unreal. Isn't it?"'

'At about the same time,' she said, 'the Master saw in a dream that an elephant had gone out to bring medicine for him. The animal was digging the earth to procure it, when he woke up. The Master asked me whether I had seen any such dream. I had seen in a dream that the neck of the image of Mother Kali was bent to one side. I asked Her, "Mother, why do you stand like that?" And the Deity replied, "It is because of this (pointing to the cancer in the throat of the Master). I also have it in my throat." '

Such experiences must have gradually prepared her mind for the coming end. To confirm this impression, as it were, the Master one day called the Holy Mother to his side and said: 'I do not know why the thoughts of Brahman are stirring my mind.' It was a hint that his consciousness was getting identified with Brahman. He took final leave of her on the 15th of August, when the Mother was standing by his emaciated body with her niece Lakshmi. All had thought that the power of speech had left him, but he whispered to the Mother: 'Look here! It seems I am going somewhere—all through water to a far-off place. You need have no anxiety. You will be just as you have been so long. Naren and others will look after you and do for you as much as they have done for me. Do have an eye on dear Lakshmi.'

The Master left his mortal body in the early hours of Monday, the 16th August, 1886, creating in the minds of the Holy Mother and the devotees a void that could never be filled by anything else on earth. But men never die in an absolute sense, much less great souls of the type of the Master. This was borne out by the following incident. After his cremation, the Holy Mother was removing her ornaments, as a Hindu widow does on her husband's death. When she was about to put off her bracelets, she had a vision of Sri Ramakrishna appearing before her[1] and saying to this effect: 'What are you doing? I have not gone away. I have only passed from one room to another.' A vision of this kind must have been very reassuring to her grief-stricken heart.

Shortly after, Balaram Babu purchased a white cloth without borders, the widow's garment, for the Holy Mother, and requested Golap-Ma to hand it over to her. Golap-Ma, thinking of the sudden reaction it may have on the Holy Mother, remarked, 'O my God! who can give this white borderless cloth to her now?' But when she went to the Holy Mother with the cloth, she found that she had already torn off the greater part of the wide red borders of her Sari. From that time onward she always used to wear a cloth with thin borders in recognition of the Master's assurance that there was no death for him and therefore no widowhood for her.

Several of the householder devotees of the Master wanted to break up the establishment at Cossipore garden immediately after the Master's passing away. But Narendra Nath (later Swami Vivekananda) and other young disciples protested against this, as it would be a great shock to the Holy Mother to be asked to leave that place so soon. They wanted that she should be allowed to stay there for a few days more, and even offered to beg food for her, if necessary. So the establishment was retained for some days and the Master's earthly relics were worshipped in that house with food offerings. On the 21st of August, the Holy Mother and Lakshmi Didi, the Master's niece, were conducted to the house of Balaram Bose. Along with them was also brought the urn containing the major part of the Master's relics. For, a dispute had in the meantime arisen regarding its disposal between some of the householder devotees headed by Ramachandra Datta and the young Sannyasin disciples. The Sannyasins wanted the relics to be in their possession, but the other party desired to install them permanently in a garden belonging to Ramachandra Datta. It was finally, decided to hand over the pitcher containing the relics to Ramachandra, but the Sannyasins in the meantime had taken away the main portion and put it in the urn referred to above. When the Holy Mother heard of this dispute, she remarked to Golap-Ma, 'Such a unique personality has passed away. But, see, dear Golap, how they are quarrelling over his ashes!'

---

1. Such experiences were repeated in her life as we shall see later on.

11. PILGRIMAGE TO BRINDAVAN

TOWARDS THE CLOSE of his life, the Master had one day said to the Holy Mother, 'You visit all those places which it was not possible for this (meaning himself) to visit.' Whatever be the significance of these words, it is a remarkable coincidence that two weeks after the Master's demise, the Holy Mother started on a pilgrimage of Upper India. It was an excellent plan to assuage her grief, and the time selected, too, was quite opportune in so far as the mood in which she then was, provided the best condition for reaping the maximum spiritual benefit from a visit to holy places.

She started from Calcutta on the 30th of August, 1886. She was accompanied by a party of devotees, consisting of Swamis Yogananda (Yogen), Abhedananda (Kali) and Adbhutananda (Latu), besides Lakshmi-Didi, Golap-Ma, and the wife of Master Mahashay (Mahendranath Gupta). As the party was proceeding to Brindavan, they halted on the way at Deoghar, Banaras and Ayodhya, all of which are well-known places of pilgrimage for the Hindus. It is said that at Banaras, while the Holy Mother was witnessing

Pilgrimage to Brindavan

the evening service of Viswanatha, she fell into an ecstatic mood. On the occasion of this visit, she also met the great Sannyasin and scholar of Banaras, Swami Bhaskarananda. Recounting her memories of him, she said in later days, 'I also went to see Bhaskarananda at Banaras, on my way to Brindavan. I was then in a terrible state of mind. It was just after the Master's passing away. When I saw him, Bhaskarananda was totally naked. But that did not produce the least self-consciousness in his mind. The moment he saw me and other women he cried out, "Don't be embarrassed, mothers. I see in you all the Mother of the Universe. Why should you feel shy?" Oh! what a great soul! Completely beyond all worldly ideas! In heat and cold alike, he always remained naked.'

While proceeding towards Brindavan, she had a unique vision of the Master. During his last illness, he had given her his gold amulet (Ishta-Kavacha), which she used to worship and wear on her arm. She was sleeping, in the train, with her arm having the amulet exposed, when the Master appeared to her in a vision and warned her of the danger of losing it. Describing the incident, she said, "While I was going to Brindavan, I saw the Master look at me through the window of the railway carriage and say, 'You have my gold amulet with you. See that you do not lose it.'" She got up at once, and put the amulet in the tin box in which she carried the photograph of the Master. Subsequently she handed it over to the Belur Math.

After Ayodhya, her next halting place was Brindavan, the holiest spot on earth according to the

Vaishnava cult. It is the place sanctified by the memories of a hundred exploits of Sri Krishna's boyhood days. It is again the one spot on earth where the heart of man, embodied as Sri Radha, loved the Divine with the reckless abandon of the most intense and unselfish form of love. The eternal sport of the Divine with the human soul, with its phases of love in separation and love in union, was enacted there on our earthly plane in the life time of Sri Krishna and the Gopis, and the pious Hindu mind believes that the same sport is going on in Brindavan for all time in a subtle invisible form.

Naturally, therefore, the sight of that place stirred the religious feelings of the Holy Mother to their depth. Besides, the association of it with the story of Radha's passionate grief at separation from her beloved Krishna, brought home to her the similarity of her own situation, and added poignancy to the sorrow that she was feeling in her heart for the loss of the Master. All her pent up feelings, having combined themselves into a passionate longing for the Divine, expressed as a torrential flow of tears that continued almost unremittingly during the early part of her stay at Brindavan. On meeting her beloved companion Yogin-Ma, who had proceeded there a few days before the Master's demise, she cried out with excessive grief, 'O Yogin dear!' and clasping her to her bosom, began to weep like a helpless child. This mood, in which love and grief blend in harmony, bringing about a gradual transformation of personality, continued for several days with her, until she had a wonderful vision in which the Master came to her and said, 'Why are you weeping so much? Here I am.

Where have I, after all, gone? Only from one room to another.'

This experience assuaged her grief very much. She began to feel the nearness of the Master more and more. The anguish of separation gradually turned into a sense of utter peace and radiant joy. Often she would fall into exalted moods in which she would walk far over the sandy banks of the Yamuna until her companions went after her and brought her back. Her temperament changed from an adult's into that of a little girl of seven or eight. How child-like in talk and behaviour she became, will be evident from an incident that Yogin-Ma records about this period of her life. One day she saw a dead body being carried to the cremation ground with the usual decoration of flowers and accompaniment of devotional music. Pointing out the procession to Yogin-Ma, she said, 'Look! How fortunate is that man to meet with his death in this holy Brindavan! I also came here expecting the end of my life, but curiously enough, I did not get even a slight fever! And I am no longer young. (In fact, she was only thirty-three at the time). See how old I am—I have seen in my own life such elderly people as my own father and my husband's elder brother!' At this childish simplicity of hers, Yogin-Ma began to laugh and said, 'What do you say, Mother? True, you have seen your father. But tell me, who doesn't do so!'

The Holy Mother's life at Brindavan was one of constant worship and meditation. As she said in later days, she and Yogin-Ma would sit together and repeat the name of God with such absorption that they knew not even when flies sat on their faces and made sores there. Brindavan is verily a town of temples, and in the course of her one year's stay, the Holy Mother visited most of them several times. In the temple of Radharamana she prayed to the Deity with tears in her eyes: 'O Lord, remove from me the habit of finding fault with others. May I never find fault with anybody!' Her prayer seems to have been answered literally; for one of the distinguishing features of her character in later life was the complete absence of this tendency. And when she found too much of this habit in those about her, she would refer to this prayer of hers and add, 'Formerly I also would see the defects of others. Then I prayed to the Master. Thus did I get rid of this habit. You may help a man in thousands of ways, but if you do him one wrong, he will at once turn his face away from you in anger. It is the nature of man to see only defects. One should learn to appreciate others' virtues... Man is no doubt, liable to err, but one must not notice it. By constantly finding fault with others, one sees faults alone.' To Yogin-Ma she said once, 'Yogin, do not look at the faults of others lest your eyes should become impure.'

Before she left Brindavan, she also did the circumambulation of the whole town and its suburbs connected with Sri Krishna's life—a pious act involving a walk of many miles, which she accomplished without any difficulty in spite of the rheumatism in her leg. In the course of her walk, Yogin-Ma and her companions noticed that she was observing the road and surroundings very carefully and that she was stopping all of a sudden at certain places. They understood that the memories of certain associations were driving her mind

Pilgrimage to Brindavan

to states of spiritual absorption. But when questioned, she said nothing except asking them to go forward.

That the Holy Mother had, during those days, many spiritual experiences that brought great transformations in her personality is certain, but she would not reveal anything about them to others. One day, however, her companions found her absorbed in Samadhi in her residence at Kala Babu's house. She remained in that state for a long time. Yogin-Ma tried to bring down her mind by repeating the name of the Lord in her ears, but it produced no effect. Afterwards Swami Yogananda came and tried the same process, which brought her mind to a state of semi-conscious experience of the world. Then she said, as Sri Ramakrishna used to do on similar occasions, 'I will eat something,' whereupon some sweets, water and betel were placed before her. She partook a little of each as Sri Ramakrishna used to do. Even in taking the betel, she threw away its tip in the manner of the Master. Swami Yogananda put to her several questions in that mood, and received replies from her as if the Master himself were answering him. After she came down to the plane of physical consciousness, she told her companions that the consciousness of the Master was upon her during that state.

The stay in Brindavan is also noteworthy for the fact that it marked the beginning of her active spiritual ministry. For here for the first time she gave initiation to Swami Yogananda. How this happened is best described in her own words. 'One day', she said, 'the Master asked me in a vision to give initiation to Yogen (Swami Yogananda).[1] That frightened me a little. I also felt rather shy. I thought: 'What is this? What will people think of it? They will say, "Mother has started making disciples so soon." But on three consecutive nights I heard the Master telling me, "I have not initiated Yogen. You do it." He even told me what Mantra I was to give him. Before that time I had never spoken to Yogen. So the Master asked me to initiate him through daughter Yogin (Yogin-Ma, her woman companion). I therefore spoke to her about it. She asked Yogen about his initiation and learned that the Master had not given him any Mantra. The Master had also appeared to Yogen and asked him to take initiation from me, but he did not dare to tell me about it. As both of us had received the Master's command, I initiated him'.

The initiation took place in this way: One day the Holy Mother was worshipping in her room. A picture of the Master and a small box containing his relics were before her. She sent for Swami Yogananda and asked him to sit near her. While performing worship, she entered into Samadhi and in that state initiated him. She uttered the holy words so loudly that Yogin-Ma, who was in the next room, could hear it.

After staying in Brindavan for about a year, the party went to Hardwar[2] where the Holy Mother consigned a part of the Master's relics in the sacred waters of the Brahmakunda. Next they visited Jaipur and Pushkar and then returned to Calcutta. On their way they halted at Allahabad where the Holy Mother immersed the Master's hair at the holy confluence of the Yamuna and Ganges. To describe the ceremony in her own poetic words, 'I came to the confluence of the Ganges and the Yamuna. The water was very calm there. Holding the hair in my hand, I was thinking of consigning it to the water, when suddenly a wave arose and carried away the hair from my hand. The sacred waters thus took the Master's hair from my hand as if to become holier by contact with it.'

At Prayag, Lakshmi Devi, who was a widow, had her head shaven clean in accordance with religious practice incumbent on widows. But the Mother did not. For, how could there be widowhood for her whose husband (the Master) was the eternal and undying Spirit? Firm in this conviction, she had continued to wear red-bordered cloth and some ornaments.

The party returned to Calcutta by August, 1887. ❑

---

1. On reliable authority it is learnt that the Master had in his own lifetime asked Swami Trigunatita to take initiation from the Holy Mother. But whether this actually took place, or whether it happened only after Swami Yogananda's initiation, no none can say definitely at present.

2. On the way to Hardwar Swami Yogananda got very high temperature in the train and got delirious. Yogin-ma nursed him, giving pomegranate juice. In the delirious condition, Swami Yogananda saw a terrible form before him, telling him, 'I would have finished you, but I am helpless. There is the order of Ramakrishna Paramahamsa, and I have to quit at once.' When departing, the figure pointed to a deity with red clothes and directed him to offer some Rasagulla to her. Swami Yogananda recovered and continued his journey with the party. From Hardwar they went to Jeypore, and there while they were visiting several shrines, Swami Yogananda cried out at the shrine of a particular goddess that was the very deity he saw in his vision in delirium. This goddess was Sitala and Rasagullas were offered to her by the party.

12. LIFE AT KAMARPUKUR AND AFTER

THE YEAR FOLLOWING the Holy Mother's return from Brindavan witnessed many adverse turns in her worldly circumstances, and formed perhaps the darkest period of her life, at least judged from the material point of view. About a week after her arrival in Calcutta she started for Kamarpukur via Burdwan accompanied by Golap-Ma and Swami Yogananda. On the way itself the life of privation that was in store for her at Kamarpukur began to cast its shadow on her. For want of money[1] she had to walk from Burdwan to Uchalan, a distance of sixteen miles. And after reaching Uchalan, while she was partaking of a little of Khichuri that Golap-Ma had prepared for her, she remarked again and again, 'Golap, your preparation tastes like nectar.' So hungry and fatigued she was.

After escorting her to Kamarpukur, Swami Yogananda came away at the end of three days while Golap-Ma stayed with her for about a month. As soon as the Holy Mother reached the village, there was an uproar of criticism among the village women, who felt scandalized at the sight of a young widow wearing bracelets and a redbordered cloth. So long as Golap-Ma was there she shielded her from their uncharitable remarks, but after she left the place, the scandal-mongers got busy again. To her great relief Prasannamayi, the aged sister of the Lahas of Kamarpukur and an intimate friend of Sri Ramakrishna's boyhood days, now came to her rescue. She silenced the critics partly by declaring, 'The wife of Gadai[2] is a veritable goddess. She is not an ordinary type of woman.'

The Holy Mother herself now decided to disarm all criticism by removing the bracelets from her wrists, but she was prevented from doing so by a vision she had of the Master. To describe it in her own words, 'While staying at Kamarpukur after my return from Brindavan, I took off my bracelets for fear of public criticism. In fact people were already talking about it. I also wished to go for bath in the Ganges, for which I have always had a special devotion. But the river is far away from Kamarpukur. Now one day I saw, to my great surprise, that the Master was coming towards the house from the direction of Bhuti's canal. He was followed by Naren, Baburam, Rakhal and many other devotees. Further I saw that from his feet sprang a stream of water which flowed in front of him in waves. I said to myself, 'I see he is everything. The Ganges has sprung from his lotus feet.' Quickly I plucked flowers from the side of the Raghuvir temple and offered handfuls of them into the stream. The Master then said to me, 'Don't take off the bracelets. Do you know the Vaishnava Tantras?' I said, 'What are they? I do not know anything about them.'

Thereupon he said, 'Gaurdasi (the same as Gauri-Ma) will come here this afternoon. She will tell you about them.' That very afternoon Gaurdasi arrived, and I learned from her that to a woman her husband is Chinmaya (Pure Spirit).'

A still greater difficulty which the Holy Mother faced at this time was the utter poverty and loneliness in which she was, as it were, condemned to live. Towards the end of his life, Sri Ramakrishna had said to her, 'After my time you go to Kamarpukur, live upon whatever you get—be it mere boiled rice and greens—and spend your time in repeating the name of God.' These words came to be fulfilled to the very letter during this period of the Holy Mother's life. She had no cash in hand. She had to take a spade and dig the earth in order to cultivate some greens to go with her daily food. Until these were fit for use, she made rice out of the paddy in the granary, offered it to the Master, and partook of it herself without any condiments. She did not have even a few paise for purchasing salt, an article which is not ordinarily denied even to the poorest of the poor.

Being ever resigned to the divine will, she never spoke of her wretched condition to anyone, not even to her own mother. On hearing of her return to Kamarpukur, Syamasundari Devi had asked her to come to Jayrambati. So she went there one day to meet her mother. Syamasundari Devi wept to see her dressed almost like a beggar woman. She asked her repeatedly to stay with her at Jayrambati, but the Holy Mother would not agree to it, nor disclose the miserable condition of her life. She only said, 'I am now going back to Kamarpukur. Let things shape themselves as God wills.'

That the story of her sufferings remained hidden from the outside world, was as much due to the utter loneliness of her life at Kamarpukur as due to her own silence regarding it. For there was no one else in the house either to keep her company or to share her woes. Ramlal, Sivaram and Lakshmi Devi, the children of Rameswar (Sri Ramakrishna's elder brother) were the other members of her family. Of these, Ramlal, who occupied the post of the chief priest of Kali at Dakshineswar, was the eldest, and it was his duty, according to the Hindu family system, to have taken care of the Holy Mother in her widowhood. But he was hostile to her and was chiefly responsible for the conspiracy that stopped the small pension she used to be given from the Kali temple. Sivaram, though affectionate, was of no practical use. Both of them stayed at Dakshineswar, and Lakshmi Devi, their sister, who often used to keep company with the Holy Mother in her Dakshineswar days, now preferred to live with her brother at Calcutta and thus deserted her in her time of need. Thus the Holy Mother was practically left alone in a hut at Kamarpukur. Mostly she had not even a woman companion to keep her company at night, except when kind Prasannamayi sent her maidservant. There was none to give her protection in times of danger, as when the mad devotee Harish attacked her. (pp. 222). The atmosphere of the village was becoming increasingly hostile to spiritual pursuit in solitude. There was the case of an Oriya Sannyasin living in that place who was molested and manhandled by a gang of village young men who led irresponsible lives and played the part of village bullies. Such elements could at any time become a menace to utterly helpless persons like the Holy Mother, and there was nothing in that village environment to give her protection. The generality looked upon her as a 'merry widow' who wore ornaments. The doors of social sympathy were thus closed to her as there was none there, except the two old ladies, Dhani and Prasannamayi, who had links with the Great Master. Her own immediate relatives, who were in duty bound to look after her, were not, as we have already seen, in any way more cordial in their attitude towards her than the village strangers. They left her in cruel neglect to spend her lonely, miserable days at Kamarpukur. Whenever her solitariness was broken by occasional visits of Ramlal and other relatives, it was only to be pestered with family quarrels over property and with unpleasant talks of people who looked upon her as a burden. During one of these visits, Ramlal abruptly left for Calcutta with the others, after making some arrangements for the worship of the family deity Raghuvir and effecting a family partition according to which the Master's small cottage was assigned to the Holy Mother as her share. The Holy Mother was thus left alone in utter poverty without even any relative to help or guide her.

Poverty and loneliness at times drove her mind to brood anxiously over her future and it was only the vivid consciousness of the Master's guidance and protection that helped her to stand the ordeal. "While staying alone at Kamarpukur,' she said in later days, 'I thought within myself, "I have no child. There is no one in this world whom I can call my *own*. What will happen to me?" Then the Master appeared to me and said, "Well, you want a son. I have given you so many jewels of sons. And in course of time you will hear many more people addressing you as Mother."' Experiences of this type, giving her a sense of the palpable reality of the Master and of the work which he intended to do through her, alone sustained her in these hours of trial.

This state of affairs did not, however, continue very long. For, in spite of the Holy Mother's silence about her sufferings, the news leaked out through other sources and reached the ears of the Master's disciples. Sometimes, at the request of the Holy Mother, Prasannamayi of the Laha family used to send an old maid servant to stay with her at nights in that lonely house. This woman carried the news regarding her life to the outside world. It soon reached the ears of Syamasundari Devi, who was very much aggrieved at her daughter's misfortune. She passed the information to her son, Prasanna Kumar, who was earning his livelihood in Calcutta, as a priest. He in turn went to Ramlal, Sri Ramakrishna's nephew and the head of the family at the time, and remonstrated with him over the neglect of his sister. He also met Golap–Ma and told her how the Holy Mother was taking food even without salt while they, the disciples of Sri Ramakrishna, were still alive. Golap–Ma at once took the matter up seriously, carried on a vigorous propaganda among the disciples of the Master—both lay and monastic, men as well as women—raised subscriptions from among them, and in the name of the followers of Sri Ramakrishna sent an earnest letter of invitation to the Holy Mother, requesting her to come over to Calcutta.

The Holy Mother was now in a fix. She was after all a widow of only thirty-four or so, and what would people think of her if she went to Calcutta at the invitation of people who were not her relations? Just to know the reaction of public opinion in the village, she made the fact of invitation from Calcutta known to her co-villagers. Of course, the village conservatives all shook their heads over it, but Prasannamayi again came to her rescue. She said, 'What do these villagers know of the wife of Gadai? Gadai's disciples are her children. It will be quite right for her to accept their invitation.' Encouraged by this venerable lady's opinion, she went to ascertain the view of her own mother at Jayrambati. Syamasundari Devi was not at first decisive, but after feeling the pulse of the village, gladly agreed to her daughter's departure to Calcutta.

So after a stay of about nine months at Kamarpukur, the Holy Mother was once again in Calcutta in April 1888 to the infinite joy of the devotees, especially of the women disciples of Sri Ramakrishna, who were feeling the need for the fostering care of some one to help the growth of their devotional life.

The disciples of the Master now began to feel that the responsibility of looking after the Holy Mother's comforts thereafter rested on them. It must, however, be pointed out that among the householder devotees of the Master, there were some who did not think very highly of the Holy Mother at first and held that women devotees were making too much of her because she was of their own sex. One of them is actually said to have remarked, 'I know Sri Ramakrishna, but I know nothing of his wife.' But hearing from Swami Yogananda, Golap–Ma and Yogin–Ma about the high spiritual moods they witnessed in her at Brindavan and other places, most of them changed their view. They now did their best to keep her in comfort, but the main responsibility of looking after her fell on Swami Yogananda and Golap–Ma until finally Swami Saradananda, by his single-handed exertion, made permanent arrangements for her comfortable stay and maintenance.

The Holy Mother's life from now (1888) till her final exit from the world in 1920 centres on the series of journeys she periodically undertook from Calcutta to her native village of Jayrambati and back, and her time, it would appear, was almost equally divided between these two places. Until 1907, when the Udbodhan Office at Baghbazar, Calcutta, was constructed by Swami Saradananda for her residence, she used to be accommodated in rented houses whenever her stay in Calcutta was long, or in the houses of devotees like Balaram Babu and Master Mahashay when it was of short duration. It was during this period, probably in 1893, when she was staying in Nilambar Mukherji's garden, that she performed the austerity known as the Panchatapa.[3]

This period of her life was also the time of her active spiritual ministry. No doubt it had in a sense begun with the initiation of Swami Yogananda in Brindavan, but it grew into the most important function of her life only after her return from Kamarpukur.

Indeed, her own spiritual genius had by this time reached its fullest manifestation, thus fitting her to continue the Master's work of awakening the spiritual consciousness of others. On her return from Kamarpukur, her intimate companions like Yogin–Ma noticed that she had become remarkably indrawn, and that a rare loveliness that was not of this earth was radiating from her face. They had occasion to witness even more tangible signs of her spiritual power during her stay at Calcutta in 1888. Yogin–Ma records that she found her in the state of Samadhi while meditating on the roof of Balaram Babu's house. Describing her experience in that state, the Holy Mother said to Yogin–Ma, 'I found in that state that I had travelled into a distant country. Everybody there was very affectionate to me. My beauty was beyond description. Sri Ramakrishna also was there. With great tenderness they made me sit by his side. I cannot describe to you the nature of that ecstatic joy. When my mind came down from that exalted mood, I found my body lying there. I thought, 'How can I possibly enter into this ugly body?' I could not at all persuade my mind to do so. After a long while, it did, and the body became conscious again.'

Another day she was meditating in the house of Nilambar Mukherji along with Yogin–Ma and

Golap–Ma. After finishing her meditation, Yogin–Ma looked at the Mother and found her seated motionless as before, absorbed in deep meditation. It took a long time for her mind to come down to physical consciousness, and when it actually regained traces of it, she began to say, 'O Yogin where are my hands? Where are my feet?' Yogin–Ma pressed her limbs and said to her, 'Why, Mother, here are your hands and here your feet.' Still it took her considerable time to become conscious of her whole body. These experiences of hers show how her mind could at will transcend the body-consciousness. The second experience described above is interpreted by many as Nirvikalpa Samadhi.

She had also another unique vision about this time. She saw Sri Ramakrishna getting down into the Ganges and his whole body dissolving into the sacred waters of that river. Narendra (Swami Vivekananda) was taking that water and sprinkling it on innumerable people with the cry, 'Glory unto Ramakrishna!' The vision created so vivid an impression on her mind that for long she felt hesitation in stepping into the Ganges with which the Master's body had become one. It also helped to fill her mind with a sense of purpose in life, which she seemed to have lost after the Master's demise. She now felt convinced that physical death did not mean discontinuity of life for the Master. He lived in his mission and he worked through those whom he made his instruments in its fulfilment. As one of the principal persons whom he had commissioned with the responsibilities of the future, she felt her life was meant to serve a great purpose.

This vision of hers synchronized more or less with the inauguration of the great preaching activities of Swami Vivekananda, and was symbolic of the wide dissemination in future of the spiritual power that the Master had brought into this world. It may also be noted in passing that with this impetus given by Swami Vivekananda to the spread of the Master's message, her own part in the propagation of it became increasingly patent; for large numbers of people began to flock to her for initiation and advice, and she became the centre of attraction for spiritual aspirants hailing from different parts of the world. But before taking up the subject of her spiritual ministry, it is necessary to consider another phase of her life that runs parallel to it, namely , her dealings with the members of her family. ❑

---

1. The special reason for the pecuniary difficulties of the Holy Mother at this time was the withdrawal of the allowance of rupees seven that she used to get from the temple management. This amount was what used to be given to Sri Ramakrishna according to the settlement made by Rani Rasamani, and after the Master's demise, Trailokya Nath, the then proprietor of the temple, continued to pay the amount to the Holy Mother for a time. But now, owing to the conspiracy of Dinanath, the chief manager of the temple, and of some of Holy Mother's own relatives who had become offended with her for petty reasons, the allowance was stopped, and she was left in her widowhood without any independent income, apart from the charity of others. The relative chiefly responsible for this was none other than Ramlal, the nephew of the Master. Towards the close of his life the Master had told Ramlal with reference to the Holy Mother: 'See that your aunt stays at Kamarpukur,' to which Ramlal replied indifferently: 'She will stay wherever she likes.' This indifference he now put into practice by active persecution of the Holy Mother in the manner described above. Narendranath (later Swami Vivekananda) pleaded vehemently with the authorities of the temple to continue the allowance but his pleadings were unheeded.

2. The pet name (the shortened form of 'Gadadhar') by which Sri Ramakrishna was known in his boyhood.

3. Panchatapa means 'austerity of the five fires.' The aspirant lights four fires, each seven feet apart in a rectangular formation. Sitting in their midst, with the burning sun above as the fifth fire, the aspirant practises prayer and meditation.

The Holy Mother seems to have performed this in order to get rid of some kind of psychic disturbance. The idea seems to have been suggested to her by a Nepalese nun, well versed in various esoteric practices. She met the nun at Banaras. Other experiences also confirmed her in this decision. During her days at Kamarpukur she used to see the figure of a girl of eleven or twelve years moving about her constantly. Sometimes the figure was of a Sannyasin with a beard, who insisted that she should perform Panchatapa. Whatever the exact nature of the vision, she consulted Yogin–Ma about it and both of them together decided to perform Panchatapa. About her practice of this austerity, the Holy Mother said, 'Fires were made on four sides with cowdung cakes, and there was the intense heat of the sun above. After finishing bath in the morning I came near the fire and saw it burning brightly. I was seized with much fear. I wondered how I could enter the place and sit there until sunset. Then as I sat there repeating the name of the Master, I felt that the fire had no heat. I practised it for seven days. It made my complexion dark like ash. After that I did not again see that figure of the little girl or of the Sannyasin.'

13. IN THE SETTING OF DOMESTIC LIFE

IN THE LATTER part of her life, whenever the Holy Mother left Calcutta for the village, she spent her time mostly in her parental home at Jayrambati, and not at Kamarpukur. Indeed, since her return from the latter place after about nine months' stay, her visits to it were few and far between. No doubt, throughout her life she held Kamarpukur in great esteem as being the Master's birthplace, and she was very enthusiastic over the idea of building a temple there in his memory. She also considered herself to be a native of that village always. For example, when, in the course of the performance of religious rites at Banaras, the priests asked the name of her village, she gave it as Kamarpukur. The Master had once said to her, 'One may beg food from others, but still one must not live at another's house. Don't pull down your humble cottage at Kamarpukur, however great might be the respect with which the devotees receive you in their homes.' And following the Master's advice, all through her life she bore the expenses of repairing and maintaining the cottage

ᙏ Udbodhan House ᘓ

ॐ Swami Saradananda ☙

In the Setting of Domestic Life

at Kamarpukur that had come down to her through him.

In spite of all this, Kamarpukur ceased to be her main rural home. Between April 1888, the date of her return to Calcutta at the invitation of devotees, and 1897, she is known to have visited Kamarpukur ten times,[1] and from this last date onwards she does not seem to have visited it at all. There were probably several reasons for her shifting from Kamarpukur. To some enquiries in later days, she said that Kamarpukur being too closely associated with the Master, it pained her to stay there in his absence. To a young devotee who attended on her, she said: 'After the Master's passing away I moved about here and there for some time. Then I went to live at Kamarpukur. But my relatives (meaning the nephew Ramlal and others) seemed to be indifferent towards me. The people of the village too were a high-handed lot. So my mother took me to Jayrambati and did not allow me to live at Kamarpukur any more.'

While loneliness and indifference of relatives formed the immediate cause of her gravitating towards Jayrambati, there was another reason for her permanent shift after 1897 till her demise in 1920. That was the domestic situation in her parental home and her intimate connection with the lives and fortunes of the members of that family. We have already seen that the Holy Mother's parental family consisted of her four younger brothers—Prasanna Kumar, Barada Prasad, Kali Kumar and Abhay Charan, who were all called 'uncles' by devotees in general. Being the eldest, the

Holy Mother had borne much of the responsibility for these brothers of hers, and therefore there was naturally a strong tie of affection uniting her with them. None of them had any of the great spiritual qualities that distinguished the Holy Mother, but grew just into ordinary men of the world, and some of them probably represented an extreme type of them. Moreover none of them prospered in life.

The good sister that she was, the Holy Mother was interested in the welfare of these brothers, and they, too realizing the warm feeling that she had towards them, always leaned upon her even after they were grown up men. And, as it frequently happens when people are not sufficiently well off in life, they tried their best to realize their sister's love in terms of rupees and paise, especially in her later days when her devoted disciples began to send money to her. There was, therefore, a regular rivalry among these 'uncles', as her brothers were called, in the matter of extracting the best they could from her, even to the extent of causing her worry and annoyance. But with that remarkable patience for which she was noted, she bore it all without a murmur and did whatever she could for their worldly welfare. Moreover, whenever she was in Jayrambati, she practically looked after the whole internal management of their household. She would not allow her aged mother to do any work, and the wives of her brothers were at first too young to take up any serious responsibility. Thus she boiled and husked the paddy, cooked for them and sometimes even looked after their children. In fact she exerted herself so much for their welfare that Girish

Ghosh once remarked that these brothers of Holy Mother must have performed tremendous austerities in their previous births to have merited so much attention from their divine sister.

After the death of Syamasundari Devi in 1906, the Holy Mother became practically the mistress of the family. But she found that, with the growth of their families, the 'uncles' were developing their own separate interests to the neglect of the common family, and that this was leading to endless bickering and quarrels among them. Finally, as the only way to restore peace, she asked Swami Saradananda to come over to her village and arrange for the partition of their ancestral properties. It was on 23rd March, 1909 that the Swami arrived at Jayrambati on this work. To arbitrate at a partition is never a pleasant duty for any one, much less for a highly spiritual personage like the Swami. But he considered it both a privilege and a blessing to be of service to the Holy Mother and to carry out any of her commands. Possessed as he was of great powers of mental detachment, he spent much of his time in talking about the Master and in editing Swami Vivekananda's Jnana Yoga, while attending simultaneously to the demarcating of landed properties and mediating in the bitter quarrels that arose in the course of partition among the 'uncles.' For example, all the documents were in the custody of uncle Kali. Uncle Prasanna, however, thought that he had an equal right to be their custodian, and in the course of a sitting of the parties concerned in the partition, he tried to snatch them away from his brother's hands. This resulted in a scuffle between them, and Swami Saradananda had to come between them before they could separate and resume their seats. Under the able arbitration of the Swami, the bickerings of the parties were finally silenced and the partition of all the properties, including houses and lands, was effected. The Holy Mother was at that time asked where she would like to stay at Jayrambati after the partition. Her reply was: 'The Master used to say, "Rats make holes and thus provide places for snakes to live in." I shall stay a few days with Prasanna, a few days with Kali and so on.' In fact, until a new cottage with a thatched roof and mud walls was built for her in 1915, she used to stay mostly with Prasanna Kumar, the eldest of the brothers. She did so because this brother had by his first wife two young daughters, Nalini and Maku, and his second wife was too young to bring them up. The Holy Mother took up the responsibility of these two young girls, and in later days one found them always in the group of relatives who formed her train when she moved from one place to another.

Partition, however, did not stop the rivalries among the brothers. For the Holy Mother was to them a common property still, and they indulged in mutual recrimination over real or supposed attempts that one or the other was making to get money from her. The way in which they worried her and her reactions to their conduct will be best illustrated by a few incidents recorded by her disciples.

On one occasion the Holy Mother arrived at Jayrambati with some disciples. One of them said to her, 'Mother, did you notice how your brothers behaved

In the Setting of Domestic Life 133

towards you? They did not even send a man to receive you when you returned to the village.' The Mother thereupon said to one of her brothers, "Why did you not send a man to help me cross the river? My children (referring to the disciples) accompanied me. You did not go yourself, nor did you send a man.' The brother replied, 'Sister, I did not do so for fear of Kali (the next brother). He might complain that I was trying to win you over to my side. Do I not know what a priceless treasure you are? But I am helpless. Please bless me that I may have you as my sister in my future births also. I do not want anything else.' To this the Mother replied, 'Do you think that I shall be born again in your family? I have had enough of it this time. To be your sister again! My father was a great devotee of Rama, and my mother was compassion incarnate. Therefore I was born in this family.'

Once, disgusted with the brothers' endless demands for money, the Holy Mother remarked, 'They always ask only for money. Did they ever ask, even unknowingly, for devotion and knowledge?'[1]

One day at about 10 a.m. she was seated at the edge of the outer verandah of her house. Suddenly her two brothers, Kali and Barada, began to quarrel about a hedge put up by the former and were nearly coming to blows. The Holy Mother, unable to witness the quarrel any longer, went herself to pacify them. She was much agitated. Now she would blame the one, and now she would restrain the other. After a while a disciple of hers and some others intervened and the brothers entered their respective homes still abusing each other. The

Mother also went into her house. She was still in an agitated mood, but as soon as she took her seat, she burst into laughter and said, 'What an illusion Mahamaya has created! Here is this infinite world, and what one calls one's own possession will be left behind at death. It is a wonder that men cannot see this simple truth.' So saying she laughed again, the laughter continuing for some time.

Among the brothers of the Holy Mother the most brilliant one, in fact the hope of the family, was Abhay Charan, the youngest; but in the end it so happened that owing to him she came to be burdened with very heavy responsibilities. Abhay Charan, while qualifying to be doctor, suddenly died of cholera in 1899, leaving behind his widow, Surabala, who was expecting a child. On his death-bed he said to the Holy Mother, 'Hereafter you look after them' (meaning his wife and the child that was to be born). Abhay was the youngest and most beloved of the Holy Mother's brothers. His unexpected death left her very sad, but the fate of his wife gradually began to cause her greater anxiety. For, this terrible calamity that befell her, augmented by the immediate demise of her grandmother and aunt, unhinged the mind of poor Surabala. In February, 1900, while she was still in that state of mind, she gave birth to a daughter who was given the name of Radharani and came to be more familiarly called as Radhu or Radhi. The loss of her husband, the strain of motherhood, and to add to these, fright caused by an attempted burglary in their house about this time, all together made poor Surabala completely insane. The question of bringing up the new born babe became a serious problem for the family. Remembering the words of her dying brother and seeing also the utterly helpless condition of his wife and baby, the Holy Mother felt the new responsibility as her own. She made arrangements for a nurse to assist the insane lady in rearing up the baby and came back to Calcutta, but she could get no peace of mind thinking of the possible harm that might befall Radhu from the neglect and eccentricity of her mother. 'One evening,' she said, 'I was worshipping in the shrine, when suddenly a veil was lifted before my vision like a curtain on the stage. I saw that in our country home Radhu was being subjected to great suffering. She was being given a few grains of puffed rice for her food. She was eating them as she rolled in the dust in the open courtyard. Radhu's mother tied her arm with threads of red, blue and other colours, just like a lunatic. I saw that other children in the family were well taken care of. At this condition of Radhu, I felt choked like a person whose head is pressed under water. I clearly felt that such would be her fate, if I did not take care of her.'

This, as the Holy Mother said later on, was the moment when Mahamaya, the great world-illusionist, seized her in her clutches; for from that time onwards Radhu became for her a source of passionate attachment, a veritable obsession in life, until towards her last days she cut this bond of affection by the power of her own discriminative faculty.

After the vision of Radhu's misery, the Holy Mother went to Jayrambati at once and took direct charge of her. Since then she never allowed Radhu to be parted from her. As her disciples noticed, she could not relish food without Radhu, and she felt her sleep disturbed unless Radhu was by her side. So strong was the bond of affection with which she came to be tied to this girl all of a sudden. In fact, she assumed the role of her mother and Radhu, too, came to look upon her as such, her own mother being addressed by her as Neri-Ma.

In course of time Radhu and her mother became the greatest source of trouble and worry to the Holy Mother. The amount of trouble and anxiety to which both these subjected her[1] would have driven even the fondest of earthly mothers to desperation and indifference. Surabala, Radhu's mother, was in the first place jealous of the Holy Mother for she found her only daughter loved the Holy Mother more than herself. Her insane imagination, therefore, discovered various evil motives in the Holy Mother's love of Radhu and with these in mind, she would abuse her in season and out of season before others. Whenever the Holy Mother put Radhu under medical treatment for her frequently recurring ailments, Surabala charged her with attempting to kill her daughter with drugs. Once, in an outburst of temper, she attacked the Holy Mother with a thick fire-brand from the oven, and only the timely intervention of some disciples saved her from serious injury. On another occasion Surabala fancied that her son-in-law had been drowned, and created a row in the family. Once she went with Radhu's ornaments to a greedy relative, who taking advantage of her helpless condition, deprived her of all the valuables, so that the Holy Mother had to intercede, and with great difficulty restore them to her. When the persecutions of this mad woman became unbearable, the Holy Mother would remark, 'Perhaps I worshipped Siva with Bilva leaves having thorns. Therefore I have got this thorn in life.'

Only on one point there was method in Surabala's madness, and that was in respect of her belief that all the money or other property that came to the Holy Mother would ultimately go to Radhu. So, it is said, when the Udbodhan Office was built as the Mother's Calcutta residence, she was delighted. Nothing pained her and upset her so much as seeing the Holy Mother make presents to others. Thus once at Banaras she severely reproached her for her liberality, whereupon the Holy Mother said to her, 'My nature is that of a child. Can I calculate so much? I give to him who seeks.'

If Radhu's mother was a thorn on the Holy Mother's side, her daughter was no less so. As she grew up, she proved herself to be weak in both body and mind. Physically she was always ailing, and mentally she was a moron. Indeed, there was a simplicity about her then as well as in her more mature years, but that was no compensation for her utter lack of understanding and discrimination. Obstinate, petulant, eccentric and intractable, she could not in the least be rectified by all the love and attention that the Holy Mother bestowed on her. Realizing this, the Holy Mother remarked sorrowfully one day, 'See how much I am entangled with Radhu! How well has Gaurdasi trained her girl and I have created a monkey!' Radhu did, indeed, love the Holy Mother very much, but for one of her temperament and level of understanding, love only meant sanction for taking extreme liberties in one's dealings with the object of love. Thus she disobeyed the Holy Mother, flouted her before others, got irritated with her for no reason whatever, abused and cursed her unsparingly, threw objects at her recklessly, kicked her, spat at her, and spoke and did things that would exhaust the patience of any other human being.

In June, 1911, the Holy Mother arranged for Radhu's marriage. But even long after the marriage Radhu would not go to her husband's house. So both she and her husband would stay mostly in the Mother's household. Even though she was now quite grown up, she continued to be of the same nature as before, and her behaviour towards the Holy Mother in no way improved. In fact, a few years later, when she was an expectant mother, she was almost on the verge of insanity. Her insolence and intractability were now at their zenith, and her general health too was very poor. It was a very anxious time for the Holy Mother. She adopted every measure, both medical and occult, for the safety of Radhu before and after delivery. Radhu came out safe through the ordeal, but that did not in any way improve matters. For she continued to be ailing in both body and mind, and the Holy Mother had, with the utmost difficulty, to find enough money for her care and treatment. Her own health was fast declining and she was approaching her end which took place about two years later, but yet it was now that she was called upon to face what was perhaps the most anxious and worrying situation in her life. The following pages from

In the Setting of Domestic Life

a disciple's diary will amply illustrate it and show her reactions to the same:

'Radhu's baby was now six months old, but still Radhu could not stand up because of weakness. She could only crawl about. Further, she became addicted to taking opium. The Holy Mother too was of late not keeping well, and was having occasional attacks of fever. She had been trying to wean Radhu from her opium habit. But Radhu was very insistent. That morning the Holy Mother was dressing vegetables, when Radhu came for opium. The Holy Mother understood it and said to her, "Radhi, you have had enough of this. Why don't you stand up? It is impossible for me to take care of you any longer. For your sake I have lost my devotion and everything. Can you tell me how I can possibly meet all your expenses?" At these words Radhu became very angry. She took from the vegetable basket a big egg-plant and threw it with great force at the Holy Mother. It stuck her with a thud and she curved her back in pain. Immediately a swelling appeared on the spot. She looked at the photograph of the Master with folded hands and said, "Lord, please forgive her misdemeanour; for she is senseless." Then she took the dust of her own feet, put it on the head of Radhu and said, "Radhi, the Master did not even once utter a word of remonstrance towards this body, and you afflict it so much. How can you understand where my place is ? You think nothing of me, because I live with you all." At these words Radhu burst into tears.

'A few days before, a devotee from Bangalore had spent some days with Holy Mother at Koalpara. He gave her a good sum of money for Radhu's expenses, and while leaving Koalpara said to her, "Mother, whenever you need money for your expenses, please inform me without the slightest hesitation." At Jayrambati her expenses increased a great deal. Swami Saradananda had written to her that, as he had to procure money from here and there, he found it difficult to supply her monthly expenses regularly. At this the Holy Mother said to the disciple, "I think Sarat has not much money to spare, otherwise he won't write like that. The other day, the devotee from Bangalore promised to send money. But how can I write to him for it? Shall I not be able to fulfil the last injunction of the Master? Look here, Radhi, I am going to lose everything for your sake! The Master said to me, "Well , don't stretch out your hand to anybody even for a paisa. You shall never lack simple food and clothing. If you beg a person even for a paisa, remember, you will be selling your head to him." '

Radhu and her mother always formed an inseparable part of the Holy Mother's retinue, whether she was in Calcutta or Jayrambati. Besides, there were also the daughters of Prasanna Kumar—Nalini and Maku,—of whom the former was unhappily married and the latter had a husband who was too poor to maintain her. They, too, therefore depended on the Holy Mother and mostly stayed with her. These girls, together with some of the young sons of her brothers, who always preferred their kind aunt to their own mothers, also formed a part of her household and often moved with her from Jayrambati to Calcutta and back. And, of course, when she was in the village, there were also her brothers, who, though loving, were always bent upon extracting whatever they could from her. The selfishness of the brothers, the mutual jealousy of the nieces, Nalini's mania for ceremonial purity, the perversity of Radhu and the insanity of Radhu's mother—all these together combined to produce a tangled domestic situation, in the intolerable atmosphere of which the Mother had to carry on her self-chosen duty without demur, with her matchless patience and divine forbearance as the forces sustaining her in all these trials. It was in such a domestic context that the Holy Mother found herself in the latter part of her life. Her conversations, recorded in the book *The Gospel of the Holy Mother*, give a realistic picture of her calm, innocent and dignified personality, as it appeared against this distracting background, and show also how, placed in such a situation, she none the less proved a source of spiritual inspiration to hundreds of people who looked to her for guidance and counsel.

It may not be out of place now to consider certain possible questions that may arise in the reader's mind with reference to the Holy Mother's domestic life described above. According to Indian traditions of ascetic life, a spiritual personage, whether man or woman, is supposed to snap the bond of that special love and affection that one ordinarily has for one's kith and kin. This being so, what justification can be offered for the Holy Mother having maintained her family connections till the end? Even if that is in any sense justifiable, how is one to reconcile her spiritual greatness with the intense attachment that she evinced in her love of Radhu? For a spiritual person is supposed to have no attachment to anything in this world. Questions of this kind are sure to arise in one's mind when one studies the domestic relations of the Holy Mother. It is therefore necessary to examine them in detail and find out their true significance.

In the first place, the Indian tradition that requires one to snap one's connection with one's family and circle of relative is applicable only in the case of Sannyasins (monks)—men who take to the fourth order of life with the usual Vedic rituals. Now the Holy Mother did not belong to the monastic order, although her life was an object-lesson in the essential principles of monastic life, namely, purity and renunciation. Her spiritual life was a natural growth, without the least influence of any kind of institutionalism. Like any other woman, she grew up in her parental home amidst many relatives, came later to associate with her husband's family, discharged her duties to all without any consideration of self, and by virtue of her own endowments and contact with her divine husband, advanced spiritually in the midst of her domestic environment. In other words, there was in her case no break between domestic life and spiritual life, and thus she felt no conflict between the ethics of the house and that of spiritual life. As a member of the family all through life, she did but perform one of her prime duties when she tried to be of some help to her poor relatives.

But even in the discharge of her domestic functions, her conduct had a remarkable feature that elevates even her worldly activity to the borderland of the highest ideal of spiritual ethics. There is no worldly love without some expectation of return. Only, in the mother's love for the offspring, perhaps, there is a large element of pure disinterestedness. But even here considerations of deriving benefits from children in future often play an important part. Thus, to love a person when that person can offer nothing in return, is itself extremely rare in this world; it is much more so when the object of love gives only kicks and abuses in return for the endless troubles and worries courted on his or her behalf. A given example of love may look apparently worldly from an examination of its setting, but if in point of disinterestedness and self-abnegation it fulfils the condition mentioned last, then one cannot help admiring it as a very high achievement of the human spirit, however alien it may be to the code of morality followed by a mere ascetic. For, a new quality, utterly absent in worldly love, has emerged in it, and by virtue of that quality it brings out all that is greatest and noblest in human nature.

The love of the Holy Mother for her relatives, it must be admitted, was of this order, even if one considers it to be of the worldly species because of its domestic associations. She had no direct responsibility for any of these relatives. Out of sheer goodness or a sense of pity she wanted to be of some service to them. Nor was there the least trace of any selfish consideration in her love. There was nothing she could expect from her brothers either in this life or in the next; much less from the eccentric Radhu or her insane mother. Extreme worry and torment were her only reward for all her solicitude. But even in the midst of it all, she went on with the discharge of her self-imposed responsibilities—calm, forgiving, sweet, loving, dignified and never forgetting the true principles of spiritual life. Her example in this respect sets before us the highest ideal of maternal love, which forms the basic virtue of domestic ethics and the one force that assures the stability of home life. For, in all other phases of love too, these elements of utter forgiveness and unselfish service, so characteristic of maternal love, are present in however small a degree, and it is by virtue of this alone that they become helpful in the domestication and, ultimately, in the spiritualization of the animal man. Therefore the home life of the Holy Mother, wherein we get a remarkable manifestation of unadulterated maternal love, becomes an integral part of her mission, and adds to the significance of her life to the vast majority of mankind. As she was immaculately pure and unselfish in the midst of all these worldly concerns, her domestic situation, which appears as a blemish to the ascetic code of ethics, only goes to enhance the spiritual worth and the ethical significance of her life.

The Holy Mother's attachment to Radhu requires also to be considered separately from her relation to the rest of her family; for, besides the ethical significance we have referred to above, it had also a spiritual purpose to serve in the fulfilment of her life's mission. We have already seen how, after the passing away of Sri Rama-krishna, the Holy Mother's mind used to dwell at a high spiritual level. The only purpose of life in the world

In the Setting of Domestic Life

which her pure and desireless mind had recognized till then was the service of the Master, and after he terminated his earthly existence, she found nothing in this world to live for. Now, a mind without desires of any kind cannot for long function through the body. Just like gold, which requires to be mixed with a certain percentage of baser metal before it can be made into ornaments, the mind too must have a modicum of worldly desires if it is to work on the physical plane. Otherwise it would be absorbed perpetually in Samadhi, and the body, in the absence of its proper unkeep, would soon disintegrate. Therefore in the life of Sri Ramakrishna we find that with the definite purpose of keeping the mind on the physical plane, he used to create by an effort of the will such harmless desires as love of association with pure souls or longing to partake of some particular sweetmeat. Now in the case of the Holy Mother too, in the absence of any worldly tie after the Master's passing away, there was a strong inclination to give up the body and seek perpetual union with the Divine. As Yogin-Ma and Golap-Ma, her companions, noticed, the phenomenon of Samadhi became more and more frequent with her, and if she were left without any worldly distraction, there was every possibility of her giving up the body early in life. But she had a particular mission to fulfil in continuation of the Master's life-work, and her body had, therefore, to be preserved until her work was over. The appearance of Radhu on the horizon of her life provided her with that element of worldly attachment necessary for the continuance of the body. In other words, love of Radhu was the mental ballast which held her consciousness at the physical level and thus helped her to minister to the spiritual needs of countless men and women.

This is not a mere fancy of her devotees, nor a theory improvised as an explanation of some unpleasant facts. It was the conviction she herself had arrived at on the strength of some very striking visions, partly premonitory in character. To quote her own words on this point: 'How the Master has entangled me through Radhu!... After the passing away of the Master, I did not at all relish anything in life. I became utterly indifferent to worldly things and kept on praying, "What shall I achieve by remaining in this world?" At that time I saw a girl ten or twelve years old, walking in front of me dressed in a red cloth. The Master pointed her out to me and said, "Cling to her as a support. Many children (disciples) will come to you." The next moment he disappeared. I did not see the girl any more. Later on I was seated in this very place (her house at Jayrambati). At that time Radhu's mother was stark mad. She was dragging some rags pressed under her arm, and Radhu crawled behind her weeping. Seeing this, I felt a peculiar sensation in my heart. At once I ran to Radhu and took her in my arms. I said to myself, "Well, if I do not look after this child, who else will take care of her? She has no father, and her mother is that insane woman." No sooner had I taken the child in my arms, than I saw the Master. He said, "This is that girl. Cling to her as your support, She is Yoga-maya, the illusive power." '

Indeed, even when the Holy Mother was alive, some of her intimate followers felt the contradiction

In the Setting of Domestic Life

between her attachment to Radhu and her position in life as a spiritual teacher. A disciple who felt this doubt in his mind once asked her plainly, 'Mother, why are you so much attached? Day and night you dote on Radhu like one entangled in wordliness.' The disciple had put the same question to her before and she had replied with her characteristic humility. 'You see, we are women; it is our nature to love our children.' But on this occasion she became excited and said, 'Where will you find another like me? Try to find one. You see, those who meditate intensely on the highest Reality become very subtle and pure in mind. Whatever they think with that mind, they think very intensely.[4] Therefore it appears to others like attachment. When lightning flashes, it is reflected in glass panes alone, not in wooden shutters.'

Once Yogin-Ma also felt a similar doubt about the Holy Mother. She thought, 'The Master was a man of such renunciation, and we see the Holy Mother behaving like a perfectly worldly person. Day and night she is restless about her brothers, nephews and nieces, I don't understand it.' Shortly after this doubt had arisen in her mind, she was one day meditating on the banks of the Ganges, when she saw in a vision the Master standing before her and saying, 'Look there! Don't you see something floating on the Ganges?' She saw a newborn baby, entangled in its entrails, being carried along by the current. The Master then said to her, 'Can anything ever make the Ganges impure? Can anything defile its waters?[5] Regard her (the Holy Mother) too in the same way. Never have any doubt about her.

Know that she and this (referring to himself) are identical.'

On these explanations of the Holy Mother's attachments, a critical mind may remark that, however good they may be in themselves, they are too subjective, and that, being of the nature of rationalization, they will be convincing only to her followers. The question will, therefore, be raised whether there are more objective considerations, distinguishing the Holy Mother's attachment from that of ordinary worldly people. The answer is, there are several such considerations, which we state in brief below:

(1) The disciples of the Holy Mother, who went to her with spiritual motives, no doubt, found her in the entanglements described in this chapter, but they found also that by association with her they themselves got rid of their worldly attachments and attained peace of mind. Several of them became monks, leaving hearth and home. How could this capacity of hers to infuse a spirit of renunciation into others be explained if we equate her attachment with the worldly attachment of ordinary people?

(2) In the case of worldly attachment we find that in proportion to one's love for a particular object, one's capacity to love others diminishes. Not only that, in pursuing the interests of such narrow and selfish love one often becomes greedy, calculating and callous to the interests of others. In the Holy Mother there was not the slightest trace of these. Renunciation, liberality and a childlike simplicity were second nature with her all through life. In fact her relatives complained that she

was too liberal with her possessions without any consideration for the future. And every one who moved closely with her found that while she doted on Radhu on the one hand, she also showed, on the other, an infinite capacity to shower sweet love and maternal tenderness on her disciples and devotees. As the Conversations in *The Gospel of the Holy Mother* amply show, no one could move with her without feeling that she was one's own mother and much more. In fact her heart was as broad as the ocean itself. The salt existing throughout the ocean may be a little concentrated in some particular area, but the very vastness of the ocean assures us that because of this concentration there is no diminution of its salinity elsewhere. So also the element of love permeating her limitless heart remained unaffected by the little concentration of it with reference to certain persons brought about by the special conditions of her life. In this respect the Holy Mother's attachments stand in striking contrast to the worldly attachments of ordinary people.

(3) Attachments always increase in intensity as one goes on cultivating them, and those who are subject to them gradually lose that power of will by which one could cut these bondages of the heart. In other words, attachment generally destroys the power of detachment. This is the rule with all worldly-minded persons. In contrast to this, the truly spiritual persons possess both the power of attachment and of detachment in an equal measure. His pure mind, whenever it takes up an undertaking, pursues it with the whole of its energy, and so also it can drop it without the least concern

when circumstances require it to do so. The Holy Mother too possessed this power of detachment in a remarkable degree. Two instances will illustrate the point.

The child of Maku, a niece of the Holy Mother, died of diphtheria at Jayrambati. In the interest of Radhu's health, the Holy Mother was then staying at the Koalpara Ashrama, situated about six miles from Jayrambati. Nera, as this child of Maku was called, was a favourite of the Holy Mother. She had made every possible arrangement for his proper treatment and nursing and was daily sending several messengers to get reports about his health. Finally, one afternoon the news of his death reached the Mother's ears. She was disconsolate and began to lament like an ordinary person. By and by it was dusk, the time for Aratrika (vespers) in the shrine. Because of the grief-stricken mood of the Holy Mother, none of the inmates of the Ashrama was disposed to do the worship. The Mother herself now got up, saying it was already late for Aratrika. Her sobbing stopped, and in a perfectly composed manner she did the worship and all the other evening duties of hers like the distribution of Prasad. For the rest of the evening she was found to be in a perfectly normal mood, and but for a few references to the excellent qualities of the child, she showed no sign of grief at all. This capacity to switch the mind from a paroxysm of grief to perfect composure is unthinkable in cases of real worldly attachment.

A still more striking example of her power of detachment is noticeable in her attitude towards Radhu during her last days. We have seen how for several years she had been doting on Radhu with an intensity of attachment that is unparalleled in worldly life. But she would say now and then, 'You see, my doting on Radhu is a delusion that I have super-imposed upon myself,' or 'My mind does not dwell on Radhu in the slightest degree. I force it on her. I pray to the Master, saying, "O Lord, please divert my mind a little to Radhu. Otherwise who will look after her?" ' The truth of these oft repeated statements of hers regarding her control even over this very intense form of attachment, was proved when she was on her death-bed. Generally the last days of a person's life, when he is fast sinking, are the times when his worldly attachments and desires express themselves with the greatest force. But in the Holy Mother's case we find that at this critical time she detached her mind completely from Radhu.[6] Worldly people generally like their beloved ones to be by them during their last moments. But the Holy Mother, who could not till then sleep without Radhu by her side, asked her attendants again and again to send Radhu and her cousins back to Jayrambati. Even when their little children approached her bed, she would ask them to be taken away from her, saying that she had once for all detached her mind from them, and that their presence by her side was even repugnant to her.[7]

These considerations are enough to make one pause and think, in place of jumping to any hasty conclusion regarding the worldly relationship of the Holy Mother. The more one ponders over it, the more is one struck with wonder at the strange synthesis of human interest and divine grandeur in her life. To the common man and woman this aspect of the Holy Mother's life has an added interest and appeal. For faced as they are with similar domestic problems, they would recognize in her a fellow-sharer of the woes of life and an exemplar of the way in which one should face them. Is it possible for one with domestic responsibilities to practise devotional life? That is a question which comes to all spiritually inclined persons who have worldly duties and responsibilities to fulfil. The Holy Mother's life is both a striking and a hope-inspiring answer to this question. Her worldly relationships constitute, as it were, the foil against which the brilliance of her spirituality gains an added significance. ❑

---

1. The Holy Mother visited Kamarpukur subsequently on the following occasions according to notes left by Master Mahashaya; end of October, 1890; in February and in July 1891; in July 1892; in January and in July, 1893; in May and in November 1895; in May and in September-October of 1897.

2. Uncle Kali once did go to the Holy Mother with such a prayer. He got a sharp reprimand one day from Girish Ghosh for his worldliness which made him look to the Mother only for monetary gains and never for spiritual advancement. Smarting under the wordy whips of Girish Ghosh, Kali approached the Mother in a reverential attitude, but the Mother put him off with the words, 'O dear Kali, what are you doing? I am the same good old sister of yours.' The worldly-minded uncle was satisfied with this, and never bothered her for higher things any more.

These brothers tried in every way to squeeze money from the Mother. Of the three, Kali with his grave countenance and eyes that got red when annoyed, was feared by every one in the family, especially the 'mad group.' He was equally avaricious. When festive celebrations had to be organised on Jagaddhatri Pooja or on the Master's or the Mother's birthday, Kali expected himself to be put in charge of them. It meant for him substantial income by way of commission in making purchases for feeding large numbers of people. The Mother for the sake of peace in the

… family group often entrusted him with such duties. This pleased him very much, but any interference with him would make him cross. Once on such an occasion he struck work for some silly reason, and by not going for food till evening, made the Mother starve the whole day.

Just in front of the Mother's house was a small plot owned by the whole family. There on the spot where the Mother was born, some devotees wanted to erect a tablet and got the stones for the same, but they could not proceed further, as the uncles would not forfeit their claims. On the same plot Sri Narayana Iyengar of Bangalore, wanted to dig a well for the Mother's use. Referring to these matters, Kali was one day speaking to Brahmachari Varada, revealing his plans and expectations: 'Narayana Iyengar of Bangalore, who is a disciple of my sister, came here the other day and promised to dig a well on our land in front of sister's house. But now he is quite silent about it. He is a well-to-do man. If he digs the well it will benefit many. And as for the price of the land, it is not so much after all. He can easily spare the money, if he has a mind to. To be able to provide for sister's drinking water—it is no small stroke of good fortune!' What the clever uncle had in mind was to knock off a few thousand rupees from Sri Iyengar for a tiny plot of land which he could not put to any use. The uncle continued; 'Mind you, Varada, if sister saved all the money she got as gift, it would come to a good amount. But on the contrary she spends everything for her brothers and Radhi. She does not amass anything. Can you say to whom she gives most?' As Brahmachari Varada kept quite, the greedy uncle changed the topic.

Referring to the same topic, uncle Kali said one day sitting in the porch of his house with the Mother, 'How long have these two stones been lying here! They have not been fixed in sister's birth place. How joyous would it be, if with Sarat Maharaj's consent, that plot is purchased and a temple put up. As for my share, Sarat Maharaj may pay as he thinks fit. I can transfer it here and now. As for the rest, you may persuade them.' Now in the small plot held jointly, uncle Kali's portion could not be put to any use, while the portions of the other brothers were under joint cultivation. Realising this situation, Kali now wanted to withdraw his original opposition to parting with his land, and his plan now was to get the maximum price for his useless plot. Till now nothing could be done to execute Sri Narayana Iyengar's proposal to dig a well there because of Kali's opposition. So the Mother now asked Brahmachari Varada to write to Swami Saradananda about Kali's changed attitude. When Kali was informed of this next day, the uncle came out with his condition. 'But, sister, I shall have to be paid something over and above the price that is agreed upon. My family is large and my income small.' Finally all the brothers demanded and got something more than their share of the total value fixed on the land. Swami Saradananda then took up the project of sinking the well. The above will give an idea of what the 'uncles' were like.

3. In the companion volume 'The Gospel of the Holy Mother' plenty of instances of this will be found.

4. This was true of Sri Ramakrishna also. Whenever he thought of doing a thing, he would be restless until he accomplished it. In his love of young disciples like Swami Vivekananda, there was an intensity unknown in worldly love. When he was separated from them for long, he felt that his heart was being squeezed like a wet towel.

5. According to Hindu belief the Ganges is holy under all conditions, however dirty and polluted it may appear from outside. There is also a chemical property inherent in the water of the Ganges, corresponding to this religious belief about it. One can keep its water even from the Hooghly near Calcutta, where it is most polluted, for any number of years; it will never get spoiled like ordinary water. Pilgrims who carry Ganges water to their homes keep it for years. Chemical examination of the Ganges water has shown that it has the property of destroying various germs in a short time.

6. For interesting details on this subject, see chap. 19.

7. To impress still more clearly the difference between the Holy Mother's attitude of mind and true worldly attachment, we draw the reader's attention to the Puranic story of the pious king Bharata. In his last days the king was living the life of a recluse, renouncing his kingdom and spending his whole time in the contemplation of the Divine. But his mind gradually got attached to a young deer which had been rescued by him from danger and was being brought up as his pet. In spite of years spent in holy living, the attachment for the deer manifested itself in all its intensity during his last moments, and he died with his mind full of anxious thoughts about its future welfare. Consequently he had to be reborn in lower levels of existence. The utter purity, non-attachment and spiritual grandeur of the Holy Mother shine vividly by the side of this example.

14. HER SPIRITUAL MINISTRY

THE ULTIMATE SPIRITUAL Principle is often described as a harmony of contradictions. Thus the Upanishads indicate it as permanence behind the impermanent, as unity in multiplicity, as sentienty amidst the insentient. It is the cause of the world, but the world neither exhausts nor contaminates It. Everything subsists in It, but not It in them. Multiplicity has its basis in It, but it fails to destroy Its unity, just as the poison in the fangs of a snake does not affect the snake itself.

The life of every great spiritual personage is an approximation to this cosmic mystery. The true spiritual type marks, as it were, the borderland between humanity and Divinity. Or rather it is Divinity manifesting Itself through the frailties of humanity—God playing the game of hide and seek through the curtain of human personality, now appearing only as man, and the next moment revealing something of His transcendent glory. Such personages are in the world, but not of it.

There seem to be two phases in the character and activities of such personages, intertwined no doubt, but sufficiently distinguishable by the stress that the one or the other receives according to time and circumstances. On the one side they look quite human and their activities resemble those of worldly men. But unaffected by this aspect, there exists in them another strand so different from anything in the common run of men, carrying with it a sanctifying influence that dissipates the darkness of ignorance from those who come in contact with them. In spite of the apparent conflict between these two phases of life, they coexist in perfect harmony in such great men, adding significance to their lives from the view-points of pure spiritual aspirants as well as of those who are in quest of worldly ideals. Such has been the case with some of the great incarnations like Rama and Krishna mentioned in Hindu scriptures.

In the life of the Holy Mother, too, this analysis holds good. In the latter part of her life, we see her surrounded by two distinct types of people—her relatives on the one hand and her disciples on the other. These two groups approached her with quite different motives, the first to gain whatever material advantages they could from her, and the second to serve her and benefit spiritually by her contact. In the preceding chapter her dealings with her relatives have been considered in brief, and in the present one her relations with those who went to her for spiritual illumination will be dealt with. It is, however, pertinent to inquire how she could fulfil both these apparently incongruous duties without detriment to either. Could it be that there were two watertight compartments in her personality, so that the spiritual side could remain

Her Spiritual Ministry

uncontaminated by worldly dealings? Ultimately this is a riddle which shades off into the mystery of the Deity—the question how He manifests Himself as the world and yet retains His pristine purity.

A harmonious mingling of the human and the divine is what gives charm and depth to the Incarnations of Divinity, and the Holy Mother was no exception to this. The one or the other of these aspects may impress a particular observer and incline him to give a one-sided picture, which may not be incorrect but is incomplete. Divinity does not preclude human excellences and limitations. Coexistence of the two without contradictions in an inextricable texture of personality-pattern is what it implies. The order of Nature has got its own course, its life patterns, which all embodied beings, including divine personages, are subject to. Thus Sri Ramakrishna says in *Kathamrita:* 'When God incarnates Himself as man, He has to behave just like any other human being. That is why it is difficult to recognise Him. He has all these—hunger, thirst, disease, sorrow, and oftentimes fear—just as men have.' In the midst of this they have the awareness of their divinity—faintly sometimes and vividly at others,—and are able, by the exercise of their will, to impart spirituality to aspirants and awaken even the spiritually dead. The life incidents of the Holy Mother recorded here and particularly the picture of her painted in the *'Gospel of the Holy Mother,'* will give a clear idea of the intermingling of these two sides of her nature, the divine and the human.

Was the Holy Mother herself aware of her own divinity, and if so, to what extent—is a question that will arise in the mind of any student of her life. It will therefore be relevant to give some statements of hers on this point. Off and on she is said to have made such statements as: 'The wisdom of God is in the palm of my hand. I can have it whenever I want;' 'In the midst of worldly activities, whenever I desire, I understand with a flash that all this is nothing but a play of Mahamaya;' 'Don't regard me as your relative; I can leave this body at once if I desire;' 'No one will be able to know my real nature so long as I am alive,' etc.

In contrast to this, when her niece Nalini's infant Neda died, she wailed like any ordinary woman. A devotee from Mysore, Sri Narayana Iyengar, asked her, 'Why did you cry like an ordinary mortal at the death of Neda?' The answer was: 'I am in the world, and have to taste the fruits of the tree. That is why I cry.' In some contrast to this there is another conversation of her depicting both sides of her nature. She said: 'People call me goddess, and I too am led to think so. Or how could you explain all the strange things that have happened in my life? Yogin and Golap know much of this. I should but think, "Let this happen" or "I shall eat this," the Lord somehow fulfils these.' A Brahmacharin was once reading letters to her. In one of these a woman had praised the mother as a goddess. At this the Mother remarked: 'Sometimes it sets me thinking that since I am merely the daughter of Ram Mukherji and there are many others of my age at Jayrambati, how can I differ from them. Devotees come to pay their respects from places unknown to anybody here. On questioning them I find they are men of importance like magistrates and lawyers. Why do these come at all?' To make her talk out, the Brahmacharin asked her: 'Well, don't you always remember your real nature?' The Mother replied: 'Can that always be so? How then could all this work be done? But even in the midst of work, whenever I want, I can get the inspiration with a little thought and thus the play of the great Maya stands revealed.'

In the case of the Holy Mother, however, even this abstract distinction between these two aspects of her mental life will have to be based on an underlying unity in their essence in so far as both of them are the expressions of the great principle of motherhood of which her whole life is a revelation. In our review of her domestic life, we have shown how the impelling force behind even her worldly attachments was her sense of motherhood—a form of love that only gives but never thinks of any return, nay, gives even when any return takes the shape of ingratitude and persecution—and how for this reason, even her worldly love bordered on pure spirituality. In her role as a spiritual teacher, too, it is the very same principle of motherhood that is illustrated, perhaps through a medium that reveals the true quality of it, with greater directness.

According to Hindu religious ideals, the relation between the disciple and the Guru (spiritual preceptor) is the most intimate and sacred. The disciple is expected to see in the Guru a channel through which divine mercy manifests itself for his redemption and, as such, to put implicit faith in his words and obey his commands without questioning. This exalted conception of the Guru entertained by the disciple makes the work of the former a very responsible one. He must be a man of great spiritual attainments, should know the purport of the Scriptures, and must be guided only by love and mercy for suffering humanity in the matter of accepting anyone as a disciple. There must be absolutely no commercial motive. He may, no doubt, accept whatever gifts a disciple offers in love and reverence, but they should never be an incentive to his spiritual ministry. He must be more like a parent—only much nobler than any parent we ordinarily come across in the world— interested mainly in giving to the loved one, not in receiving any corresponding advantage from him.

Such being the conception of the Guru among the Hindus, there have been few so qualified as the Holy Mother for discharging the onerous responsibilities connected with it. By virtue of her long preparation for this work under Sri Ramakrishna, the direct command he had given her to continue his spiritual mission and her own great spiritual attainments, she was eminently fitted to play the role of a Guru. Besides these qualifications, it was her inherent quality of motherhood, which blossomed to its full proportions about this period— rendering her so selfless, forgiving, kind and anxious to serve,—that distinguished her among the great spiritual teachers of the world.

The idea will be clear if one remembers her own words on the responsibilities she undertook when she initiated anybody as a disciple. 'The power of the Guru is transmitted through the Mantra to the disciple,' she said once. 'That is why at the time of initiation the Guru

Her Spiritual Ministry

takes on himself the sins of the disciple and suffers so much from physical maladies. It is extremely difficult to be a Guru for he has to take the responsibilities for the disciple's sins. He is affected by them. A good disciple, however, helps the teacher. Some disciples make quick progress, and some do it slowly. It depends on the tendencies of the mind acquired by one's past deeds. That is why Rakhal (Swami Brahmananda) hesitates about giving initiation. He said to me, "Mother, as soon as I initiate a disciple, I feel physically ill. The very mention of the Mantra makes me feel feverish." '

Probably for the above reason, Swami Brahmananda used to be very sparing in the matter of giving initiation. Hence the vast majority of devotees who sought initiation were sent to the Holy Mother. For, as far as she was concerned, her motherly love and tenderness for all never allowed any such consideration of personal suffering to stand in the way of giving refuge to those who went to her. Referring to this quality of the Holy Mother, Swami Premananda once said, 'We are sending to the Holy Mother the poison we could not ourselves take. She is giving refuge to everybody, accepting the sins of all, and digesting them.'

It was her conviction that the great physical sufferings that she had to undergo in life due to illness, were of a vicarious nature, being the effects of the sins she had taken from her disciples. An unsympathetic critic will, of course, pronounce this statement to be a mere rationalization. But there are other incontrovertible facts of her life which show that such powers were present in her. As in the case of the Master, the utter purity of her life, both physical and mental, had endowed her organism with an extreme sensitivity to anything that was unholy and sinful. Thus it was noticed that when certain people, evidently with sinful propensities, proceeded to touch her feet, the feet would shrink back even against her will, as if by reflex action. Often her disciples saw how she suffered from a burning sensation due to the indiscriminate touch of people. In 1916, when she attended the Durga Puja at the Belur Math, people without number prostrated themselves before her and touched her feet. A little later, Yogin-Ma saw her washing her feet again and again with the Ganges water. She remonstrated with her, saying, 'Mother, what is it that you are doing? You will catch cold.' To this the Holy Mother replied, 'Well, Yogin, how can I explain it to you? Some people touch my feet, and that refreshes me wonderfully. Again there are others whose touch gives me a terrible burning sensation. I feel it like the sting of a wasp. Only by applying the Ganges water do I get some relief.'

Another disciple records a striking example of this phenomenon at Jayrambati. The disciple who was then attending on her had gone out. On returning, he found the Mother lying on a straw mat in the verandah. Seeing the disciple, she said to him, 'A rather elderly man came here with L—. Seeing him from a distance, I entered my room and sat on the bed. He was very anxious to salute me by touching the feet. Though I protested and shrank back, he touched my feet by force, as it were. From that time I am almost at the point of death through an unbearable pain in the feet and the stomach. I washed my feet three or four times; still I cannot get rid of this burning sensation. Had you been here, you would have understood it by a sign from me and forbidden him to touch my feet.'

In Calcutta also disciples often noticed such occurrences, especially on certain holidays when the general public was allowed to salute her. But when she spoke of her suffering to any, she would add, 'But don't tell it to Sarat (Swami Saradananda). Then he will stop people from coming.' So compassionate was she that in spite of her suffering she did not like to deprive others of the satisfaction and relief they derived from her contact.

In the light of this indubitable fact it is intelligible how she could vicariously suffer for her disciples. Indeed, prompted by that motherly love for all, she considered it her proud privilege to suffer for others. Once at Koalpara, when a disciple hesitated to touch her feet, thinking it would cause her suffering, she said, 'No, my child, we are born for this purpose. If we do not accept others' sins and sorrows and do not assimilate them, who else will do so? Who else will bear the responsibilities of the sinners and the afflicted?' During her last illness, when her body had become very much emaciated and she could no longer get up without being helped, her monastic disciples were speaking amongst themselves about her extreme suffering. One of them said, 'If the Mother recovers this time, we shall not allow her to give initiation any more. She is suffering so much because of taking upon herself the sins of so many types of people.' On hearing this, the Holy Mother smiled and said, 'Why do you say so? Do you think that the Master came only to take Rasagollas[1]?' Greatly concerned to know that the Mother would suffer by initiating disciples, a devotee once said to her: 'Mother, it is sad you have got rheumatism because of your acceptance of the devotees' sins. I have an earnest prayer to make: don't you suffer for my sake. Ordain it so that I myself may suffer the consequences of my own work.' The mother replied quietly, 'How can that be so, my boy, how can that be so? You keep well and let me suffer.'

This desire to serve the spiritually sick and needy was an active passion with her and not a mere passive sentiment. It is said that she was often found unhappy at Jayrambati if new devotees failed to come any day. On one such day Swami Gauriswarananda heard her complaining to the Master: 'This day too is going in vain. No devotee has turned up today. Did you not tell me, "You will have to do something or other every day?" ' She kept on saying to the Master with tears in her eyes: "How is it, Master? Will this day go in vain?" And the Mother's face brightened when three devotees came the next day. This gives us an insight into the dynamic nature of that redeeming love which prompted her ever to court suffering in the service of others, all of whom she looked upon as her children.

Urged by this maternal love, she used to initiate people regardless of the immediate condition of her own health. Ill or well, when anybody went to her in a suppliant mood, her tendency was to satisfy him without any thought of her own convenience. Once she was suffering from malaria at Jayrambati, and at the order of

Swami Saradananda her attendants were not allowing anyone to approach her for initiation. A devotee from Barisal arrived, eager to see the Mother, but the disciples would not let him into her presence. This led to an altercation, hearing which the Mother came to the door and asked a disciple why he was not letting the gentleman in. On being told of Swami Saradananda's prohibition, she said sharply, 'Who is Sarat to prohibit? I am born for this purpose. Eat something today. I shall initiate you tomorrow.' For, the devotee had gone there with the determination that he would eat only after initiation.

On another occasion, she was at Calcutta, just convalescing after severe illness. No devotee was admitted into her presence then, but an exception was made in the case of a devoted Parsi youth coming from far away. This young man, as was natural, asked her for her blessings. At once she said to the disciple attending on her, 'Shall I initiate him?' The disciple raised objections and said, 'How can you do it in your present state of health? What will Sarat Maharaj say if he hears of it?' The Mother then asked the disciple to go and ask Swami Saradananda about it. The Swami, however, replied, 'What shall I say? If the Mother desires to have a Parsi disciple, let her have one. There is no use telling her anything against her wish.' On going back, the disciple found that she had already made arrangements for initiation. Later on she expressed great satisfaction at this young man's spiritual potentialities.

Thus, under the influence of maternal love, she gave initiation to one and all who went to her for blessings. Often she felt that many were unworthy, but her grace was so abounding that she would generally brush aside all considerations of fitness. As she said once to a disciple, 'My child, several among those who come here are up to anything in life. No type of sin has been left undone by them. But when they come here and address me as mother, I forget everything and they get more than they deserve.'

On account of this extreme liberality and motherly eagerness to serve, the circle of her initiated disciples was very large. Evidently the majority of these received initiation, not because of any special merit or qualification of theirs, but only through the Mother's infinite kindness. So they were not seen to develop into outstanding spiritual personalities. Bearing this in mind, Yogin-Ma one day said to her humorously, 'Look at the Master's disciples. Each one of them is a spiritual giant. But what about your disciples, Mother?' To this Holy Mother replied, 'Is it to be wondered at? He picked out the best types, and with what care he selected them! And towards me he has pushed all this small fry, coming in their hundreds like ants! Don't compare my disciples with his.' Further she spoke thus to a disciple, regarding the significance of her initiation: 'Whatever I have to give, I give at the time of initiation. If you want peace immediately, practise the spiritual disciplines prescribed. Otherwise you will achieve it only after the fall of the body.'

Some of the disciples attending on her felt that this liberality of hers in the matter of initiation was not quite desirable. There were instances of her giving initiation

Her Spiritual Ministry 167

to boys of ten and twelve even against the protest of her associates on the ground that they would not even remember the Mantra after a few days. Once one of her disciples therefore questioned her thus: 'Mother, you give initiation to so many people, but you can't keep all of them in mind. You don't even give a thought to what is happening to them. A Guru has to look after the spiritual unfoldment of the disciple. So it is better that you initiate only as many as you can remember.' To this her reply was, 'But, my child, the Master never forbade me to do so. He had instructed me on many things, could he not have told me something about this as well? I give the responsibility of my disciples to the Master. Everyday I pray to him saying, "Please look after the disciples wherever they may be." Further I received these Mantras from the Master himself. Through these one is sure to achieve perfection.'

But it is known for certain that she did concern herself with the spiritual welfare of her disciples in a more active sense. Daily she used to do Japa in very large numbers, and from her own words one understands that this was for the sake of her disciples. During her last illness, though she could not sit up for meditation, she was none the less seen to do Japa. It was also noticed that she would wake up at 3 a.m. Observing this, a disciple asked whether she was not sleeping well at night. Her reply was, 'How can I, my child? All these children come to me with great longing and take initiation, but most of them do not practise Japa regularly. Why regularly? They do not do anything at all. But since I have taken their responsibility, should I not see to their welfare? Therefore I do Japa for their sake, and pray to the Master constantly, saying, "O Lord, awaken their consciousness. Give them liberation. There is a great deal of suffering in this world. May they not be born again!"'

When the Mother reassured a faltering devotee of her constant support, the devotee enquired: 'Do you have to work for your sons wherever they may be?' The Mother replied: 'I have to work for all.' The devotee further asked: 'You have so many children. Do you remember them all?' The Mother admitted that she could not recollect them all, and then explained, 'I do Japa for those whom I recollect. And for those I do not remember, I pray to the Master thus: "I have many sons in many places. Do you please look after those whose names I do not remember, and graciously grant that they may prosper."'

Among the hundreds of people who approached her for initiation, there were very few whom she refused. Their number may not be more than a dozen. And in these cases it is impossible to say what exactly guided her decision. Probably it was due to a feeling that these people sought initiation from her only with a view to avoiding payments to their family gurus; for there were instances when she insisted as a condition of her giving initiation, that the disciples would continue, or even enhance, the financial contribution to their family gurus, and show them the same respect as before. Or her refusal may have been by way of a test, which these unfortunate souls failed to stand. For we know from the following instance that she considered tests of this kind to be legitimate on the part of a spiritual teacher. A young man, placed in very poor circumstances, went twice or thrice to Jayrambati for initiation, but could not, unfortunately, succeed owing to the Holy Mother's illness. So he wrote complaining, 'Please do not refuse me any more. It is with great difficulty that I go over there. I want to know whether the next time I come, I shall get initiation or not.' In reply the Holy Mother said to a disciple, 'A person, whoever he may be, must go back if I am not well. Even if I am well, I cannot invite people to take initiation. People get facilities and opportunities according to their past Karma. A person comes here several times, but does not get the opportunity to see me, either because I am ill or for some other reason. It is his bad luck. What shall I do? You may say that it means a great deal of expense for him, and everybody does not have money. But a Guru may turn away a person seeking to be a disciple, time after time. He who is really eager for the blessing of the Guru, however, will come to him even by begging. The truth is this: He who is really anxious to cross the ocean of the world will somehow break his bonds. No one can entangle him. Financial difficulties, awaiting a reply, the fear of going back with unfulfilled desire—these are mere excuses.'

There are at least two known cases of people failing to get initiation from her for reasons that look providential. A gentleman named Navadwip Chandra Roy Varman brought two young men for initiation with the Mother's permission. By the time the first was initiated, the other had fled away and could not be traced anywhere. Afterwards the young man said that his mind was seized with an inexplicable fear which made him take to his heels. Another similar case was that of Sri Chandramohan Datta, an employee of the Udbodhan office. He had free access to the Mother, as he did marketing and other odd jobs for her. Once some of the senior Swamis told him, 'You go so often to the Mother and get Prasad from her and eat it. Why don't you ask her to give you salvation?' 'It is the easiest thing for me to do,' replied Chandramohan with bravado. 'I shall immediately go to the Mother and return in a trice after making the request.' When he went to the Mother, she was at worship. Chandramohan approached her and stood within the sight of the Mother. He found that his entire body was seized with a shivering, and when the Mother, on seeing him, asked him what he wanted, he could not at first reply. Then by force of habit, he blurted out, 'I want Prasad,' and the Mother pointed out by sign where Prasad was kept. It took an hour's time for Chandramohan to get over that nervousness.

Her motherly love was expressed not only through the liberality with which she gave initiation to spiritual aspirants, but also through the extreme tenderness, sweetness and forbearance that characterized her dealings with the devotees in her everyday life. The consciousness of universal motherhood was so powerfully operative in her that there were cases of devotees, who had lost their mothers in early days, finding even the very physical likeness of their mothers in her. It may be a subjective experience, but still it is significant in so far as they very subjectivity of it centred on her. While such experiences fell only to the lot of a few, almost everyone who went to her felt that they received from her such love and attention as equalled or even surpassed what their earthly mothers were capable of. Thus when devotees went to her at Jayrambati, she would, so long as she was in health, herself cook for them, serve them, and even insist on removing their leavings. There have been several instances of her washing and drying the bedsheets of devotees every day unknown to them, so that it was a matter of surprise for them that their sheets were found white and clean in spite of use for several days. When they protested against such action on her part, or against her serving them on their arrival by fanning and washing their feet, she would silence them by the effective reply, given in a tone of utmost sincerity and with overflowing feeling, 'What after all have I done for you? Am I not your mother? Is it not the privilege of a mother to serve her child in every way—even to clean its dirt with her own hand?' There was absolutely no exaggeration in this expression of motherly sentiment, for even this extreme form of service she is known to have performed at Calcutta, when the baby of a lady devotee soiled a carpet in her room. She insisted on cleaning the carpet herself, despite the protests of the devotee who felt greatly embarrassed by her action.

At Jayrambati it was not unusual to see her go from door to door in the early morning for some milk, may be to feed a sick devotee or to prepare tea for another who found it impossible to begin his day without a cup of that beverage. When any devotee fell ill, she nursed him with as much solicitude as a mother would do. At Jayrambati a young disciple who suffered from itches in the hands was fed by her day after day by her own hand. Sometimes in expectation of the arrival of some beloved disciple, she would preserve for him the cakes or sweets prepared in the house on the previous day. For, to feed the devotees was her greatest delight. She would not allow anyone who went to her during meal time to go without food, so much so that it was a constant cause of complaint to Golap-Ma, who did the housekeeping in her Calcutta residence, that she was always required to provide meals for people without any previous notice. Golap-Ma would complain to her, 'You entertain here anybody and everybody who comes to you calling "mother", "mother!"' And to devotees who went to her at times other than meal time, she would give sweets, fruits, water and at least two rolls of betel. Though they were trifles, she would give these things with such great affection and warmth that the recipients' hearts would be filled with joy and they would feel great attraction for her. Whenever a devotee took any offering to her, be it even common things like betel leaves, she would express heartfelt delight at it, irrespective of all consideration of its value. When any dainty came to her, she was in the habit of reserving it for the devotees, and seldom partook of it herself. Thus the special sweets, for instance, sent to Jayrambati for her by Swami Saradananda, would be reserved for distribution among the devotees, both morning and evening. Of all such presents, one part would go to

Simhavahini, another to Dharma Thakur, another for some other deities, yet another to neighbours and relatives, and the rest to the devotees—for herself she would hardly reserve anything. She was the mother of all, and her nature was to give, never to preserve anything for herself.

Once a disciple attending on her had to go out to a neighbouring village on business and could return only late in the afternoon. As he had not taken his meal, the Holy Mother too did not take her food at the usual time and waited for his return. The disciple on arrival remonstrated with her for fasting when her health was so bad. But her reply was, 'You have not taken your meal; so how could I?' The disciple concerned felt that such loving solicitude could not be expected even of one's own mother.

When the devotees went to her village home at Jayrambati, she always insisted on their staying there and taking rest for at least two or three days. For she would say, 'People have to stand so much hardship to come over here. It is easy to visit Gaya or Banaras, but not this place.' Often the number of such devotees would go up to ten or twelve, and they would be arriving at her house at all odd hours, sometimes even at midnight. To feed and maintain all of them was too much of a drain on her slender resources. Yet she was all warmth and cordiality when they went to her, and she personally looked after all their comforts both as regards food and accommodation. The one cause of worry for her was that in that out-of-way village she could not give any delicacies to the devotees, and so she was very particular about keeping some specially preserved food for their use. And when any devotee took leave of her, it was always a moment of sorrow for her, as it is for any mother at the time of parting from her child. She would, on such occasions, follow them for some distance, and sometimes with eyes wistful and moistened with tears, watch till they were out of sight. While staying in Calcutta in rented houses on the banks of the Ganges, there have been occasions when at dusk she would stand outside the house in the rain, only to watch a devotee who had just taken leave of her, crossing the river in a boat. Thus every detail of her conduct towards devotees was impressed with the tinge of her motherly love.

Not only in acts of love and tenderness but even in the way in which she stood the importunities and indiscreet conduct on the part of devotees, she showed herself to be more than a mother to them. In the last few years of her life the number of people who used to visit her in Calcutta was so large that it was a great strain on her to meet them all. It is said that when she got tired with this rush of people in the city, she went to her village home, but even there she had no rest as her relatives pressed her with their never-ending demands for pecuniary help. Besides, knowing that at Jayrambati one had greater access to her than in the city, many devotees from Calcutta would go over there, some of them arriving at odd hours, even at midnight, without any consideration for problems of accommodation and food, of which she was very particular.

Her Spiritual Ministry

Reference has already been made to the great physical suffering that the Holy Mother had to stand owing to the touch of impure souls. Besides this, on holidays and festive occasions hundreds of people came and offered flowers and cloth at her feet by way of worship while she was required to sit for hours like an image to accept them. In Calcutta, many devotees who sought her, especially women, went for the fulfilment of their worldly desires, may be to ask her blessings so that they might have a child, or have some illness cured, or have their financial condition improved. The Mother used to listen patiently to the tales of woe and suffering that even such people brought to her, and it is said that many supplicants of this type also had their desires fulfilled through her blessings.

But the most troublesome devotees were those whose spiritual fervour was in excess of their common sense. One or two examples of this kind are worth mentioning in order to show how much torment she had to suffer at their hands. One day at the Udbodhan Office, the Holy Mother had just finished her daily worship, when a devotee carrying some flower in his hand came to see her. At the sight of the stranger she wrapped herself with a sheet and sat down on her bedstead, with her feet resting on the floor. The devotee offered the flowers at her feet and saluted her. Then he sat in front of her and began to do breathing exercises! As the other inmates of the house were busy with their work, there was no one by her side at that time. The devotee continued his breathing exercises, and the Holy Mother, sitting in that position with her whole body covered up, began to feel uncomfortable. Just then Golap-Ma happened to come. She understood the whole situation. She roused the man and rebuked him sharply, saying, 'Do you think that you are before a wooden image and would awaken life in it by your breathing exercises? Have you no sense? Don't you see the Mother is feeling warm?'

Another day a devotee, while saluting the Holy Mother, forcibly stuck his head against her big toe. It hurt her very much and see cried out in pain. Those who were by her side asked the person why he did so, and his reply was that he had purposely pained her, so that she might remember him on account of that pain! The devise adopted by another devotee for the same purpose was to bite her toe while prostrating. Still another queer person was once about to pull her leg upto his chest and be blessed that way.

One can estimate from the account given above what an amount of patience and forbearance was required to stand all these eccentricities of the devotees. There was nothing she had to gain from them. Nor had she the least interest in being lionized by society. All the worship and praise that the devotees bestowed on her produced no impression on her mind. In these respects she was a true follower of Sri Ramakrishna, for whom money was no consideration in judging one's personal worth, and honour and publicity were matters of utmost abhorrence. Thus pure maternal love, irrespective of all considerations of the worth or fitness of the object towards which it was directed, was the only

Her Spiritual Ministry

motive-force behind her long and arduous work as a spiritual teacher.

It is now necessary to deal with another subject connected with the Holy Mother's spiritual ministry, namely, her ways of imparting instruction to disciples and guiding them in their spiritual life. One of the most remarkable features of this phase of her life was her catholicity. It is definitely known that she never imposed the ideal of Sri Ramakrishna on anyone, although she recognized the value of a true understanding of him in the spiritual growth of her disciple. Before she gave a Mantra to a disciple, she generally consulted the religious traditions of his family, whether it was Vaishnava, Saiva or Sakta, as also his own spiritual inclinations. There were cases of disciples who pleaded ignorance regarding the religious traditions of their family, denied preference for any form of the Deity, and gave her the entire responsibility of selecting an ideal for them. In the case of others, it was not always that she acted according to their traditions or inclinations. She would also meditate and see whether the intuition of her mind coincided with what they apparently thought to be their path and chose an entirely new Mantra when she considered it necessary. Thus it was not any stereotyped method that she followed in initiating people, her unerring insight into the spiritual tendencies of men was her guide.

It is generally true to say that she initiated disciples under the spur of a felt inspiration. Formalities and even language played very little part as intervening factors. She used to say, 'It is the Master who sends these candidates. I am nobody. It is the Master who graciously blesses them. I am only his instrument.' When she was in the South, not knowing any language other than Bengali, she could not talk with devotees. They went to her with such words as 'Mantra, please' or 'Instruction, please.' But without any exchange of words, she was able to give each of them the correct Mantra that suited his or her particular religious tradition. As to how that inspiration functioned in her, she used to say: 'As soon as I want to impart a Mantra to some people, there arises in the mind such thoughts as 'Give this' or 'Give that,' whereas in other cases, it appears as though I know nothing and nothing seems to come up. I keep on sitting. Then after long cogitation I can visualize the Mantra. In the case of good aspirants the Mantra springs up instantaneously.'

Sometimes people, already initiated by a guru, went to her again for initiation. She generally discouraged this, but if the candidate was very earnest and persistent, she agreed. About such a case she said, 'I cannot bear anybody's tears. I pray to the Master to strengthen their faith, and through his direction I give them initiation in addition to the Mantra already received by them. This additional Mantra is given for fresh stimulus and strength in order to increase their faith in the name of God.' There was the case of a family guru threatening a disciple with a curse for having taken initiation from the Mother, but she assured him that no curse can ever affect her disciples. But she was particular that people did not evade paying their annual

Dakshina (votive donation) to their family Gurus after taking initiation from her.

There were others who had been long ago initiated by her, but had for some reason or other felt doubt about the correctness of their understanding of the Mantra. A certain lady in that predicament went to her three years after initiation to get her doubt cleared. The Mother said, 'Well, my daughter, did I give you this particular Mantra?' The disciple agreed that it was what she had been repeating and the Mother thereupon assured her of its correctness. Another person named Rasiklal Roy was not able to tell the hereditary Mantra of his family when the Mother wanted to know it at the time of initiation. After a short silence, the Mother gave him initiation into a Mantra, saying that it was his family Mantra. The disciple found on enquiry that the Mother's intuition was correct.

In these moments of introspection she often saw the spiritual future of the disciples. A remarkable instance of this from the life of Swami Nikhilananda may be mentioned here. He took initiation from the Holy Mother when he was a college student and had no idea of becoming a monk. After initiation it is customary to present some fruits, flowers, cloth and money to the guru according to one's capacity. The disciple concerned placed before her some fruits and flowers with a rupee. She then said that she did not accept from monks any money as gift. The disciple reminded her that he was not a monk but a student who led an ordinary life. Still she did not accept it on the same ground as before. Thrice the disciple reminded her, and every time she gave the same answer. A few years later, this disciple actually became a member of the Ramakrishna Order. Evidently she divined his future at the time of initiation.

In case her intuition showed her that the family tradition or the apparent inclination of a disciple was not in the proper line of his spiritual evolution, she did not hesitate to put him on the right track, though it might be entirely new to him for the time being. We many cite here an example of this, also from the life of another distinguished monk of the Ramakrishna Order, Swami Virajananda. When he took initiation from the Holy Mother, he had already been repeating a Mantra and was deriving much peace and bliss from it. He found, however, that the ideal and the instructions she gave him at the time of initiation were totally different from what he was till then following with so much benefit. He felt rather bewildered on account of this and communicated his feelings to the Holy Mother. But to this she said in reply, 'This is better.' These few words of the Mother had miraculous effect on the disciple. He felt an immediate transformation in the spiritual attitude he was cultivating. The feeling of hesitancy to accept the Mantra given by the Mother altogether disappeared, and he felt there was perfect harmony between the new ideal and his spiritual past. This experience convinced him of the value of a true guru—of how such a guru could set an aspirant on the right track and appease the conflicts and struggles within his mind.

Another incident from the life of the same disciple reveals the great competence of the Holy Mother as a teacher of men. This disciple was once seized with an intense spirit of renunciation and yearning for God, subsequent to the demise of a great spiritual luminary of the Ramakrishna Order, whom he respected very much. Thenceforth, he spent about a year and a half in an Ashrama far from the haunt of men, observing silence and devoting fourteen hours a day to Japa and meditation. This strenuous discipline ultimately told on his nerves. Gradually he felt as if his mind was refusing to work, and began to experience a sense of vacancy in the brain. He, therefore, gave up the practice of meditation for a time and devoted himself to scriptural studies. By this change he did not feel any relief as far as the condition of the brain was concerned. So he left for Calcutta, where the senior Swamis of the Belur Math put him on nourishing diet and had him treated by a renowned Ayurvedic physician. Even this did him no good. It struck him just then that he should consult the Holy Mother. She was then in her village. He, therefore, went to Jayrambati and explained to her his condition. When she heard of the nature of the meditation he had been doing, she shuddered and told him that he was following methods of meditation which one should adopt only in the highest stage of spiritual practice. She then gave him some simple directions for meditation, and by following these he soon felt his nerves getting soothed and his complaints all disappearing.

To cite another instance of a similar nature, a gentleman named Shyamacharan Chakravarty of Rangoon after studying Swami Vivekananda's Raja Yoga, began practising Pranayama for about three hours a day. As a consequence he began to experience an intolerable buzzing sound in his ears, which made it impossible for him to attend to his work at the office. As all attempts at treatment proved ineffective, he took leave and went to Calcutta. Visiting the Belur Math, he came to know of the Holy Mother and went to meet her at Jayrambati. It is said the very atmosphere of Jayrambati rid him of the intolerable experience of ringing sound.[2] After meeting the Mother, he told her of his desire to practise Pranayama and other such Yogic disciplines. Her reply was, 'What energy have you stored up in your body and mind qualifying you to undertake these practices?' 'Have I then no way out?' asked the devotee. 'I shall tell you whatever has to be done,' replied the Mother, and soon after initiated him, instructing him to do Japa twice daily. Shyamacharan, who believed in intense and assiduous practice of Sadhanas, was not satisfied with this, and asked why he should not do Japa thrice and also wanted more practices to be recommended. The Mother again repeated her instruction to do Japa twice a day and said, 'It is all that is required for you.' She knew everyone's capacity and limitations. Such examples show how this simple, uneducated and unostentatious lady knew all the profound secrets of spiritual life and was ready to help her disciples when they got stranded on the spiritual path.

It has been noted before that she never forced the ideal of Sri Ramakrishna on anyone. But she seems to have held the view that in the case of those who took initiation from her, spiritual advancement would be accelerated if they accepted the true spiritual identity of Sri Ramakrishna. Once an old man went to the Holy Mother with the notion that Sri Ramakrishna was a saintly person, and that the Holy Mother, being his spiritual consort, would have some of his powers. He had no idea about Sri Ramakrishna's being a divine incarnation. When he was brought in for initiation, the Holy Mother at once understood his mentality and called out to Yogin-Ma, 'O Yogin, this man does not accept the Master. What am I to do?' Yogin-Ma said in reply, 'Initiate him. The Mantra you give will never be fruitless.' He was given initiation, and it was noticed that through her grace he became a great devotee of Sri Ramakrishna in a short time.

Her attitude in this respect may be explained this way: The spiritual progress of those whom she initiated was guided not merely by their effort but also by the connection they established with Sri Ramakrishna through her. The great austerities performed by the Master were not for his own sake but for the good of the world at large. For it is not within the power of ordinary human beings, with their many weaknesses and limitations, to strive independently and escape from the hands of Maya. They require the help of a redeeming power to supplement their little strength. In the spiritual energy generated by Sri Ramakrishna's austerities lies that reserve of power which aspirants can make use of for their upliftment. But it is only by accepting him whole-heartedly that they can get into touch with the spiritual energy accumulated by him. Otherwise they would be excluding themselves from it.

In a few cases she is known to have diverted the tendencies of people from evil ways by an effort of her will. Thus she cured a disciple, who was an inveterate drunkard, of his bad habit; changed the mind of a girl who was trying to seduce a young man; and converted to the path of holy living a young wife who was heading towards ruin in a fit of revenge against her husband who had taken to an exclusively religious life against her will. But she did not effect such conversions very often. When some disciples asked her for an explanation of this, contrasting it with the example of Sri Ramakrishna who had effected many such striking cases of conversion, her reply was that it was not given to her to do so, as her spiritual ministry was to be long and extensive. In effecting such conversions one had to spend on a few the spiritual energy that was meant for the many. According to her the earthly life of the Master was cut short because of the tremendous amount of spiritual energy he had to spend on men of exceptionally evil dispositions.

There are many devotees of the Holy Mother who claim to have had experiences of a highly mystical type in the course of their relationship with her. Some had seen her in dream as a Goddess in human form, though they never had occasion to see even a picture of hers before. Others had received either full or partial Mantra and spiritual instruction from her in dream, and at the time of their initiation were astonished to find that the Mantra she gave them in the waking state tallied exactly with what they had got in dream. Still others claimed that they were rescued from great dangers during

Her Spiritual Ministry

critical situations in their lives by the help she rendered them either in dream or in the waking state. She did not, however, validate a Mantra only because it was got in dream or in any supra-normal way. It had to tally with her own intuition. In many cases it tallied, in some it did not. When it did not, she either supplemented it or positively changed it. There is an example of her prohibiting a devotee named Kusumkumari Aich from using a Mantra she got in dream, as it would have led to her ruin. This lady was for long desirous of going to the Mother for initiation, but circumstances always stood in the way. In the meantime she got a Mantra in a dream, which somehow she felt did not suit her. She now managed to go to the Holy Mother, and on her narrating her whole history, the Mother said: 'Some one is trying to encompass your ruin and to that end has given that Mantra in the name of three deities. Try to forget those words as early as you can. Now that you have come here you need have no fear.' And the Mother initiated her in a new Mantra.

A unique example of the way in which the Mother gave her protective guidance to disciples in mysterious ways is provided by the following incident concerning Girish Chandra Ghosh, a leading literary man and artiste of those times, and an ardent lay disciple of Sri Ramakrishna. Now Girish Chandra was also among the staunchest of Sri Ramakrishna's householder devotees. But like many others among them, he did not at first think very highly of the Holy Mother's spiritual greatness. Some years after Sri Ramakrishna's passing away, he went on a visit to Jayrambati along with some of the monastic disciples of the Master, seeking consolation from grief due to the demise of his three year old son[3] with many mystic associations. That was the second occasion when Girish was taken to the Holy Mother's presence. After prostrating himself before her, he looked at her once, and immediately withdrew from there and sat in the outhouse in very serious and introspective mood. His companions were astonished at this transformation of Girish. At last Swami Niranjanananda approached him and asked him the reason for it. Girish thereupon wanted him to inquire of the Holy Mother, whether she was not the person who had appeared to him in dream in his nineteenth year. In reply the Holy Mother sent him the information that she was. Then Girish gave out the story to his fellow-disciple. At the age of nineteen he was suffering from a severe illness. The doctors had given him up for lost. In that condition he dreamt one night that the whole sky was lit with a celestial effulgence. It gradually proceeded towards him and assumed the form of a Goddess. Girish, it must be remembered, was in those days a rank atheist. The Goddess approached him and said, 'Well, my child, you are suffering terribly. Aren't you?' Then she put something into his mouth, resembling the consecrated food of the Puri temple, and vanished. After that Girish gradually recovered from his illness. He had often tried to make out who that figure might have been, but could get no definite clue. So he had surmised that it must have been the figure of his mother whom he had lost in his early childhood. But the day on which he saw the Holy Mother, he was surprised to notice the likeness of that Goddess in her. Doubting Girish asked the Mother twice more for confirmation of her identity, and she gave the same reply. On the last occasion she said: 'I am truly your mother—mother, neither by virtue of being your Guru's wife, nor because of any assumed relationship, nor by way of empty talk, but truly your mother.' Thenceforth he looked upon the Holy Mother with great reverence and used to say that through the grace of Niranjan (Swami Niranjanananda) he had recovered his 'mother'. Thenceforth Girish Chandra Ghosh became very intimate with the Mother. On several occasions he went to Jayrambati, and the Mother would look to all his comforts, including personally procuring milk for his morning tea from neighbours, and soaping and drying his bed sheet every day , unknown to him. She would also prepare delicious dishes for him, and feed him sumptuously sitting by his side. At Calcutta, he was a frequent visitor at the Mother's house. One day when he came to take leave of her when she was about to depart for Jayrambati, he addressed these memorable words to her: 'Mother, when I come to you, I feel like a little child coming to its own mother. Had I been a grown up boy, I would have served my mother. But it is quite different now. It is you who serve us, and we receive your service. You are going to Jayrambati to serve the people there, even by cooking food for them in the village kitchen. How can I serve you, and what do I know about serving the Mother!' And to the people standing around he said with a voice choked and face flushed: 'It is difficult for human beings to believe that God can incarnate in a human form like our own. Can you realize that you are standing before the Mother of the Universe in the form of a village woman? Yet she is the Mother of the Universe—Mahamaya, Mahasakti—appearing on earth for the salvation of man and at the same time exemplifying the ideal of true womanhood.'

Whatever might be the significance of these uncommon experiences, the Holy Mother, as we have seen, was most simple and human in her everyday life, without the least touch of mysteriousness or occultism about her. Excepting the wisdom she manifested, there was nothing out of the way about her. Her tendency was always to encourage the disciple to seek for knowledge, devotion and dispassion, and not to be always waiting for visions and occult phenomena. According to her, if psychic experiences came, it was well and good. But, as she once said to a disciple who felt sorry for not having had any vision, these experiences were not of much consequence. They were only by-products of the spiritual life. Its essence was in something else. As to her conception of true spiritual evolution, she once said in her simple and yet expressive way, 'What else does one obtain by the realization of God? Does one grow a pair of horns? No. One's mind becomes pure and, through the pure mind, knowledge and illumination are awakened.'

Even in her manner of initiation she was very unconventional, reducing ritual and ceremonial to the very minimum. Generally speaking, she followed the established rules, and in addition observed certain conventions of her own. She generally did not give initiation at Varanasi, on the ground that it was Siva's

Her Spiritual Ministry 189

place and that He is the only Guru there. She also did not initiate people on the Master's birthdays. But no convention or rule sat too rigidly on her and, when circumstances required, she had no hesitation to relax every one of them in the matter of initiation and in worship in general. Thus she relaxed in many cases the rule prohibiting religious observance, worship etc during days of mourning after death, the menstrual period of a woman and such other periods of ritualistic impurity. She permitted some to do their worship etc. after taking tea, and allowed non-vegetarians to continue their accustomed food habits. In the matter of initiation, she generally did it after her morning worship. The candidates, too, had to approach her beforehand. But she is often known to have overlooked all these conventions and initiated aspirants at any hour and under any condition. Once she initiated a person during the period of mourning, considered to be a time of defilement, saying, 'There is no connection between the spirit and the body. The talk of defilement due to death is meaningless.' Sometimes she is known to have given initiation in the verandah or under the eaves of her house. A young devotee, who was a police suspect because of alleged implication in the nationalist movement, and who could not therefore be accommodated in her house at Jayrambati, was initiated by her, sitting on straw for a seat in the centre of an open meadow. Once she initiated a man in the compound of a railway station, an umbrella serving as the roof and the rain water collected in the depression made by a cow's hoof as the water for purificatory purposes. She had sometimes offered to give initiation to certain well-qualified aspirants even without their asking. Small boys of eight and ten who persistently and piteously pleaded for initiation had been blessed by her in spite of the opposition of her companions like Golap-Ma on the ground that they were very immature. One day she initiated a person standing where she was, on that person clasping her feet and weeping, with prayer for initiation in his mind. She initiated a girl friend of her early days while she was resting on her bed. Thus conventionality did not stand in the way when she felt the urge to bless people for reasons best known only to herself.

There were some people who created situations by coming for a re-initiation. About them she said once to a devotee: 'Sometimes people of little faith and of unsteady mind come for initiation. I mentally read their history from their very appearance and behaviour and ask them whether they were previously initiated by someone else. If they reply in the affirmative, I tell them, "Strange, you have come for initiation again! You have no faith in the Mantra given by your Guru. What is a Mantra but the holy name of the Lord?" When they are persistent and they implore with tears in their eyes, I pray to the Master for strengthening their faith, and through his direction give them initiation in addition to the Mantra already received by them. This additional Mantra is given for fresh stimulus and strength in order to increase their faith in the name of God.'

Generally initiation by her took only a very short time. On this point Swami Saradananda was once

Her Spiritual Ministry

questioned by a disciple, as to how it was that the Holy Mother took only two or three minutes to initiate a disciple, while he took about half an hour. To this the Swami replied that the very touch or will of the Holy Mother was sufficient assurance that the disciple had been surrendered to, and accepted by the Master, whereas in his case some time must be spent in meditation before he received that assurance. The speed and spontaneity with which the Mantra to be given appeared in her mind, was probably another reason.

Besides giving Mantra to people, the Holy Mother also used to give the vows of Brahmacharya (celibacy practised by a novice) and Sannyasa (renunciation of the world) to the members of the Ramakrishna Order. In such cases, what she used to do was to convey to the disciples the inner spirit for which these institutions stood, and symbolize her having done this by giving the Brahmacharin's dress or the Sannyasin's ochre cloth to the disciples. She would then ask them to go to Swami Brahmananda and perform the appropriate ceremonies with the chanting of holy texts.

Thus she had a very large number of disciples both monastic and lay. She would often seem to be very tender and specially considerate to the latter class, seeing that they had to face innumerable worries and difficulties in the world. Her heart, so full of motherly sympathy, could not help doing so. She also told certain householder devotees, perhaps to appease some conflict of ideals in their mind, 'Is the ochre robe everything? You will attain spiritual realization without all this. What is the need of taking the ochre cloth?' She would also sometimes point out how the ochre robe became only a source of vanity for some and say that it would be far better to be like herself, wearing the white dress of the householder but observing Sannyasa in practice. There were also occasions when she asked unmarried young men to marry and settle down in life with the remark, 'Why can't one lead a good life if one is married? The mind alone is everything. Did not the Master marry me?'

Such statements have led some to think that the Holy Mother stood more for the ideal of the householder than for that of the monk. This, however, is a hasty conclusion. For, Sri Ramakrishna and the Holy Mother have, by the many-sidedness of their lives, set the ideals for men and women of all countries and in all stations of life. Still it may not be wrong to state that, more than in the life of the Master or any of his disciples, one finds in the Holy Mother the fulfilment of the ideal of inner Sannyasa—of being *in* the world but not *of* it. But that is not to say that she minimized the importance of the ideal of Sannyasa. We have seen how, when she went on pilgrimage, she visited the great Sannyasins in those places. Once while she was staying at Kamarpukur, perhaps on the second occasion after the Master's passing, a Sannyasin visited the village. She built a hut for him, gave all necessaries for his daily food, and went to salute him every morning. In later days when Sannyasins of the Ramakrishna Order visited her, she would ask Radhu and her other nieces to salute them. Once a householder devotee quarrelled with a monk and used harsh words. The Holy Mother advised him

Her Spiritual Ministry 193

never to do so, but always show respect to monks; for, she said, 'One word or one thought of a monk may injure a householder.' She once snubbed her niece Nalini very severely for speaking slightingly of the monks. One day, while a monastic disciple was sitting before the Holy Mother, a woman devotee passed that way, touching the back of the disciple with the corner of her cloth through carelessness. At this the Mother said very sharply, 'What have you done? He is a monk and your have touched him with the edge of your cloth! You must be respectful to him. Take the dust of his feet.' Another day a much-respected lady devotee of the Master had some exchange of hot words with a Brahmacharin at the Udbodhan Office and went away in anger, saying, 'If he stays in this house, I cannot remain here.' When it was reported to the Holy Mother, she was not at all sympathetic towards the lady devotee's attitude and said, 'Who is she? A householder! She should not have taken offence with a monk in this manner. Let her go away if she pleases. The monks have renounced everything for my sake and are staying here.' She would often remark to her disciples, 'Ah! With whom shall I live if there are no self-renouncing Sannyasins about me?'

The following incident is also a striking illustration of her deep regard for the monastic ideal and the appreciation she had of its value in developing the spiritual life of certain types of aspirants. A young disciple of hers, having made up his mind to adopt the monastic life, went to her for permission to do so. At first she tried to dissuade him from that course and cross-questioned him with a view to knowing his real intentions. But on being convinced of his earnestness, she said, 'What is there in the worldly life? What an inordinate attachment people have for it! See how out of one so many come out, and how one's attention and energies are all dissipated! Is it possible for a person placed under such conditions to attain spiritual greatness? Have you not seen crabs? The mother crab peeps out of her hole again and again, and then goes down. She struggles hard repeatedly to free herself, but fails. And why? Because of her attraction for her numerous progeny living in the hole. This attraction drags her into the hole in spite of all her efforts. Such is the case of those who are immersed in worldly life.'

In fact, the Holy Mother respected both the ideals— that of the Sannyasin and that of the householder—but disliked the vanities of the followers of either. Whether accompanied by the garb or not, renunciation was the essential thing. Provided that was present, both the ideals took one to the highest goal. But her conversations in the Gospel of the Holy Mother show that she always encouraged a person to lead a celibate life, if she found him fit for it. In the case of girls too she would recommend celibacy to such of them as were drawn to the ideal of complete renunciation. One day a devotee requested the Holy Mother to order her daughter to marry. But the Holy Mother replied, 'Is it not a misery to remain in life-long slavery to another and always dance to his tune?' She said that though there was some risk in being a celibate, if one was not inclined to lead a married life, one should not be forced into it and subjected to lifelong worldliness. She characterized this as intolerable oppression, but in the case of those for whose spiritual evolution she found the married life more suited, she certainly recommended that course, without creating any conflict of ideals in their minds. She would say to them, 'Do you not see everything in this world in couple--two eyes, two ears, two hands, two feet and so on? So also the male and female principles!'; or 'Everything is in the mind. Don't you see that the Master married me?'

In the matter of social relationship, however, she always insisted that the householder must show due regard to the Sannyasin, and she herself set the example in that respect. ❑

---

1. Rasagollas are a kind of high class sweets of Bengal. Her meaning was that it was not to enjoy life but to work for the good of others that Sri Ramakrishna and she were born.

2. On the holy vibrations of the atmosphere of Jayrambati, at least when she stayed there, and its transforming effect on men, there is a significant saying of hers. A devotee named Naresh Chandra took to her two persons for initiation, one of them specially recommended and sent by Swami Dhirananda. The Mother felt they were extremely impure and at first refused to initiate them on grounds of her health at the time. She was afterwards persuaded to initiate them, but she said, 'But what of their extremely impure aura? Well, ask them to live here for three nights. That will purify them. For this is verily Siva's domain.'

3. This three year old boy of Girish, born in 1888 shortly after the Master's demise, was believed by Girish to have had the Master's special blessing. The boy was very fond of the Holy Mother and she, of him; whenever she saw him, she would fondle him and seat him in her lap. In 1890 when the Mother was staying at Sourindra Thakur's house at

Baranagore, Girish went there with the boy. The boy, who had not yet learnt to speak, was very anxious to see the Holy Mother. He made people understand the same by his gestures and incoherent utterances. He was taken up to the Mother and he prostrated himself before her. When he was brought downstairs, he urged his father to go up, at which Girish burst out crying; 'O my dear, how can I see the Mother? I am veritably a sinner.' But because of the boy's insistence he had to go upstairs with the boy in his arms. Trembling all over with emotion, he fell at the Mother's feet, saying: 'Mother, it is because of this child that I have now a glimpse of your blessed feet.' He did not see her face. Probably she was veiled. This boy died soon after, and it was seeking consolation upon this bereavement that Girish now went to Jayrambati with others, under the prompting of Swami Niranjanananda.

15. GLIMPSES OF HER PERSONALITY

THE HOLY MOTHER was about medium height and quite well-built for an Indian woman. In her early days she was not stout, but towards middle age she showed a tendency to be so. But as she grew older, she again became slim, and it was in that period that most of the devotees had occasion to meet her. In her complexion and general appearance, too, there was a marked difference between her early and later days. On being questioned about her appearance in her youth, she described it as quite pretty. It is said that, when she returned to Calcutta from Kamarpukur for the first time after the Master's passing away, Swami Premananda's mother was very much struck by her pre-possessing appearance and asked her, 'Mother, wherefrom did you get such exquisite beauty and charm?' Surabala, her insane sister-in-law, used to say that, when she saw her first, the Mother would appear radiant as she sat in meditation. But this was in her 'pre-Radhu' days, when she used to be in highly exalted spiritual states and spent all her time in meditation and devotional practices. After the coming of Radhu, when, to quote the Mother's own words, 'Maya laid her hands' on her, such external expressions of her inner beauty ceased altogether.

When most of her disciples saw her, she was in a declining state of health owing to age and frequent attacks of malaria. Her general appearance had by then deteriorated to a great extent. Her complexion at that time was somewhat dark, but even then there was in it a mellowness and subdued glow, lending an exquisite grace to her form. A monk who saw her at the age of forty describes her as having in her countenance the delicacy and tenderness of a maiden, as speaking only words of sympathy and compassion, as possessing an inexpressible celestial luminosity in her looks, and as conveying to one and all the impression that she was one's own mother. It was in fact a subtle grace and quiet dignity, rather than any extra-ordinary physical beauty or awe-inspiring majesty of form, that marked her out from others. But this was evident only on careful scrutiny and owing to her plain looks and unassuming manner, a superficial observer unacquainted with her could never pick her out from the company of other women. Once, while she was in Banaras, a Marwari woman came to see her. The Mother was then seated with Golap-Ma who had a rather imposing appearance. The woman took Golap-Ma to be the Holy Mother and went towards her to make prostration. She thereupon pointed out the Mother to her, but the Mother, out of a spirit of mischievous fun, directed her to Golap-Ma as the saintly woman she was seeking. Golap-Ma once more showed the Mother to her, but the Mother was bent on misdirecting her once again. This went on a few times until Golap-Ma called out to the woman in an excited tone, 'Can't you distinguish between a mere human face and the face of a divine being?' These words at once drew the woman's attention to that subtle and elusive charm in the Mother's face—to that gentle dignity and incorporeal beauty which we associate with the expression of Gods and Goddesses. Indeed, only comparisons drawn from the conception of divine agencies can adequately convey an idea of the sublime expressiveness in the lines and curves of the face of one whose whole life had been dedicated to the pursuit of holiness and the practice of forbearance, innocence and loving service.

This combination of gentleness, dignity and grace gave her that maternal pose which no one who went to her failed to notice. It inspired reverence in one's mind without creating the least sense of inaccessibility. One felt the utmost freedom in her company, but one also got a feeling of elevation and an apprehension that one was before a presence that was something more than merely human. Many persons who went to her with a list of questions felt no inclination to ask them when they were actually before her; for they found their doubts dissolving in the sense of peace and exaltation that her presence conveyed. To restore faith and courage in the wavering, to inspire confidence in the weak, to disperse the clouds of despair and depression, were powers which her personality always carried with it. But all this was not done by any sort of aggressive influence, such as we associate with a militant personality. It was more through that sense of consolation which the loving touch of a mother conveys to an ailing child. For even the most wicked disciple felt that he was near and dear to her, that she had no eye for his failings, that there was no error too grievous for her forgiveness, and that if he would but open his heart, her overflowing sympathy and assurance of divine protection would heal the wounds of his soul. When she was requested by a direct disciple of the great Master not to allow a certain young disciple to come to her presence on account of some misconduct on his part, she remarked, 'If my child gets covered with mud or dust is it not my duty to cleanse him and take him on my lap?' When a woman who had led a bad life went to her in a mood of sincere repentance and made an unreserved confession of her sins, she embraced her with great warmth of feeling, uttering these words of assurance, 'Don't despair for whatever you have done. You will get over all your sinful tendencies.' She also gave initiation to that woman.

More instances are not wanting which made the 'mother' in her overcome even all the accepted standards of moral respectability. There was an educated young disciple of hers who used to visit her frequently, and was also conducting a religious centre in his village. The young man got involved with a widowed girl—an offence of double sacrilege according to the prevailing moral codes. Several puritans tried to persuade the Mother not to allow the young man into her presence. Though she was visibly moved by this lapse of the young man, her reply to such requests was:

Glimpses of Her Personality

'How can I, who am his mother, forbid him to come? Such words will never come out of my lips.' The young man continued his visit. He also brought the girl one day. Though she reprimanded her for enticing the young man, her behaviour towards her was as affectionate as to any of her daughters. To mention another similar incident, while she was at Koalpara, a sweeper woman came to her in a completely distracted mood because her paramour had suddenly deserted her, leaving her completely stranded. No moral prudishness stood in the way of the Mother giving a helping hand to the woman. She sent for the man and, by her very gentle and motherly persuasion, reconciled the couple.

A unique feature of her maternal love was its constitutional disinclination to notice the faults of others. In this respect she combined in herself the nature of a loving mother and that of an innocent child—the mother in her making her too big-hearted to count the error of her children as of any significance, and the child in her, insulating her vision from the perception of evil by her utter innocence. We have already referred to her prayer at Brindavan to have the fault-finding tendency blotted out from her. Her prayer was literally answered. For, it is said that even if any action proceeding from the smallness of men happened to meet her eyes as she passed by, her gaze, with its characterisitic innocence, as of a little girl, would take no notice of it. Golap-Ma was once scolding a maid-servant. When the Holy Mother asked her the reason for it, she said in a pique, 'Mother, what is the good of telling you? Your cannot see the defects of others.' To this the Mother replied in a mild voice, 'Well, Golap, there is no want of people to see the fault of others. The world will not come to a standstill if I am otherwise.' The secret of that tremendous patience and forgiveness which she displayed in her dealings with her kinsfolk and disciples was this combination of motherliness and childlike innocence in her character. To pardon the erring was an instinct with her. It was not unoften that novices who were threatened with dire consequences by the heads of centres took refuge at the Mother's feet and escaped punishment through her intercession. Of course she impressed on them also the need for obedience and discipline in the monastic Order. In several cases her way of forgiveness, fortified by a motherly reprimand, worked much better than drastic methods. There was the instance of Brahmachari Nagen (junior) of Belur Math, who was afraid that Swami Shivananda, the then manager of the Math, might expel him from the Math for some grave mistake. He escaped to Jayrambati to seek shelter with the Mother, who interceded on his behalf and saved him. About this Swami Shivananda remarked: 'How is it, my boy! You went to the High Court directly to complain about us?' This incident is only one among several others, and is specially cited because of its connection with great personages.

Her attitude of kindly forgiveness extended even to servants guilty of misconduct. Once Swami Vivekananda ordered a servant of Belur Math to be dismissed for stealing. The man went to the Mother, then staying at Bosepara Lane, for shelter. That evening when Swami Premananda went from the Math to pay his respects to the Mother she interceded on behalf of this man: 'Look here, Baburam, this man is very poor. It was his poverty that forced him to steal. Should Naren on that account drive him out? The world is full of misery. You are monks and realize very little of it.' No need to say, the man was taken back.

It has been repeatedly emphasized that the Holy Mother's life and personality form a striking revelation of the universal principle of Motherhood. The expression of this quality in her was not restricted to her relationship with her disciples and relatives. It extended in a general sense to her attitude towards all. Her heart was very sensitive to the woes and sufferings of those round about her and, as she herself said, she often lost herself in compassion. No one in distress went to her without being helped with food, clothing or money according to her capacity.

In Jayrambati there was a woman named 'Bhavani's mother' who had none to look after her in her old age and sickness. She found a refuge in the Holy Mother, and it was the Mother who looked after her till death.

There was another woman in her village belonging to the Banerji family, who was suffering from a foul cancer in the ear. Everyone including her kith and kin avoided her. Her pitiable condition came to the Holy Mother's notice, and when a young disciple from the Koalpara Ashram went to visit her one day, she reported the matter to him with much feeling. At this the disciple suggested that he would like to take the patient to the Koalpara Ashram for nursing. The Holy

Mother was thrilled with joy to hear this, but the next moment she controlled herself and told him that he could take her there only with the permission of the president of that Ashram. So the disciple went to Koalpara and came back next day with a cart, after getting the necessary permission. He noticed that on seeing his arrival for taking away the woman, the Holy Mother's face was lit up with an expression of joy and exaltation that he had never seen in any other face. That day he had a glimpse of what is meant by disinterested love.

The Holy Mother also evinced keen interest in the flood and famine relief operations of the Ramakrishna Mission and always encouraged her disciples to cooperate in such activities. Whenever anyone returned from relief work, she would make detailed enquiries about the suffering of the people and the extent of the relief given. Her heart was always moved by stories of human suffering.

Her motherly love obliterated every vestige of the vanity of position from her and endowed her with a readiness to do even menial services to others and to silently forgo her own comforts and conveniences so as to save trouble for others. It has already been seen how forgetful of self she was in the service of her disciples and relatives. Once Akshay Kumar Sen, a disciple of hers and the author of the metrical biography of Sri Ramakrishna entitled *Ramakrishna Punthi*, sent some vegetables to Jayrambati with a coolie woman. As it was evening when she arrived, she was allowed to spend the night at the Mother's house. Being a malaria patient, she got at night high fever with vomiting. Before others had got up, the Holy Mother went into her room early in the morning and saw the place strewn with the vomit. At once she herself removed the dirt and washed the room with water. There were others in the house to do this work, but she knew that they would scold the woman severely and she wanted to save her from it.

At Jayrambati a disciple once noticed that the Holy Mother was removing her bed into the kitchen during nights. On enquiry he learnt from her that she had been doing so for some days past, as she found her room too uncomfortable. Though the Holy Mother asked him not to worry about it, the disciple went into her room and found the cot and other things full of bugs. Immediately he set himself to cleaning them. He was, however, astonished to note that the Holy Mother had never told anybody about it, because she preferred herself to be inconvenienced rather than trouble others for her sake.

It was not only the erring and the sinful that found consolation in her love, but even those who were held in dread by society for their wickedness. None was excluded from her motherly sympathy. When her house at Jayrambati was being built, they employed a number of Muslims of a neighbouring village as labourers. Originally their profession was to rear silkworms, but owing to foreign competition they were thrown out of employment, and they took to robbing and dacoity as their means of livelihood. So when they were employed for the construction of the Holy Mother's house, there was regular consternation among the villagers. But afterwards they remarked that through the Mother's grace even these dacoits turned into devotees. Actually, one day one of these Muslims brought some bananas to her and said, 'Mother, I have brought these for the Master. Would you accept them?' The Holy Mother accepted the offering very gladly. A lady devotee, who was standing by, thereupon told her, 'I know these people are thieves. Why do you accept their things for the Master?' She replied to her in a solemn tone, 'I know who is good and who is bad.'

Among these Muslims, there was one named Amjad whom the Mother took into her house for a meal. He was seated in the verandah and Nalini, her niece, was serving him. Owing to caste scruples, Nalini was standing at a little distance from him and throwing the various items of food into his plate. At this the Holy Mother remarked, 'If you serve a person in this way, can he eat with relish? You give the things to me, I shall serve him.' After he had finished eating, the Holy Mother herself washed the place where he had taken food. Nalini was shocked at this and exclaimed, 'O aunt, you are going to lose caste.' The Holy Mother snubbed her with the remark, 'Keep quiet. Even this Amjad is my son, exactly in the sense that Sarat (Swami Saradananda) is.'

Even this example does not represent the limit of her all-embracing love. For in spite of her upbringing in a very restricted environment, her maternal instinct led her to a level of thought which would not allow any considerations of race or country to interfere with the free play of her universal love. Once, during the time of the Durga Puja, she asked a disciple to purchase some cloth for the children of her brother. He purchased only cloth of Indian make, but the women of the family did not approve of it and made suggestions as to what they wanted. The disciple, out of patriotic feeling, replied in an excited voice, 'But what you want are all foreign cloth. How can I buy them?' The Holy Mother was present there. She said with a smile, 'My child, they (the Western people) too are my children. I must accommodate everyone. Can I ever be exclusive? Buy the things they want'[1]

This was not a mere passing sentiment with her, but a conviction which she used to reiterate whenever occasion arose. When the disciples spoke to her about many people in the West accepting Sri Ramakrishna's teachings after Swami Vivekananda visited those parts, she would remark, 'Those people are also my children. What do you say?' In later days Western devotees like Sister Nivedita, Mrs. Ole Bull, Sister Christine, Sister Devamata and others came to India from time to time. In spite of her early training amidst rigidly orthodox surroundings, she mixed with them all very intimately, at times even eating and sleeping with them in the same room.

Indeed, this breaking of the bonds of caste was another achievement for her maternal consciousness. She was not a breaker of caste in the manner of social reformers. For it was never her intention to give a violent shock to anyone by breaking long-established traditions. What happened was that before her maternal love the impediment of narrow rules and restrictions automatically gave way. We have already seen how in the case of the Muslim labourer and the Western devotees she broke the rules of caste. Often she would place articles of food from her plate in the hands of disciples of a lower caste and continue to eat without washing her hands. There has been an occasion when she offered to the Master rice cooked by a non-Brahmin disciple and partook of it herself. Even the so-called untouchable caste were not excluded from the pale of her liberality. Once at Jayrambati a sweeper brought her a straw-ring for supporting water jars. She asked him to keep it in the verandah of the house. But her sister-in-law, who had strong caste prejudices, began to make a fuss and abused the man for touching things belonging to their house. The Holy Mother however consoled the man, saying that he had done nothing wrong, and also gave him some money for refreshments. Such conduct on the part of a high-class Brahmin lady of her position was in those days considered sacrilegious from the point of view of strict caste etiquette. Her all-embracing heart, however, broke the bonds of these restrictions, but not as a deliberate revolt against established social conventions or in an attitude of contempt towards them.

Her motherly heart embraced even sub-human species in the sweep of the love it radiated. To a pointed question of Brahmachari Rashbihari, she replied that she was the mother of even all lower creatures. Not unoften she would be moved by the bleating of a calf out of hunger or solitariness, and she would sit by its side for long, fondling or feeding it. Persecuted cats of the household found shelter at her feet. And once, when she left Jayrambati for Calcutta, she specially asked

Brahmachari Jnan, their chief persecutor, to cook rice specially for the cats and charged him: 'Don't beat the cats; even in them I am.' The Brahmachari thenceforth began to bestow special attention on them.

The spirit of motherhood thus shone through the various phases of her life and character. In fact, her whole life is a revelation of this cosmic principle, wherein humanity and divinity meet. Man's highest conception of God can only be in terms of the noblest sides of his own nature. Hence motherhood—which marks the peak of human character in the achievement of love, forgiveness, selflessness and service—has rightly been held as the perfect symbol of Divinity. To those of the present generation, the Holy Mother is the most illustrious example of the expression of this principle in human terms, and as such they may see in her an embodiment of Divinity. In the light of this explanation one can understand the import of her words, 'Sri Ramakrishna left me behind to manifest the Motherhood of God to the world.' Once a monastic disciple told her, 'Mother, after having seen you, people will no more respect the various Goddesses.' Her significant reply was, 'Why not? They are all my parts.'

While appreciating the human quality of her motherhood, it is befitting to remember that there was also a cosmic dimension to her motherhood as hinted in the above statement. This kind of self-revelation of her Divinity, even in a theocentric sense, did occur occasionally in conversations with devotees and disciples, although generally she hid herself under a human veil. Such self-revelations occurred either unconsciously or in her talks to some very worthy persons, but there was never any tinge of self-glorification in it. To her nephew Sivaram, she declared that she was Kali and blessed him by putting her hand on his head in an exalted mood, when the latter in an intensity of spiritual longing questioned her persistently on her identity and finally implored her, holding her feet and shedding copious tears. Once in her Dakshineswar days she asked Yogin-Ma whether she offered dry Bilva leaves in her worship. On her admission, she said, 'This morning during my meditation I saw you offering dry Bilva leaves to m.....' She stopped suddenly and blushed without completing 'me'. Swami Tanmayananda once prostrated himself before her and placed her feet on his head, to which the Mother objected, explaining that the Master dwells in the head as Siva seated on the thousand-petalled lotus. To this the Swami said, 'If the Master is Siva Himself, who are you?' The Mother replied unhesitatingly, 'Who else could I be? I am the Divine Mother.' At Koalpara she put the Master's picture and hers side by side and worshipped both. Once when the devotee Vaikuntha took leave of her at Kamarpukur, she said suddenly, 'Vaikuntha, call on me,' and at once corrected herself by adding, 'Call on the Master.' But Lakshmi Devi, who was present there, asserted that what came out of her mouth first was the fact and asked Vaikuntha to stick to that command. The Mother indicated her tacit agreement with the interpretation through her silence. Once Prof. Gokul Das De found the Mother sitting on the lowest step of the Ghat on the Ganga wrapt in meditation. In very low tone, not

Glimpses of Her Personality

audible from that distance he chanted verses from the *Chandi* in salutation of the visible Mother before him. The Mother opened her eyes, looked at the devotee and raised her hands in benediction, accepting her oneness with the Chandi invoked in those verse. Yet such acts of self-revelation were few and far between; and occurring, as they did, in the midst of her vastly preponderating role as universal mother in a human sense, they may look to some as vague and ambiguous. The Mother herself gave her explanation in her reply to a woman who asked her bluntly, 'Why is it that we do not see you as the Goddess?' The Mother's reply was: 'Can all and sundry do so, my dear? There lay a diamond on a flight of steps of a tank. Every one who went by it for bath took it for an ordinary stone, rubbed his or her feet on it as they went their way. At last a jeweller came, and he recognised it to be a precious stone.' The parable conveys the idea that only those who had a real eye for matters divine and spiritual, had the fitness to see that aspect of hers. From others, it remained hidden. But its revelation through the vestment of humanity was common to all.

Another very striking feature of her personality was her reverence for what she called the 'Master' (ie Sri Ramakrishna), to her the equivalent of God as man. It has already been mentioned how, during the life-time of Sri Ramakrishna, he formed the centre of all her thought and activity. Even after his physical disappearance, a sense of his presence as a living, palpitating reality continued to be the ground work of her earthly consciousness. It has been pointed out before that the Master appeared to her in a vision and told her that death for him meant only passing from one room to another. She had verification of this fact in the vision she had of him and in the help and guidance she received from him at all times of crisis in her life.

This experience of hers was not a mere subjective feeling, but a fact guaranteed by other objective considerations. She had heard from the Master himself, as recorded in her conversations, that even after his passing, he would continue to live in his subtle body in the hearts of his devotees for three hundred years to come, after which he would appear on earth once again. This statement has to be understood in the light of the fact that the Master was not an ordinary soul born on earth to reap the fruits of his own Karma, or to attain personal salvation, but a Divine Incarnation come to fulfil the need of humanity as a new guide and helper in its spiritual struggle. An Incarnation therefore does not pass out of the sphere of the cosmic scheme when his physical body perishes, as an ordinary enlightened soul (Mukta-purusha) does at death. The Incarnation survives in his subtle body and continues to serve as a medium for the expression of Divine mercy of which his personality is an embodiment. He continues to do so until he takes another physical embodiment, inaugurating a new age in the life of mankind. Those who serve the cause of the Incarnation and commune with him in sincere devotion and self-surrender, can contact his personality and receive his protection and guidance in their spiritual strivings. The sense of presence which the

Holy Mother had with regard to Sri Ramakrishna is only an illustration of this truth.

The Master's presence was a reality to her in a very intimate sense. One found this from the way in which she did his daily worship and offering, which had a uniqueness of its own. Her worship looked more like the actual service of the Master and direct communion with him rather than a ritualistic procedure. In fact she employed no rituals at all. The things for offering such as flowers, sandal paste and fruits were all prepared either by herself or someone else. She was very particular that this was done with scrupulous neatness and precision, exactly as one would do for the reception of a living person. Her actual worship consisted only in placing the flowers before the Master with loving devotion and in meditation for a while, which took in all about half an hour.

It was the way in which she made the food offering that, more than anything else, conveyed a sense of her intimate perception of the Master. After arranging the food, she would address the Master as one would a living person, and say, 'Please come and take your food.' At Jayrambati she was often heard to tell the Master on the Jagaddhatri Puja days, 'O Lord, finish your meal a little quickly today. I have to attend the Jagaddhatri Puja.' This behaviour of hers would be puzzling until it is understood that she actually used to visualize the Master partaking of the food. She used to say that he took it in three ways. Either he actually partook of the offering, or a ray of light from his forehead touched the food, or he only indicated his acceptance without actually partaking of the food. Never would she be satisfied until she found the Master accepting the food, and no food would she herself take unless it was accepted by him.

A remarkable example of this took place when she was once invited by a family of devotees at Calcutta, well-known among the followers of Sri Ramakrishna. Though devoted, the reputation of that family was not all clean. Now, when the Holy Mother went there, she was requested to offer cooked food to the Master in the family shrine. Being very much pressed, she agreed to do so. But as she said later on, she found the Master reluctant to accept the food; for he could accept no food other than what came from pure souls. Finally, after much prayer, he just touched a bit of the payasa (a kind of porridge) to his tongue. That day the Holy Mother was observed not to eat anything from the rich variety of dishes served to her. With some difficulty she swallowed a little payasa. For she could not bring herself to eat anything that the Master had not taken.

Even when she travelled long distances, she would not take food without offering it to the Master. She would break the journey at some convenient place, cook the food, offer it to the Master and then partake of it. A striking event, illustrative of her non-ceremonial devotion and living contact with the Master, took place once on her way to Jayrambati. Arrangements had been made for cooking rice in an earthen pot. But in the act of getting the pot down, it dropped from a disciple's hand and broke, throwing its contents out. All were perplexed as to what they would offer that noon, but not the Holy Mother. She gathered the clean rice from the top layers, and offered it to the Master, saying, 'O Lord, you must be satisfied with this today.' She knew that the Lord she worshipped was a living presence, one near and dear to her, who did not stand on any ceremonial considertation.

Another instance, illustrating how the Master was a living presence to her, will not be out of place. In the procedure of worship followed at the Udbodhan Office, it was customary to pick the best of the offered flowers, remove the water from them and decorate the photograph of the Master with them when he was put to sleep. One day, while the Holy Mother was taking rest in the afternoon, she dreamt that the Master had got up from bed and was on the floor. Surprised at this, she woke up, approached the Master's bed, and saw the photograph covered with ants. Evidently the ants had come from the flowers, and her dream indicated that they disturbed the rest of him who was a living presence to her. Thenceforth she instructed the Swami who assisted in the shrine to dispense with the decoration.

To all those who went to her in a mood of repentance or with true spiritual aspiration, she conveyed a little of her vivid sense of the Master's presence. She assured the Master's grace and protection to them, and helped to create in them a conviction of the same. But she claimed no power for herself. To her the Master was everything, and she was his humble instrument. She had obliterated herself in him. So also, never by word or action did she convey the slightest trace of self-assertion with regard to him. Ordinarily she never showed that her earthly relation with him gave her any special claim on him. He was the same to all, and devotion was the only condition of realizing his presence.

While the idea described above is comparatively easy to understand, it should not be misconstrued to mean as mere faith in the personal survival in a deified form, or as exhausting the many-sidedness of her relation with the Master. The conception has much more profound depth than appears at first glance. That the Master came and that he is ever present even now after his physical disappearance, is an assurance of his eternal existence. For she identified him with the Universal Being and all His manifestations. When the Master passed away, she exclaimed: 'Ah Mother Kali! Have you left me!' She told Sudhira Devi one day: 'I was in such a state at one time that I could not even drive away an ant from the food-offering because of the conviction that the Master himself was eating it.' To several devotees she said, 'The Master is everything—he is the Guru and he is the Chosen Deity.' To a devotee, Surendranath Bhowmik, who felt some incongruity in worshipping the Master as a male form but addressing him at the time of dedicating the fruits of his Japa as 'O great Goddess', the Mother replied, 'He is both the great God and the great Goddess. He is in all the deities and he dwells in all creatures. You may call him the great God or the great Goddess.' To another lady devotee she said, 'He is everything; He is both the Purusha and the Prakriti. Everything flows from him.' She maintained that in the Master all the deities dwelt and that they could all be worshipped in him and with his name.

If the Mother then looked upon the Master as the Universal Being fit to be worshipped as all deities, and herself as his humble votary and disciple, there is an esoteric sense in which she was identical with him, with a distinction that does not amount to a difference. Side by side with the acceptance of the Master as one with the supreme Divinity, she also spoke of him as the redeemer, the one Entity that incarnates from age to age for the redemption of mankind and of herself as his Sakti accompanying him in all his incarnations. As such, they were the obverse and the reverse of the same coin, and not merely the Deity and the devotee, or the Guru and the disciple. It is this notion that some of the early lay disciples of the Great Master failed to grasp and which came to be corrected later with deeper understanding as illustrated in the relationship of Girish Chandra Ghosh with her. It was again against this tendency to make an absolute difference between them that Swami Premananda declared that those who do so will not make any progress in spiritual life. A man with a devotional insight into the Master's life can easily understand that they are the warp and woof of the same web. The vision that sees her only as a follower or a votary, the Guru's wife, is as mistaken a notion as setting her as a parallel personage in exclusion of him.

There were, however, moments when, under the influence of higher moods or by way of confiding some secret to a devoted disciple, she would speak of her higher nature and of her divinity. In such moments she would compare herself to Lakshmi, the divine consort of Narayana, speak of herself as the Mother of all beings, or admit her capacity to confer liberation on any one. A few illustrations will make the point clear. To Swami Kesavananda who expressed his sorrow at not having seen the Master, she revealed this secret: 'He is here in this body (her own) in a subtle form. The Master himself told me that he dwells in me in subtle form.' Another striking undertone of her sense of identity with the Master is the following experience of three devotees: These three together were paying their respects to the Holy Mother at the Udbodhan Office. The Mother arranged Prasad for them in three leaf plates, and before handing them over to the devotees, touched them with the tip of her tongue, so as to make it her Prasad too. At this one of them blurted out, saying, 'Mother, I don't take anybody's Prasad except the Master's.' The Mother replied impassively, 'Then don't eat it.' A little later, better sense dawned on the gentleman. The significance of the Mother's act now became clear to him, and he approached her again, saying, 'Mother, I have now understood your meaning. You and the Master are the same, identical.' With the same impassiveness as before, the Mother replied, 'Then eat.'

Thus even in this sense of identity, she never minimised the Master's importance in the unified conception of them both. She was a part and parcel of him, an eternal and uneliminable essence in his being, always going with him and never having an existence separate from him. If, without understanding this, any one equated her with the Master or even distantly suggested the displacement of him by her, she reacted very sharply. When a disciple once said in answer to an enquiry, 'Mother, with your blessing, I am quite well,' She reprimanded him, saying, 'Why do you drag me in everywhere? Can't you mention the Master's name? All that you see belongs to the Master.'

Generally she displayed only this attitude of a humble votary, ever living in the presence of the Master, serving him—an attitude that would appear to some as in conflict with her theophanic oneness with him. She did so, probably because this human role was much more significant for men at large, as it would set for them a pattern of devotion that they could try to imitate or follow. So very often, as soon as statements about her divinity came out of her mouth, she would change the topic and try to give the impression that they were slips of the tongue. For, unlike ordinary people, who want to appear much bigger than what they are, her tendency was always to hide her own greatness and appear as a common person. When anybody spoke of her, in her presence, as a divine being, she would at once stop such flattering words and say with the utmost sincerity that she was what she was, only because the Master had given her shelter at his feet. The veil with which she always hid her face in public seemed to be symbolic of this more profound veil of modesty with which she loved to hide her own towering greatness. It was for this reason that Sri Ramakrishna in fun likened her to a cat that loved to hide its real colour with ashes.

As in spiritual gifts, so was she great in her intellectual qualities. Though uneducated in the modern sense, she was the heir to a great culture both by birth and training, and her extensive travels, varied contacts and experience in administration, both spiritual and secular, endowed her with a broad outlook, refined manners and penetrating intelligence. Thus the stateliness of her courtesy and the openness of her mind were almost as wonderful as her sainthood. Sister Nivedita, who made these observations, found in her an 'instant power to penetrate a new religious feeling or idea,' which she must have cultivated by her association with Sri Ramakrishna. When Easter music was sung before her by the Sister and another Western devotee, she evinced swift comprehension and deep sympathy with those resurrection hymns, unimpeded by any foreignness or unfamiliarity in them. Again when the same disciples described a European wedding to her, she was exceedingly delighted on hearing the marriage vow, 'For better, for worse, for richer, for poorer, in sickness and in health—till death us do part,' and characterized them as 'dharmic words, righteous words!'

Her intelligence also was equally remarkable. She could grasp complicated situations with the utmost ease and arrive at sound judgements with extreme swiftness. An example of this has already been seen in the way she responded when the Master tested her with the gift of ten thousand rupees that the devotee Laxminarayan wanted to settle on him. The following incident furnishes another example. One day when the Master was going to a religious festival at Panihati, a few miles from Dakshineswar, with some devotees, the Master inquired through Yogin-Ma if the Holy Mother desired to accompany, adding that she might come if she liked. At once she understood that he had some reservation in his mind, and did not join the party. Later on, the Master spoke highly of her intelligence in having divined his thought; for he feared that if light-hearted people saw them together on the scene of the festival they would sarcastically remark, 'Look there, the "Hamsa" and the "Hamsi" (female swan) are going.'

In later days a disciple who was conducting a charitable dispensary complained to her, 'Even people with means come to our dispensary for medicine, though it is meant only for the poor. Should we give medicine to those who have resources?' After a minute's reflection she replied, 'My child, all are poor in this part of the country. If, even after knowing the object of your dispensary, people go there begging for medicine, you should supply it, provided you have the resources. Any one who begs is poor.'

Once the head of the Koalpara Ashram complained to the Holy Mother that he no longer had control over his workers because they had learnt to think for themselves, and moreover, when they went to her or to Swami Saradananda, they received every attention and nice food. And he requested her to send them back to him with proper instruction. At this she replied, 'How foolishly you talk! Our essential point is love. It is through love alone that the spiritual family of Sri Ramakrishna has grown and developed. Besides, I am their mother. So how could you criticize in my presence the way in which they were fed and clothed? Alas, how much did I weep and pray to the Master for my children! That is why you find everywhere Ashramas and monasteries through his blessings. After the passing away of the Master his disciples renounced the world, found a temporary shelter and for a few days lived together. Then one by one they went out independently and began to roam hither and thither. That made me very sad. I prayed to the Master, saying, "O Lord, you have been embodied in human form, and you spent the period of your earthly existence with a few disciples. Now has everything ended with your passing away? In that case, what need was there for your embodiment entailing so much suffering? I have seen in Brindavan and Banaras so many holy men living on alms and having the shades of trees for shelter. There is no lack of Sadhus (holy men) of that type. I cannot bear to see my children, who have renounced all for your sake, wandering about for want of simple food and coarse clothing. It is also my prayer that my children should live together, clinging to you and your teachings, and people afflicted with the sufferings of the world should come to them and get peace of mind by hearing from them your words. That is why you incarnated yourself in a human form. My mind becomes restless, seeing my children roam about here and there." ' This remarkable reply shows what an insight she had into the secret of administering the monastic organization of Sri Ramakrishna, and what important part she played in its formation quite unknown to others. Many more such instances of her intelligence will be found in the companion volume—*'The Gospel of the Holy Mother.'*

Glimpses of Her Personality

She had also a very large reserve of courage and resourcefulness, which no one would at first credit her with. Her general bashfulness and motherly tenderness hid these qualities of hers, and it was only when critical situations in life faced her that she would allow this side of her nature to show itself. These qualities became manifest in a remarkable manner in connection with the 'dacoit father' episode.[2] To cite another instance: Once when she was staying at Jayrambati, Girish Chandra Ghosh went to see her with the intention of taking Sannyasa with her consent, but the Mother, in very mild terms, refused him permission. Girish, however, would not accept the verdict so easily. He began to argue his case vehemently for about half an hour, and as he was a man of great mental powers and violent emotions, his pleadings were likely to demolish the resolution of any ordinary person. But the Holy Mother, in spite of all her apparent mildness, had the nerve to stand them and stick to her conviction.

Another incident of the same type occurred in connection with a mishap that befell Swami Vivekananda. While travelling in Kashmir, the Swami was cursed by a Mohammedan Fakir who was displeased with him, because a disciple of his had contracted an admiration for the Swami. The curse had its effect. The Swami felt very much mortified at this, especially thinking that Sri Ramakrishna could not protect him from a Fakir's black magic. When he next met the Holy Mother, the Swami told her about these happenings. He was in a fit of pique, and as he represented his grievance against the Master on this account, his face flushed, and he became very excited and vehement. The Holy Mother, however, did not lose her presence of mind. She calmly consoled him saying, 'Well, my child, we read that even Sankaracharya suffered from the effects of a similar curse. It is all the same whether the ailment occurs to your body or to that of the Master. Moreover, the Master did not come to destroy anything; he came only to fulfil. He had respect for all forms of knowledge, and believed even in omens.'

The most remarkable manifestation of her courage and presence of mind, however, took place during her Kamarpukur days, when she was attacked by a devotee of the Master named Harish who had turned insane. To describe the incident in her own words: 'Harish was then staying at Kamarpukur for a few days. One day, when I was entering the house after visiting a neighbour, he began to chase me. He was then in a distracted state of mind. He had lost his senses on account of his wife. There was then no one else in the house. I did not know where to go, and ran quickly behind the barn. He would not, however, leave me. I ran and ran round it seven times till I got exhausted. Then my true self came out. I threw him to the ground, pressed my knee on his chest, drew out his tongue and slapped him hard on the cheeks until my fingers became red with slapping. He began to gasp for breath.'[3] Thus her mild and motherly personality had unsuspected potentialities within it.

The Holy Mother was thus endowed with diverse qualities of head and heart which would have made one great in any situation. Her greatness, however, consisted not so much in being so gifted, which many others too could be, but in keeping herself above the vanity attendant on it. Besides, she was being literally worshipped by hundreds as a veritable embodiment of divinity, and many distinguished monks and citizens of Calcutta were at her beck and call. All the great Sannyasin disciples of Sri Ramakrishna held her in reverence. They were all men of high culture and spiritual attainments. Yet when they were to take any decisive step in their life, or in the management of affairs, they considered the Holy Mother's opinion to be of the highest importance. Even Swami Vivekananda decided on his visit to the West only after he had ascertained her view. Swami Premananda would regard a word from her as a divine command and obey it implicitly. It was noticed that when Swami Brahmananda went to her, his frame would shiver with a high spiritual emotion.

Even Sannyasins who had no connection with the Ramakrishna Order and were utter strangers to her showed the highest reverence to the Holy Mother. Once a Dandi Sannyasin came to pay his respects to her. Now, Dandi Sannyasins are generally very orthodox. Excepting to their Gurus and men of their own rank, they do not show special regard to any other, much less to a woman. But this Sannyasin, probably hailing from western India, had come to Calcutta only to meet the Holy Mother. From some scriptural discussions he had at the Udbodhan Office, it also turned out that he was an erudite scholar who could speak fluently in Sanskrit and had a thorough grasp of the Vedanta and other systems of philosophy. When he was taken to the

Mother's presence, he approached her with great fervour to make prostrations. But she, with her characteristic humility and regard for Sannyasins, felt much embarrassed and requested him not to do so. In spite of it he prostrated himself before her, recited verses from the *Saptasati* in praise of her with great devotion, and prayed for her blessing here and hereafter. The Mother then asked a disciple to give some mangoes to the Sannyasin. Only three mangoes could be found in the store, and these were presented to him. When the Sannyasin had left her presence, she asked the disciple to search for more ripe mangoes, as she wanted to give him more. The disciple got one more and took it to him. As he handed it over to him, he was astonished to hear the Sannyasin remark with great delight, 'Oh, I am very glad to receive this. At first when the Mother gave me three mangoes, I thought she gave me only the Trivargas—the three-fold ends of Dharma (virtue), Artha (wealth) and Kama (desire). Now I find she has given me also the fourth end—Moksha (liberation).'

But no amount of honour, praise, or worship elated her in the least. She was hardly conscious that all this was being done to her. To her spiritualized vision, all that was hers, or was due to her, went to the glorification of the Master and not of herself. Hence she always remained the innocent village maiden that she was when she tramped her way from Jayrambati to Calcutta—simple, unostentatious, guileless and ever ready to serve. But it must be noted that hers was no affected simplicity. For behind her virtues there was no trace of the ego. Just as a perfume manifests its fragrance and a full-blown lotus its beauty without any conscious effort on their part, so did all her virtues, including her very simplicity, manifest themselves spontaneously.

To sum up, the main strands that enter into the complex make-up of her personality are her Divinity, her motherliness, her absorption in the Master, her artlessness, her simplicity, and her holy innocence which overshadowed her many gifts of both head and heart. Taking into account all these colours in the spectrum of her personality, Swami Premananda once spoke thus of her glory: 'You have seen with your own eyes, how this Mother, who is in reality the great Goddess ruling over those who wield the destinies of kings and emperors, has yet chosen to become a poor woman, plastering the house with cow-dung, scouring utensils, winnowing rice and clearing the leavings of the devotees after their meals. She undertakes all these tasks to teach the householders their domestic duties. What infinite endurance, limitless mercy and absolute absence of egotism are there!' And again he speaks thus on the same theme in a letter: 'Who has understood the Mother? There is not the least trace of splendour. The Master had at least the brilliance of wisdom. But what about the Mother? For her even that glow is wanting. What a great power is that! The poison that we cannot assimilate we pass on to the Mother. The Mother takes on every one on her lap. Infinite power! Limitless mercy!... She is giving shelter to all, eating everybody's food, and assimilating all. Remember the mercy of the Mother, that infinite compassion of the Mother in weal and woe, in success and failure, in famine and pestilence, in wars and revolutions. Glory unto the Mother!'

No picture of the Holy Mother's personality can be complete without a brief account of her daily routine and habits. Whether she was at the Udbodhan Office or at Jayrambati, she invariably got up at 3 a.m., just as she used to do in her Dakshineswar days. As the first auspicious sight for the day, she would have a look at the Master's photo in the shrine, which was also her living room wherever she was, for she never liked to be separated from him. She then prayed to the Master for leave to attend to her daily duties, and sat in her bed telling beads till about 6 o'clock when she woke up the Master and made the first offering. After this, if she were at Jayrambati, she would, as the mistress of the house, busy herself with cleaning the rooms and cutting vegetables for the day's cooking. Devotees noticed that she appeared specially affectionate and gracious as she sat cutting vegetables and conversing with them on various topics. So long as her health was good, she used also to take part in the more strenuous items of household work like scouring utensils, carrying water from the tank and husking paddy. The arrangements for worship, such as cutting fruits and collecting flowers, were generally done by her personally, sometimes assisted by her nieces or devotees. Every day she made about a hundred (some say two hundred) rolls of betel. Between eight and nine she performed the worship and gave initiation to people, if there were any who desired it, and then distributed the offered fruits and sweets among the devotees and members of the house. She was very particular that the worship should be finished by ten at the latest, and she would become impatient if the monastic disciple to whom she entrusted the work at times, caused delay; for it would then be too late for the devotees to take Prasada (consecrated food). After the worship she took her breakfast which consisted of sugar-candy water and a little of the offerings, if any were left; for whenever she distributed them, she gave away everything without keeping anything for herself. She then went into the kitchen and relieved the cook who would then go to take breakfast and attend to her personal needs. Thus she would herself cook most of the things for the Master's food offering. She had no objection to offer whatever was prepared for the day, but she took special delight in making those dishes which the Master had particularly liked. The distinctive characteristic of her cooking was that she would use salt, spices and red pepper very sparingly. After 11 o'clock she finished her bath, and by half past twelve made the noon offering to the Master. All the members of the house then sat for food. In her earlier days the Holy Mother would serve food to all the devotees, and herself sit for the meal only after they had finished. As this habit delayed her meal time considerably, she was later on persuaded to desist from it. She would, therefore, see that the devotees were seated and served, and then herself sit down for the meal. After the devotees got up she would send them her Prasada for which many of them would wait. It was generally a mixture of several things taken from her plate, and sometimes of milk and rice.

She then conversed with the devotees for a while, and before 2 o'clock retired for her siesta.[4]

She used to rest till 3 o'clock, after which she woke up the Master at about 4 p.m. Then she sat in a corner of the room, doing Japa without rosary and talking with the devotees who went to see her. Towards the evening she came out and sat in the verandah. Sometimes she worked in the kitchen in the evening too, to save the cook from over-work. At dusk, after doing the Aratrika, she took a bit of offered sweets and reclined on her bed in an indrawn mood, perhaps doing Japa. The last offering to the Master came off at 7 p.m., and half an hour later the devotees all sat for supper. At night the Mother took two or three pieces of Luchis, a little curry and a pint of milk. Before eleven she retired for the night.

In Calcutta also her daily routine continued to be almost the same. She used to take her bath a little earlier, for which purpose she went to the Ganges on alternate days, accompanied by Golap-Ma. Her physical work too was less, as Golap-Ma and Yogin-Ma looked after the household management. Sometimes in later days even the worship, excepting the offering of food, would be entrusted to some monastic disciple. But in spite of relief from regular duties, her life at Calcutta was much more strenuous; for, devotees would go to her at all hours of the day for initiation, for getting their doubts cleared, or for unburdening their hearts. Even after 2 p.m., when she rested, quite a number of women devotees would gather round her; for they had to return home by 4 or 4.30 p.m. The Holy Mother would, therefore, talk to them, lying in bed. In the afternoons, men

Glimpses of Her Personality 231

devotees are allowed to see her after half past five, when the women assembled would be asked to retire to an adjoining room. As the men came in to make obeisance to her, the Holy Mother would be seated on the bedstead, her feet resting on the floor, her face veiled, and her whole body covered with a Chaddar (sheet). If any devotee made enquiries about her health or other matters, she would reply either in low tones or just by the movements of her head or the hand. Those who had to ask her any questions waited till the others had gone out. If the devotee was intimately known to the Mother, she would directly answer his questions in a subdued voice. In case he was a stranger or was an elderly person, she would reply indirectly in very low tones, and the disciple attending on her would communicate the reply distinctly to him. On Tuesdays and Saturdays, as well as on special festive occasions, the public at large was allowed to approach her and make obeisance. They were generally very strenuous days for the Holy Mother.

She required very little food and sleep. She went to bed at about 11 p.m. and got up by 3 a.m. Sometimes on moonlit nights she would get up even earlier, thinking that her usual time had come. As mentioned before, she had three meals a day, but her breakfast and supper were very light. Owing to rheumatism, she used curd and cold things of that type very sparingly. Her main condiments consisted of thin soup of black lentil and poppy seeds roasted in a ladle. Among the things she liked were fried vegetables, preparations made of tender leaves of pulses and radish, Sandesh of the less soft variety, and cakes soaked in syrup of sugar. In later days she used to take a kind of green called Amrul, prescribed by the physicians as a precaution against dysentery. Of all edibles she had a partiality for mangoes, curiously preferring those that had a tinge of sourness in them. Once a devotee purchased mangoes without tasting them, and when they were served at the dinner time, all found it impossible to take them. But everyone was surprised to hear the Mother remarking, 'Ah! these are fine mangoes. They are a little sour.'

In her dress the Holy Mother was very simple. She draped her body with one long piece of cloth like all Bengali ladies of the old generation. She never used any frock, stitched garments, or footwear. Once a devotee presented a fine frock to her, but she used it only twice or thrice and then put it aside. As she was simple and guileless in nature, so was she plain and unsophisticated in food, dress and daily habits.

Before concluding this chapter, it is relevant to cite a number of small events in the Mother's life and her remarks on several topics, revealing the versatility of her personality and her liberal outlook on problems of life. Human sentiments always weighed with her more than social respectability. The following is a striking example. In front of the Mother's house at Calcutta, a man was living with his mistress. Respectable society shunned such relationships. The woman once fell ill. It was found that in spite of this irregular relationship, the man attended on the woman with all care. Coming to know of it, the Mother said to a woman in great appreciation: 'How splendidly the man is attending on that

Glimpses of Her Personality   233

woman. I never saw the like of it before! This is real service, this is real love.' Mother's catholicity was extremely puzzling to that socially conservative lady to whom she addressed these words. The lady's reaction was: 'Oh fancy! Serving a mistress! I cannot think of it!'

There was also a vein of girlish simplicity and innocent frivolity often in her talk and behaviour, which made her company delightful. Some examples will illustrate the point. During her early visit to Calcutta, she mistook the hissing sound in water pipes caused by air pressure, as the hissing of a snake within and got frightened. Often she used to narrate this to others and laugh at herself. The wire loop of an old type of hurricane lantern was too much for her to manipulate for taking out its shade for cleaning, and she used to speak of it as a complicated mechanism! Her estimation of mechanical skill once provoked the laughter of all present when she remarked: 'Oh, the daughter-in-law of such and such a family can wind a time-piece!'

Though the Mother was liberal in her outlook on all questions concerning human welfare and dignity, she none the less followed the local customs and shared the common beliefs and habits of the people of the place. Some instances will shed interesting light on her personality. She was advised by Golap-Ma to apply oil when she went for bath to the Ganga. But she would not, saying, 'If I do so, others will follow my example; and it is not proper to dip oneself in the holy Ganga with oil rubbed over the body.' When returning from the Ganga after a bath, she would pour water at the wayside banyan trees and salute them. She would not undertake a journey to outside stations in March-April (Chaitra), as some old traditions prohibited it.

A lady disciple once questioned her whether there was any justification for Hindu women considering themselves impure during their monthly period and keeping aloof from cooking, worship and sacred functions in general. The Mother in reply quoted what the Master had told her on this subject: 'You won't incur any sin thereby. Would you explain which part of the body is impure—skin, flesh, bone or marrow? Know that purity and impurity reside in the mind; there is nothing impure outside.' Then she added: 'Yes daughter, it is permissible if one has the requisite devotion to the Master. ...You can do worship. But if you feel any compunction, then don't do it.'

Radhu was once slapped by her husband Manmath for throwing a towel at him. At first the Mother sympathized with Radhu, but when the other ladies remarked that Radhu was wrong and deserved slapping, the Mother innocently remarked, 'Well, I had no such problem with the Master, and so I am inexperienced in such matters.' She sometimes played the part of a petulant girl and entered into disputes with children at their level. Once she was rolling Chapatis along with a boy assistant, Rammay (the later Gouriswarananda). Nalini, her niece, praised Rammay's rolling at the expense of the Mother. The Mother at once stopped rolling and said, 'I have grown old in this work, and he is just a suckling from whose throat milk will come out if pressed! I shall roll no more.' Rammay also stopped, saying that, if the Mother did not roll he too would not. In the end a reconciliation was effected.

When in the course of advancing years, it became impossible for her to cook for all, an old Brahmin lady was engaged to cook. The Mother called her 'aunt.' At a Durga Puja celebration, after the image was immersed, the Mother went to bow down to the 'aunt,' as juniors generally do to seniors. The woman protested, saying, 'Ah! This is unthinkable. You are the Mother of the universe, and all salute you. How can you think of saluting me, an ordinary woman?' But the Mother was not dissuaded by this protest. She did bow down to the cook, saying, 'It won't do. You are my "aunt," and I must bow down to you.'

In the Mother's house there was a parrot which received the Mother's attention everyday. After washing and cleaning the cage and feeding the bird, the Mother would say, 'Dear Gangaram, now talk,' and the bird would say, 'Hare Ram, Hare Ram; Ram Ram Hare Hare: Hare Krishna, Hare Krishna; Krishna Krishna Hare Hare.' From the Brahmacharins it learnt to address her as 'Mother,' and occasionally it would cry, 'Mother, O Mother!', which meant it was hungry. The Mother would respond, 'Here I am, my son, here I am,' and would go and feed it.

Once Sister Nivedita and Sister Christine, who had just learnt a little Bengali, wanted to demonstrate their skill in it and addressed the Mother in Bengali, 'Mother divine! You are our Kali.' The Mother responded with an innocent smile and quipped 'Ah! I can't be Kali before you. I shall then have to put out my tongue!'

Towards her last days at Jayrambati, 'aunty' Bhavani, a distant cousin of hers, had come to see her. The 'aunt's mother was sick, and the Mother gave her two good pomegranates to feed her. Just then a good quantity of fruits, sent by some devotee of Ranchi, arrived. The greedy 'aunt' could not help coveting it. She remarked with a deep sigh: 'Alas! At first it was I who was proposed to be married to Paramahamsa Deva. My father did not give me in marriage to him, because he thought he was mad. Ah! If my father had accepted the proposal, all these things would have come to my house!' All had a hearty laughter at the greedy 'aunt'. The Mother did not join the laughter, but put on a friendly smile, enjoying the funny situation, and said to the 'aunt,' 'Then take as much as you want of these fruits. They are yours.'

About Pranayama she told a disciple practising it: 'You may do it, just a little. It is no good heating the brain by too much practice of it. And if the mind settles down of its own accord, where is the need for Pranayama?' And about Yoga Asanas she said: 'You may practise after taking into consideration both sides of the question—on the one hand, there is the chance of the mind becoming too much body-conscious by their practice, and on the other, total giving up of the practice may ruin the health.'

A devotee, not finding peace of mind by making Japa, wanted to stop Japa and other practices. He had also heard that it is harmful if one fails to make Japa after receiving the Mantra. So he went to the Mother and wanted to return the Mantra to her. At this she said, 'Now look at this! I lose my sleep in the thought of you all, and the Master has blessed you long ago.' Tears rolled down her cheek as she spoke. She continued, 'Then you need not make Japa of the Mantra any more.' Brought to his senses, the devotee felt utmost remorse for his thoughtless act and cried out, 'O Mother, will you take away everything from me? What shall I do hereafter? Am I then condemned to hell?' The Mother at once consoled him, saying, 'What! You, who are my son, to be damned! Whoever has come here, whoever is my son, is already redeemed. Destiny dare not throw my children into hell. Entrust your future to me and be free from anxiety.'

A devotee asked the Mother about initiation: 'Why should one take initiation and repeat a Mantra? Instead of doing the Japa of a Mantra, one can go on repeating any name of God. Won't it be sufficient?' The Mother replied: 'The Mantra purifies the body. A man becomes holy by repeating the Mantra. The Mantra is necessary for the purification of the body, if not for anything else.'

Comparing Japa to a tree coming out of a small seed, she said: 'How small is the seed of the Lord's name! And yet from it sprouts in time divine moods, devotion and love.' At another time she said: 'Through Japa and austerity the bondage of karma is cut asunder, but God cannot be realized except through love and devotion. Did the cowherds get Krishna by Japa and meditation, or by practising a sense of their closeness to him, which enabled them to address him intimately, "Come here, dear," "Take this dear," "Eat this, dear," and so on?'

From an exalted point of view she said to another disciple: 'These Mantras and the like are nothing, my daughter. Devotion is all.' And to another: 'You talk of having done so much Japa or so much of work! Nothing will avail. Who can achieve anything unless the Mahamaya opens the way? O creature, surrender yourself, just surrender yourself. Then only will She be gracious and clear the way for you.'

She never encouraged people to undertake rigorous forms of austerity amounting to torture of the flesh. Old-time Brahmana widows of Bengal were expected by custom to fast during day, and be satisfied at night with liquid diet and fruits. To one who was practising such rigorous rules of life, the Mother said: 'You should take Chapatis or Parothas at night. Take these after offering them to the Master.' Kshirodbala Roy, a widow from childhood, was in the habit of observing Ekadasi, eschewing all food except some sago at night. Coming to know that sago is a ceremonially impure food, she gave up even that and began to fast totally. On hearing about it, the Mother persuaded her to take sago. She had clipped her hair the way widows did and Yogin-Ma and Golap-Ma were arguing with her against this practice of orthodox widows. Strangely enough the Mother came to her help and said: 'It is good that she has done so. If one has hair, there creeps in a sense of luxury and one spends much time caring for the hair. However that might be, my daughter, you have crossed over the bridge of hair and reached here. You have reached the goal for which all austerity is practised. So I tell you, don't practise austerities any more.' She discouraged another fasting widow from her exaggerated notion about fasting, saying: 'If the soul hungers for food, that should be offered. Else you incur sin. The soul cries out saying, "She has deprived me of food." ' She also permitted some of her disciples to do their spiritual practice or worship after taking tea or snacks. She used to say: 'Call on God when the body is calmed with a little food.' Here we get a wonderfully harmonious blend of conservatism and liberalism.

This does not, however, mean that the Holy Mother herself threw the healthy rigours of austerity to the winds. She herself observed Ekadasi, but took Luchis as food. She took no fish or meat. Nor did she wear any bodice or jacket, and her clothing was one long piece of cloth with thin border. She always kept an air of austerity about her. A woman once went to seek the Mother's benediction on her husband who was seriously ill. She was dressed in all her finery. The Mother dismissed her quickly and remarked: 'See, how she has come in, all perfumes and fripperies, when she should have been observing vows.'

Once while instructing a woman devotee that human gifts are ephemeral, and that one should not therefore beg from men, not even from one's father or husband, she said, 'When the Master gives, it overflows all limits. The Master's gift knows no limitation. He that begs gets nothing; and he that begs not, gets everything.'

Her attitude towards money was one of non-attachment combined with practical wisdom. She had no allergy to touch money or precious metal as the

Master had. Whenever money or ornaments came into her hand, she touched them to her forehead by way of paying obeisance to Goddess Sri, whom wealth represents. When someone contrasted this behaviour of hers with the Master's, she said, 'To compare me to the Master! My son, I am after all a woman! The Master himself went so far as to make me wear gold ornaments.' She had, however, no attachment for it and did not bestow much attention on it. In her Dakshineswar days a sum of rupees two hundred, which some one had given for her expenses, came into her possession. She kept it in a provision container until she was taken to task for such carelessness with money. It was characteristic of her to refuse to accept a balance amount of seven rupees and a half from a disciple from the ten rupee note that she had given him for purchasing a blanket for a poor woman. The cost of this blanket was only rupees two and a half, but the Mother was under the impression that she had given only rupees five, and only the balance of it, after deducting the cost of rupees two and a half, was due to her. She would not receive what she considered excess in the refund offered. She was asked whether she knew the total amount in her box. She said she did not, because she kept no account. The Brahmacharin had at last to confront her with the question wherefrom he could have got this surplus money unless she had given him a ten rupee note. This made her accept the refund. In her earlier days, whenever money orders came to her, her brothers received them and surely they must have helped themselves to these remittances considerably. In later days a monastic

Glimpses of Her Personality 241

attendant received the money orders and put the amount in a box, from which she asked people to take money as and when required. She had to meet a lot of expenditure after Radhu came into her life and relatives began to lean on her more and more. Remittances too came from disciples very liberally. She spent on others whatever money came into her hands, and kept no account.

But because of her non-attachment, she should not be considered a fool in money matters. When the local village council imposed a tax of rupees four on her house, she protested and had it rescinded next year, saying, 'I am here now and can afford to pay the tax. But in future some monk or Brahmacharin may be in charge. Living on the support of others, he will find this tax a hardship.'

There is the story of procuring 'pure milk,' illustrative of her shrewd prudence. In order to get pure milk for Mother, Swami Jnanananda offered to give double the market price to a milkman at Jayrambati. Hearing this, the Mother protested, saying, 'What are you doing? Here milk is available at one pice a pound, and by offering double to the milkman, you are raising the price of milk and making it very dear to the poor people. As for milkmen, it is a part of their trade to add water whatever price you give. Higher cost will only be an inducement for them to add more water and earn more money.' When some of this 'pure milk' was brought to the Mother one day by a Brahmacharin, to the horror of all, they saw a small fish in it—an evidence of water not being added, to be sure! The Ashrama inmates wanted to throw away the milk, but the Mother said that others could take it without offering it to the Master.

One day Nalini was higgling for a long time with a woman pedlar of blankets to reduce the cost of a blanket from one and a quarter, to one rupee. At last the Mother interfered and scolded Nalini for detaining there a poor pedlar, who had to go from house to house, for a paltry sum of four annas. She further added that Nalini required no blanket, and that the one purchased should be given to a very poor disciple, Kshirodbala, who was present there, and who, in spite of her poverty, would not beg of anyone for a blanket even in that cold winter.

To quote one more instance of her practical wisdom: her disciples felt that a pedlar woman bringing vegetables to Jayrambati was charging a bit too high and they wanted to dismiss her. But the Mother interfered and said, 'Don't do so. She is mindful of our needs. Don't you see that she is able to procure for our mere asking all our needs even when none is available locally? She is our friend in need. She is my store-keeper.' Such wise and practical outlook on money matters in spite of her non-attachment is remarkable.

When the fourteen clauses of the Peace Treaty, as adumbrated at the close of the First World War by President Wilson of America, were explained to the Mother by a disciple, she remarked: 'Their protestation is only lip-deep (*mukhastha*). If it had come from their hearts (*antastha*), it would have meant a world of difference.'

She was against all forms of callous waste, even of trivial things. For example, some one threw away a fruit basket after emptying it. Mother saw that it was a good and serviceable one. She had it brought to her, washed it and kept it for future use. A disciple was about to throw away some well-prepared Khichuri, when the Mother protested. She found a beggar woman who was very glad to receive it. And she added, 'Each should have his due. What men can eat should not be wasted on cattle. What cattle can eat, should be thrown away to dogs. What cattle and dogs cannot eat, can be thrown into ponds for fish to eat. Nothing should be wasted.' ❑

---

1. Later on this disciple noticed that whenever the Mother wanted foreign goods, she would not ask him to procure them. She would send someone else. For she always respected others' sentiments. Besides, this shows that she approved of the nationalist spirit; only it was too narrow for her who was the mother of all.

But she did feel terrible indignation at some of the high-handed acts of certain police officers in suppressing the nationalist movement. Once two young women of the District, who were expectant mothers, were arrested on suspicion and made to walk a long distance to the police station. The news agitated the Mother very much, and with great indignation she said, 'Is this due to the Government orders, or to the ingenuity of the police official? We had never heard of such oppression of innocent women in the times of the good Queen Victoria. (Like many people of the old generation, the Holy Mother seems to have been an admirer of Queen Victoria to whose rule she referred now and then). If this has been done under the orders of the Government, the sin of this unrighteous act will tell on them. Were there no men nearby to rescue the poor girls?' Shortly after, she was glad to hear the news that the women were released.

For the information of those who favour the extensive use of home-made cloth, we may also mention here that she wanted some disciples to start a weaving factory instead of merely crying out patriotic slogans. She herself expressed a desire to spin if she could get a spinning wheel.

2. See pp. 93-96 *et seqq.*

3. Harish was a devotee of Sri Ramakrishna, who used to frequently visit the Baranagore monastery of the Ramakrishna Brotherhood in the early days. It is said that his wife, afraid of his tendency towards a life of renunciation, sought to deter him from it with drugs and charms, which eventually made his mind deranged. In this deranged condition he once visited Kamarpukur, and the Mother, coming to know his condition, wrote to the Math, asking that some one should come and take him away. Accordingly Swamis Saradananda and Niranjanananda started for this purpose. It was just before their arrival that the above mentioned incident took place. The Mother's words: 'Then my true self came out' are given a mystical meaning by many. They believe that the Mother, being a manifestation of the Divine Devi, could take any form she wanted. In this instance, the consciousness of Bagala, one of the Maha-vidyas, must have been on her, as Bagala is said to have killed an Asura in the same manner as the Mother now punished Harish. This punishment had a salutary effect on Harish. He fled to Vrindaban, and gradually his mental equilibrium was restored. Apart from these mystical implications, this incident, together with that of the 'dacoit father,' reveal certain most unsuspected features of the Mother's human character and personality also.

4. She cleaned her teeth four times a day with her favourite tooth powder made of burnt cocoanut leaves and tobacco leaves.

16. MORE PILGRIMAGES

THE HOLY MOTHER undertook several pilgrimages since the one to Brindavan immediately after the Master's passing (1886), described in chapter 11. These stretch over a period of twenty-five years and chronologically relate to different parts of her life.

About the month of April 1888, she went to Gaya with Swami Advaitananda (Gopal Senior). Sri Ramakrishna had asked her after the demise of his mother to go to Gaya and make funeral offerings in her memory. She took this opportunity to fulfil the Master's wish. On this occasion she also visited Bodh Gaya, the place of Buddha's enlightenment, situated a few miles away from Gaya proper. There she saw the well-known Hindu monastery of Bodh Gaya, and there the sight of provision for the comfortable accommodation and feeding of the resident Sannyasins evoked a characteristic desire in her motherly heart. The poverty and uncertainty in which the Master's own disciples were then living came to her mind in striking contrast, and she prayed to the Master with all the fervour of her motherly solicitude for similar arrangements being made for her monastic children. This was the prayer from which the monastic Brotherhood of Sri Ramakrishna gradually took shape as an organized body with the monks staying in Ashramas and centres of work.[1]

Towards the end of the same year (November 1888), the Holy Mother visited the famous temple of Puri with a party including Yogin-Ma, and swamis Brahmananda, Yogananda and Saradananda. They were accommodated at Puri in a house belonging to Balaram Bose's family. Now, Balaram Bose's brother, Harivallabh Bose, a famous advocate of those days, was a very influential man in those parts, and the priests of Puri held him in great respect. As the Holy Mother and party were his guests, Govinda Singari, one of the prominent priests of the place, wanted to show special honour to her by taking her to the temple of Jagannath in a palanquin. But she told him, 'No Govinda, you lead me to the temple, and I shall go after you just like a humble, destitute beggar woman to see Jagannath, the Lord of the Universe.'

As Sri Ramakrishna had not visited the temple of Jagannath in his lifetime, she took his photograph to the temple covered with her cloth and showed it to the image. She stayed for about four months at Puri, often visiting the temple at the time of the morning and evening services, and spending much time in meditation at the shrine of Lakshmi.

Recounting her experience of Jagannath, she said afterwards, 'I saw Jagannath seated like a Person of leonine bearing on His precious altar, and I was serving Him as an attendant.' Regarding the identity of

Jagannath, she had a dream in which she felt that the image was really the emblem of Siva seated on the altar made of a lakh of Salagrams (an emblem of Vishnu).[2]

The next time she went on pilgrimage was in 1894, when she visited Banaras and Brindavan for the second times, accompanied by her mother and brothers, besides Swami Yogananada, Golap-Ma and Yogin-Ma. Towards the end of November 1904, she went again to Puri along with her mother, her mad sister-in-law Surabala, her niece Radhu, and her brother Kali and his family, besides Swami Premananda and several devotees of the Master. During her stay at Puri she got a very painful boil on the leg. It was so painful that she would not allow anyone even to touch it. Coming to know of it, Swami Premananda made an arrangement with a doctor, who was a devotee of hers, to come with a knife and open the boil. The doctor approached her apparently to make prostration, but while doing so he quickly opened the boil. Although at the moment the intensity of pain caused annoyance in her mind towards the persons involved in the plot, she was very grateful to them when she felt relief after the operation. Subsequently her health improved, and she could therefore visit all the holy spots at Puri, circumambulate the temples and bathe in the sea twice. She spent two months in joy and peace in the holy city, reputed for its salubrious climate.

On one occasion she also paid a visit to Vishnupur,[3] situated about twenty-eight miles away from Kamarpukur. Vishnupur was once the capital of a flourishing kingdom, and the pious Vaishnava kings of the place had erected many beautiful temples, now mostly lying in ruins. Sri Ramakrishna looked upon this place as very sacred and asked the Holy Mother to visit it, saying, 'Vishnupur is "concealed Brindavan." You should go and visit the place some day.' Her visit to the place was in fulfilment of his command.

In December 1910, the Holy Mother started for Kothar in the Balasore district of Orissa en route to Rameswaram, the famous place of pilgrimage in the South. She stayed for about two months at Kothar, the headquarters of Balaram Bose's estate in Orissa. One Devendra Nath Chatterji, postmaster of Kothar—who had once accepted Christianity, and now, repenting of his action, wanted to come back to Hinduism—got reconverted there with the Holy Mother's approval. After certain purificatory ceremonies, one of the Holy Mother's monastic followers gave him the sacred thread and the Gayatri Mantra, and the next day he was initiated by the Mother herself.

Towards the close of February she started for Rameswaram with a party of eight, and reached Madras, halting on the way at Berhampore for a day. Swami Ramakrishnananda, a disciple of the Master and the founder of the first Ramakrishna Math in South India, accorded her a cordial reception. She stayed in Madras for about a month and gave initiation to several people. Though, for want of a common language, she could not speak freely with the large number of ladies who visited her, yet on account of her sympathetic understanding they could make themselves understood to one another. After her return to Calcutta she said to a

More Pilgrimages

disciple by way of her reminiscences of Madras, 'Many people visited me there. The women of those parts are highly educated. They asked me to deliver a lecture. I said to them, "I do not know how to deliver lectures. If Gourdasi had come, she would have been able to do so." '

Starting from Madras, with the party strengthened by the inclusion of Swami Ramakrishnananda in it, she halted at Madurai for a day and reached Rameswaram the next night. She spent three days in that great place of pilgrimage. By the order of the Raja of Ramnad, she was given facilities of worship which are never given to any pilgrim, however exalted his position in life may be. At Rameswaram, unlike in the temples of North India, no one except the officiating priests is allowed to enter the sanctum sanctorum or to touch and worship the image. But by the special order of the Raja of Ramnad, who was a great devotee of Swami Vivekananda, not only the Holy Mother but all the women of her party were allowed to go into the shrine and worship the Siva image for three days.

An incident of great mystic significance took place when the Mother worshipped the Sivalinga one day. The image, which is normally covered with a golden cap, was uncovered for the Mother to do Abhisheka (ceremonial washing) with Ganga water. Brahmachari Krishnalal, who was in attendance, is reported to have heard the Mother soliloquizing one day after the Abhisheka, 'It is just as I had left it.' And at once the Mother corrected herself saying, 'Some meaningless words escaped my lips.' Some months after, when one

Kedar Babu of Koalpara asked her in Calcutta about her experiences at Rameswaram, she again said, 'He is just as I left Him, my son.' Golap-Ma, who was passing by, also heard these words and, when she began to proclaim the hidden meaning of it, the Mother again tried to wriggle out of the situation, saying, 'Why? I was only trying to say I was delighted to see the image.' Golap-Ma would not, however, accept such an explanation, and proclaimed that the Mother had admitted that she was the same as Sita who witnessed the installation of the Siva image at Rameswaram by Sri Rama while returning from Lanka, and that her words sprang from a sudden flash of memory of what took place in her previous incarnation as Rama's consort, Sita.

Recounting her experience of Rameswaram, the Holy Mother said afterwards: 'Sasi (Swami Ramakrishnananda) procured for me one hundred and eight *bel* leaves made of gold to worship Siva at Rameswaram. When informed of my coming, the Raja of Ramnad ordered his officer there to show me his buildings and treasures. He further gave the order that if I liked anything, it should be presented to me. But what did I want there? Unable to come to any decision, I said, "Sasi has arranged for everything I require." But unwilling to hurt the feelings of the officer, I added, "If Radhu wants anything, let her ask for it." I said to Radhu, "You may take whatever you need." Then as diamonds and other precious stones were shown, my heart began to tremble. Eagerly I prayed to the Master, "O Lord, please see that Radhu does not crave for any of these things." Radhu at last said, "What shall I take? I do not care for

More Pilgrimages

any of these things. I have just lost my pencil. Please buy one for me." I heaved a sigh of relief. Coming out I bought her a pencil for half an anna from a shop in the street.'

Leaving Rameswaram, she came back to Madras where she attended the celebration of the Master's birthday that year. Towards the close of March 1911, she left for Bangalore, where a branch of the Ramakrishna Math was already in existence. She was given a very cordial and respectful welcome by Swami Nirmalananda, the President of the of the local Ashrama. She was accommodated in the Ashrama building itself, while a tent was put up in its compound for the rest of the party. Even without any public announcement large numbers of people came to see her there. Referring to this she said in later days, 'What a crowd I met in Bangalore! People began to shower flowers as I got down from the train. Flowers lay high on the road. The message of the Master has spread everywhere; therefore so many people come.'

One day when she returned to the Ashrama from a short afternoon visit to the cave temple of Gavipur, the whole front portion of the Ashrama was crowded with visitors, all of whom solemnly prostrated themselves before her as she alighted from her carriage. The Mother was visibly moved by the silent, respectful and spontaneous adoration of this concourse. She stood there still for some moments, extending her hand in solemn benediction. The whole atmosphere was charged with an elevating spiritual vibration that filled the hearts of the audience with peace. Later in the Ashrama hall also large numbers of people went to make prostrations to her on all the days of her stay there. No words were exchanged as they sat before her in large numbers and, when she expressed her sorrow at not being able to speak to them at least a few words of solace and exhortation, they replied: 'No, Mother, words are not needed! Our hearts are full by your very presence!'

One day she sanctified the hillock of rocks at the back of the Ashrama by performing Japa on it in the evening. Hearing that the Mother had ascended the small hillock and was sitting there, Swami Ramakrishnananda ran in hot haste to see and adore her as the Parvatavasini (Resident of the Mountain). He prostrated himself before her, chanting verses from the text of *Devi-Mahatmya* and the Mother blessed him, placing her hands on his head.

On her way back to Calcutta she halted for a day at Rajahmundry for bath in the holy Godavari, and for a couple of days at Puri. She reached Calcutta on the 11 April 1911. Soon after her return, she paid a visit to the Belur Math, where she was given a very impressive reception by all the monks and devotees, headed by Swami Brahmananda. Fully covered with a white sheet and accompanied by her women companions, the Mother walked solemnly from the gates like a white and animated holy image between the lines of adoring devotees chanting holy Mantras from the Chandi and occasionally bursting crackers as is done during holy festivals. In the Bhajan that followed in the Math hall, Swami Brahmananda got lost in Samadhi for long. He could be brought down only by the chanting in

More Pilgrimages

his ear of certain divine names suggested by the Mother.

One more pilgrimage she undertook in her lifetime, and that was in November 1912, to Banaras for the third time. She was accompanied by a large party consisting of a few senior Swamis of the Ramakrishna Order, some relatives and several devotees. She was accommodated at Lakshmi Nivas, a newly built house belonging to a devotee, very close to the Ramakrishna Advaita Ashrama.

She stayed this time in the holy city for two months and a half. So she could on this occasion visit at leisure all the important temples and other places of interest in and around the city. After making her obeisance to Viswanath and Annapurna, the principal Deities in Banaras, she visited, on the third day of her arrival, the Ramakrishna Mission Sevashrama, one of the premier philanthropic institutions under the Mission and an important centre of medical relief in the city. After seeing the different wards, she was highly satisfied and made kind enquiries about how it was started and by whom. Finally she expressed her appreciation of the work in these significant words: 'The Master is present here, and Mother Lakshmi (Goddess of Prosperity) too is abiding here in all Her glory... The place looks so nice that I should like to stay here permanently,' And as soon as she went back to her residence, she sent a sum of ten rupees as her donation to the institution.

As regards the shrines she visited, she said about the Siva images known as Vaidyanath and

Tilabhandeswar that they had sprung from the earth and not been made by the hands of men. About the image of Kedaranath she said, 'This Kedar and the Kedar in the Himalayas are related to each other. If one visits this, one really visits the other. This Deity is a very Living Presence.'

One day she went to visit Sarnath, the ruined site of an important centre of Buddhist learning and religious activity in ancient days. On seeing there some Westerners looking at the relics of Buddhism in speechless wonder, she remarked, 'These are the people who built this place in a previous birth. And now they are amazed at their own doings.'

While returning from Sarnath, the Holy Mother narrowly escaped a very serious accident. On the return trip Swami Brahmananda had exchanged his carriage with that of the Holy Mother. As they proceeded, the horses of the carriage in which the Swami was seated ran amuck, thus upsetting the carriage and causing considerable injury to the Swami. Referring to this incident, the Mother said, 'I was to be involved in the accident, but Rakhal (Swami Brahmananda) diverted it and made himself the victim of it. Otherwise the consequences would have been disastrous.'

The Holy Mother visited two well-known monks in Banaras. One of them belonged to the sect of Nanak and lived on the banks of the Ganges. The other was the celebrated Chameli Puri, who was a junior contemporary of Tota Puri, the preceptor of Sri Ramakrishna, and who belonged to the same monastery as he. When Golap-Ma inquired of this monk as to who had been supplying him with food, the monk replied with great force and earnestness, 'It is the Goddess Annapurna who feeds me. Who else would?' The Holy Mother was highly pleased with the answer. Returning home, she said to her disciples, 'The face of the old man is constantly in my mind. It is just like that of a child.' Next day she sent him some oranges, sweets and a blanket. When asked if she would visit other holy men in the city, she said, 'I have seen that holy man (Chameli Puri). What need have I to visit others? And what other holy man is here?'

She returned to Calcutta on the 16th January 1913. ❑

---

1. About this incident she said as follows; 'Ah! For this I have shed tears and prayed to the Master! And only then through his grace has this Math come into existence now. When the Master left the body, the boys gave up the world and gathered together round a rented shelter for some days. Then they scattered about independently and went on roaming about here and there. Then I felt intensely sad and prayed thus to the Master: "Lord, you came, disported with these few and then went away; and should everything end with that? If so, where was the need for coming down and undergoing so many travails? I have seen in Banaras and Brindavan many holy men who get their food by begging and shift their residence from the shade of one tree to that of another. There is no dearth of holy men of that type. I shan't be able to bear the sight of my sons, who came out in your name, going about begging for food. My prayer is, that those who leave the world in your name may never be in need of bare sustenance. They will all live together holding to your ideas and ideals; and the people afflicted by the worries of the world will resort to them and be solaced by hearing about you. That is why you came. My heart is pained to see them wandering about." After that Naren began gradually building up all this.'

2. It is to be noted that the Holy Mother's intuition is in many respects in agreement with historical finding. At present the image is considered to be that of Vishnu or Krishna. Many historians are of the opinion that this was originally a Buddhist temple, and when the temple fell into the hands of the followers of Sankaracharya, the image was converted into the emblem of Siva, and still later, when the Vaishnavas got control, they converted it into a Vishnu image.

3. This is a station on the Eastern Railway and pilgrims going to Jayrambati and Kamarpukur used to get down here, and cover the remaining distance by bus.

17. HER LATER LIFE

IT REMAINS NOW to take a rapid survey of the main incidents of the Holy Mother's life since she began to stay among the devotees in Calcutta from 1888. Her pilgrimages falling in this period, as also the several small incidents of her daily life revealing phases of her character and personality, have already been dealt with, and only a few noteworthy events of her later life remain to be recorded.

On the 12th November 1898, the day of the annual Kali Puja, she paid her first visit to the monastery at Belur that was being built by Swami Vivekananda after his return from the West. A few months earlier (probably in April), shortly after the site of the future monastery was acquired, she had been taken to the site. She then went round the place in the company of the monks, besides several foreign disciples and devotees of Swami Vivekananda like Sister Nivedita, Mrs. Ole Bull and Miss MacLeod. The Mother pronounced her benediction at the end of her visit saying; 'At long last the boys have a place to stay—the Master has cast his benign look on them.' By the time of the visit on 12th of

November, the buildings were probably nearing completion but the installation in the monastic shrine had not yet taken place. It has already been mentioned how the Holy Mother's heart felt very sorry that her monastic children had neither a fixed abode nor sufficient food, and how she prayed to the Master that they might be provided with both. The sight of the new monastery must, therefore, have gladdened her beyond measure. On the day of her visit, she herself swept and washed a room in the Math and performed the worship, installing her own picture of the Master. Referring to the site of the Belur Math, the Mother said on the occasion of one of her early visits to the place: 'Of a truth I always saw as though the Master lived on the land on the other side of the Ganga (that is, opposite to Dakshineswar)—in a cottage just where the present monastery and plantain trees are.'

The new buildings of the Math were completed by December 1898. On the 9th December Swami Vivekananda carried the relics of the Master on his head to the new Math at Belur, where he installed them and performed worship and Homa for solemnizing the occasion. The new monastery came to be occupied by the monks early next year, and in the October of 1901 Swami Vivekananda had the Durga Puja celebrated on a grand scale at the new Math. The occasion was memorable in the annals of the Math, both because it was the first worship of that type to be done there, and because the Holy Mother was present on all the five days of worship, which was done in her name.

Her Later Life

The years 1898 and 1899 were in certain respects years of joy for the Holy Mother, for these marked the construction of the permanent Math building for her monastic children at Belur. But this period was also noted for the sad bereavements she had to suffer in quick succession. As mentioned before, it was toward the middle of 1899 that the youngest and most beloved of her brothers, Abhay Charan,[1] met with premature death, leaving behind tremendous domestic responsibilities for the Holy Mother to shoulder. A little earlier, on the 28th March of the same year, had passed away Swami Yogananda, one of the most illustrious of Sri Ramakrishna's monastic disciples and the Holy Mother's attendant and guardian for the past twelve years. His death left the Holy Mother so disconsolate that it affected even her health.

In fact, the Swami, as already mentioned, was among the earliest of her disciples, and had accompanied her to Brindavan and to Kamarpukur. After his return from those places, he subjected himself to austerities at Banaras. In those days he took a vow of possessing no money, and all his time, except two or three hours of sleep, was devoted to meditation. To reduce the time spent on procuring food, he would collect a number of Chapatis by begging once in three or four days, keep them tied up in a cloth, and take a portion of them powdered every day. This rigorousness told upon his delicate health. He got a severe attack of dysentery and had to return to the Math. He was much emaciated, but his face looked healthy and luminous. His eyes, indrawn and reddish in tinge resembled the 'divine eye' described by Sri Ramakrishna and in spite of his physical ailments, he remained always witty and jovial. In Calcutta he generally stayed at Balaram Babu's house, as he got better facilities for diet there. Whenever the Holy Mother came to Calcutta, he attended on her. He then stayed in a room at the entrance of her house, did all the outdoor work connected with her establishment, received gifts from the devotees for her, admitted visitors according to her convenience, and did everything to make her stay comfortable. Even when he was seriously ill, he continued to do his service to the Mother. He passed away prematurely, leaving the Holy Mother to bemoan his death with an intensity of sorrow which few earthly mothers are capable of[2]. She is said to have remarked in her sorrow, 'Now one brick has fallen from the building; the others will follow.'

In later days the Holy Mother used to speak of him thus: 'No one loved me like Yogen. If anyone gave him eight annas, he would put it aside, saying, "Mother may need it for a pilgrimage." He attended on me constantly. The other disciples of the Master therefore used to tease him for staying among women.'

Again the years 1905 and 1906 were rendered unhappy for the Holy Mother by the sad loss of several close relatives and the consequent devolution of more heavy family responsibilities on her. In April 1905 her uncle Nilmadhav, who was living under her care in his old age, passed away. She engaged herself unsparingly in nursing this uncle who was very dear to her. Nilmadhav's death was followed very shortly by that of a sister-in-law, the wife of her brother Prasanna. The

Her Later Life

lady, who was staying with the Holy Mother at Jayrambati, had a sudden attack of what looked like cholera. There was no medical aid available in the village and she died in a few hours, attended only by the Holy Mother. She left behind two very young girls, Nalini and Maku, who had thenceforth to be looked after by the Holy Mother. Along with Radhu they became the Holy Mother's charge, and we find them always as members of her household.

Crowning all these bereavements came the death of her own dear mother, Syamasundari Devi, endearingly called 'grandmother' by devotees. Aged about seventy, she had seen all the ups and downs of life, and had played her part heroically even when faced with utter poverty and destitution. She had lived to see her daughter Sarada rising in people's estimation, from the wife of an eccentric man to a goddess worshipped by people occupying the highest positions in life. From the head of an unknown village family, she (Syamasundari) was now the mistress of what she called 'a household of God and godly people,' and the 'grandmother' of the innumerable spiritual children of her divine daughter. Simple, diligent, hardworking and kindly, she engaged herself all through the day, in spite of age, in every kind of household work—tending cattle, feeding labourers, husking paddy and entertaining the many devotees who either visited, or camped in, their house to meet the Holy Mother. Even on the last day of her life, sometime in February 1906, she had helped in husking paddy and had made some purchases for the house. After that she felt very weak, lay down in the verandah, and called out: 'I am dying, I feel my head reeling.' All the occupants of the house, including the Holy Mother, hurried to her side. As a last sacrament the Holy Mother gave her the sacred water of the Ganga to drink, and performed Japa touching her head and chest. The lady quietly passed away, leaving the Holy Mother and a host of grandchildren, both spiritual and secular, to bemoan her death. Swami Saradananda made very grand arrangements for her obsequies.

Another bereavement that the Holy Mother had to stand within six months of this was the passing away of the old venerable lady, Gopal's Mother, one of the Great Master's disciples, whose spiritual relationship with him forms a most thrilling chapter of his life-story. In her very advanced years, she was transferred from her solitary cottage to the premises of the school run by Sister Nivedita. The Mother had met her there once in 1904. In her dotage she had lost all memory and could not generally recognise others. She, however, recognised the Holy Mother and addressed her as 'daughter-in-law.' In April 1906 she met her again when she was on her deathbed. The old lady addressed her as 'Gopal' this time, and stretched her hands, as if she wanted something. The lady in attendance on her interpreted that she wanted the dust of the Mother's feet to be put on her head. Ordinarily the Holy Mother, who looked upon her with the reverence due to a mother-in-law, would not allow this to be done. But now she permitted this for reasons too mysterious for us to understand. Soon after, the venerable lady passed away.

Her Later Life

In 1907 the Holy Mother attended the Durga Puja celebration held at the house of Girish Chandra Ghosh, the great Bengali dramatist and a prominent householder disciple of Sri Ramakrishna. She was then in poor health owing to malaria, and it was only the earnestness of the great devotee Girish and his sister that brought her from Jayrambati to Calcutta to attend the festival. Ever since his mystic experiences connected with the Holy Mother's spiritual identity, Girish looked upon her as the veritable embodiment of the Mother of the Universe, and the prospect of her presence at his worship therefore filled him with ecstatic joy. The Mother was accommodated at Balaram Babu's house and visited Girish's place to attend worship. The first two days of the ceremony passed smoothly. The worship in fact took a twofold form. While the worship of the image was going on, streams of devotees who went to see her at her residence and at the place of Girish Ghosh, continuously offered flowers for long hours at the feet of the living Mother in the shape of the Holy Mother. The strain of the first two days' experience told upon her declining health, and she had to announce her incapacity to attend on the third day which was the most important day of worship. This was terribly depressing news for Girish and he felt that without the Holy Mother's presence, the worship of the Goddess, which he had organized with great effort and at great expense, would be nothing more than a pageantry. When the clouds of disappointment were thus gathering in the devotee's mind, the Holy Mother, by divine intuition, as it were, changed her mind and, just when the most auspicious moment of the worship was to begin, announced herself at the entrance of Girish's house. The news of the Holy Mother's arrival revived the drooping spirit of devotees and poured new enthusiasm and fervour into their hearts. On the third day also the Mother received the flower offerings of her innumerable devotees, including the actors and actresses of the theatre conducted by Girish Chandra Ghosh.

The same scenes of spiritual fervour and enthusiasm, as on the occasion described above, were witnessed whenever the Holy Mother graced the Durga Puja celebrations held at the Belur Math by her presence. To attend the Puja at Belur in 1912, she camped there for about a week. When she arrived at the gate of the Math at the close of the Bodhan ceremony (awakening of the Deity), the monks and devotees, headed by the great Swami Premananda, unhorsed the carriage and drew it through the Math grounds. On successive days hundreds of devotees made flower offerings at her feet. Swami Brahmananda worshipped her with one hundred and eight full-blown lotuses, and her devotee and disciple, Dr. Kanjilal, danced before the image of the Deity with gestures and postures like a mischievous imp, to entertain the Divine Mother, as it were. She was again present at the worship of Durga held in 1916. We get an impression of the exaltation she created by her presence, in the following extract from a letter of Swami Shivananda: 'Owing to the presence of the blessed Holy Mother amongst us, this year's Puja has been a direct worship of the Divine Mother, unlike the usual one through the consecrated image. Although there was continuous rain and wind on all the three days, no part of the celebration suffered, thanks to the Mother's grace. We were astonished to note how even the rains stopped whenever it was time for devotees to take Prasad (consecrated food), sitting in the unprotected courtyard. Afterwards we learnt from Yogin-Ma that whenever rain seemed imminent at about the meal time, the Holy Mother would sit down to make Japa of Durga's holy name, praying, "Mother, save us. How can these devotees take Thy holy Prasad in this pouring rain?" And Mother Durga did, indeed, save us.'

The 23rd of May 1909, was an important date in the Holy Mother's life. For that was the day on which she stepped into her newly built Calcutta residence, generally known as the Udbodhan Office. Ever since she began to visit Calcutta in 1888, she was being accommodated either in the houses of devotees or in rented buildings. Evidently this was inconvenient both to herself and to those who went to see her in increasing numbers. Besides, with the passing of years her entourage of dependent relatives, devotee-companions and disciple-attendants increased in number, making it too inconvenient and expensive for any individual devotee to accommodate. Taking all this into consideration, Swami Saradananda, who had taken up the Holy Mother's charge some time after Swami Yogananda's demise, raised a loan of about eleven thousand rupees and constructed this new building as the Holy Mother's Calcutta house. Towards November 1909 the Swami added another hundred sq.ft. to the compound at a cost of one thousand eight hundred rupees, and the building was enlarged to its present size in 1915. It is also called the Udbodhan Office, because the *Udbodhan*, the Bengali organ of the Ramakrishna Movement, is being published from there since its opening. For the remaining eleven years of her life, the Holy Mother lived in this house whenever she was in Calcutta. The northern hall on the second storey of it formed her living room as well as the shrine. She lived[3] in this house along with a few of her inseparable relatives, her monastic followers and some of Sri Ramakrishna's woman disciples who formed her attendants and companions.

During this long period of eleven years, the Holy Mother's time was divided between her Calcutta residence and her rural home. It was the period during which the vast majority of her disciples met her and received her blessings. It was also the period when she found herself burdened with the responsibilities of several indigent relatives. The devotees found in her a veritable goddess and went to serve her and receive her benediction, while the relatives, as we have already seen, surrounded her either because they were helpless in the world without her protection, or because they could utilize her presence for deriving financial advantages. In the chapters depicting her dealings with both these groups of people, it has been shown how the demands of these conflicting relationships lost their disharmony under the sanctifying influence of her sense of universal motherhood.

Her life in her village home was a strenuous one. She had to shoulder the main responsibilities of the household herself, and that was rendered onerous because it consisted not only of her inseparable relatives, but also of several others who camped in her village home. In Calcutta her movements were very restricted and she was inaccessible to men devotees except at fixed times. In the village, however, she moved in and out of the house very freely, and devotees could see her almost always. So, many devotees flocked to Jayrambati, and the Holy Mother used to feed and accommodate them in her own house. Being aware of the higher standards of comforts prevailing among her Calcutta visitors, she strove her best to provide them with every possible amenity, though it often meant very heavy physical strain on her. She went about collecting milk and vegetables for them, often cooked special dishes to feed them, and attended on those that happened to fall ill. As the welcome she gave to these spiritual children was whole-hearted and spontaneous, she went through all this strenuous experience with the utmost joy and satisfaction, although the devotees themselves felt embarrassed at the trouble they were giving her unknowingly. It was indeed a sad day for her when the house was without any devotee-visitor, and she considered such days as days spent in vain.

Among the devotees and disciples who served the Mother in her village home, special mention has to be made of the inmates of the Koalpara Ashrama. Koalpara was a village on the way from Jayrambati to Vishnupur, from where one could take a train to Calcutta. The Ashrama practically sprang into existence as a midway house for the Holy Mother to halt on her way to, and from, Jayrambati, and the inmates of that Ashrama looked upon themselves as an outpost to guard and serve the Mother in her village home. Often the young Brahmacharins did a lot of manual labour in the Mother's household whenever there was construction work or a religious festival there. They procured vegetables for her, ran errands, and were always at her beck and call. The Mother too had a very soft corner in her heart for them. She did her best to give a spiritual turn to the life of these young men who were at that time moved powerfully by the nationalist movement. She called Koalpara her 'parlour,' and had a cottage built for her in the Ashrama premises. She also spent some days in that cottage when Radhu's health required a retreat in an absolutely quiet place.

Besides the visiting disciples and devotees, the Mother's household in her village home consisted mostly of her relatives—brothers, their wives, nephews, nieces and their husbands, all of whom looked upon her from an angle of vision totally different from that of the devotees. The brothers teased her with their quarrels for money, the nieces worried her with their freaks and eccentricites, and their husbands taxed her with their demands for ceremonious attention which their relationship as sons-in-law in the family entitled them to. Drawing attention to this marked contrast between the attitudes and behaviour of these groups, the Mother once remarked, 'See, I have many children (disciples). When they come, one can serve them food in hand or on leaves, as one finds convenient. But should any of them (the relatives and the sons-in-law) come, what a number of cups and dishes one will have to get! If you don't, there will be bitter complaints.'

The peace of her village home was in these days occasionally disturbed by another type of people. These were officers of the Police Department who were on the lookout everywhere for people implicated in the nationalist (Swadesi) movement. Those were days when the political life of Bengal was lashed into violent activity owing to the partition of the Province. An important feature of this phase of the national movement was the boycott of foreign goods, especially cloth, and a vigorous propaganda for Swadesi or indigenous goods. The wearing of indigenous cloth thus became a symbol of political agitation in the eye of the police. A strict watch was therefore kept on all sympathizers of the movement. Among the Mother's disciples there were several who were under internment for being deeply implicated in the movement. The frequent visits of such persons made the Mother's place suspect in the eyes of the police. Very often police parties would visit the house, causing great unpleasantness to her, and take note of men and things there. She was however relieved of much of this trouble after a high police officer was brought to her house to study the real state of affairs. Thenceforth the police vigilance was slackened into mere noting of names of persons who came to, and went from, the place.

The quietness, the freedom and the unconventionality of village life was very much to the Mother's liking, and she often spent there long periods, sometimes extending over a year. But ill health arising from the strain of household work and the malarial tendencies of rural Bengal, as also the necessity of expert medical consultation for Radhu's frequent ailments, often forced her to migrate to Calcutta and spend long periods at the Udbodhan Office, the city residence built for her by Swami Saradananda. In Calcutta her movements were considerably restricted, but she was free from financial responsibilities and the burden of domestic duties. Swami Saradananda shouldered the former and Golap-Ma the latter. None the less her days were busily occupied with the service of the Master and the reception of devotees. On all days and at all times she was accessible to women devotees, and there was a constant stream of them, some seeking help and inspiration in spiritual life, others with prayers for attainment of worldly goods, and still others for confessions and consolations to relieve their distressed hearts. Men devotees too were admitted, but only at particular times of the day, and they probably had not the same freedom of association with the Mother in Calcutta as in her village home. That was why many of the intimate men devotees flocked in large numbers to Jayrambati in spite of the difficulties of journey and stay.

Though the rural surroundings of Jayrambati were more to her liking, life in Calcutta had its own attraction for her. Calcutta offered her the opportunity of living with some of her old associates—the great monastic disciples and women devotees of Sri Ramakrishna, some of whom took upon themselves the duty of being her attendants and companions whenever she was in

Her Later Life

Calcutta. A life of the Holy Mother will be incomplete without at least a brief account of these attendants and companions who played so important a part in her life. Frequent references have been made to them in the course of this narrative, and one of them, Swami Yogananda, the great monastic disciple of Sri Ramakrishna, who attended on the Holy Mother for twelve years, has already been dealt with. Among the other disciples of the Master, Swami Adbhutananda, known also as Latu, had served her in earlier days, and in later times Swami Trigunatitananda took for a short period the place left vacant by Swami Yogananda.[4] Afterwards the responsibility of the Holy Mother was taken up by Swami Saradananda, otherwise known as Sarat Maharaj, who played a very important part in her life.

The Swami was one of the twelve young disciples of Sri Ramakrishna who left their home and studies with a view to serving their great Master in his last illness. After Sri Ramakrishna's demise, he, like his fellow disciples, devoted himself to severe austerities. Swami Vivekananda had great confidence in him for his deep spirituality, his intellectual powers and his administrative capacity. So he was first sent as the Swami's successor to preach Vedanta in England and America (1895), and a few years later (1898) he was recalled and appointed Secretary of the Ramakrishna Math and Mission, a position which he retained till the end.

Sometime after Swami Yogananda's passing away, he took up the responsibility of looking after the Holy Mother, besides attending to his onerous duties as the Secretary. The work of attending on the Holy Mother was not a light one. As she herself put it, 'I shall have no difficulty so long as Sarat lives. I do not see anybody else who can shoulder my burden.' For it involved a good deal of expense, besides looking after the eccentric and infirm relatives of the Holy Mother, for whom she had a responsibility. In spite of many difficulties, the Swami discharged this task so much to the satisfaction of the Holy Mother that he won her whole-hearted love and confidence. If anyone spoke of her going to Calcutta when the Swami was not there, she would say, 'There can be no question of my going to Calcutta when Sarat is not there. To whom shall I go? Suppose I am in Calcutta and Sarat says that he wants to go elsewhere for a few days. Then I tell him, "Wait a little, my child. First of all let me leave this place, and then you may go."' She used to speak of him as her Vasuki, the mythical snake, who protected her with a thousand hoods. In her last days she was heard to remark. 'I am tired of this life. I shall now depart, taking Sarat in my arms and carrying him wherever I go.' It is said that the Swami wept like a child on hearing this.

The Swami's devotion to the Holy Mother found expression in his reverential attitude towards all womankind, and in his active interest in the working and progress of the Nivedita Girls' School. Besides, it has found embodiment in architectural form—first as the Udbodhan Office, which he constructed for the Holy Mother's residence in Calcutta,[5] and next as the Holy Mother's temple at Jayrambati, which he built after her passing away. His devotion has also received literary commemoration in his book *Mother Worship in India*

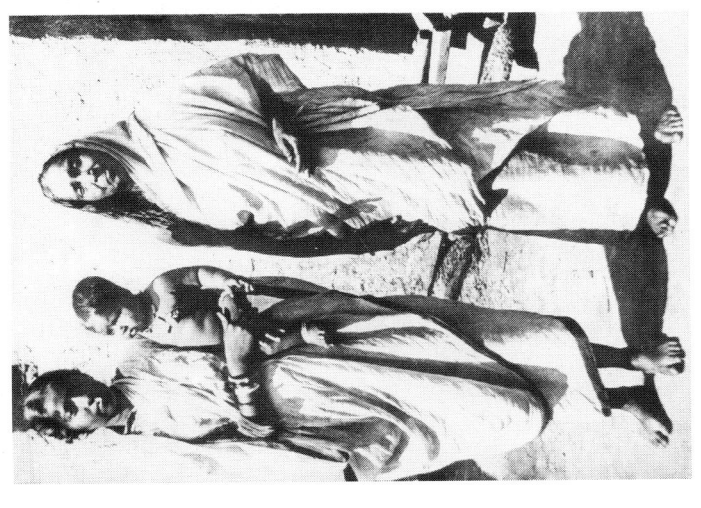

ಌ With Maku and Neda, 1918 ಌ

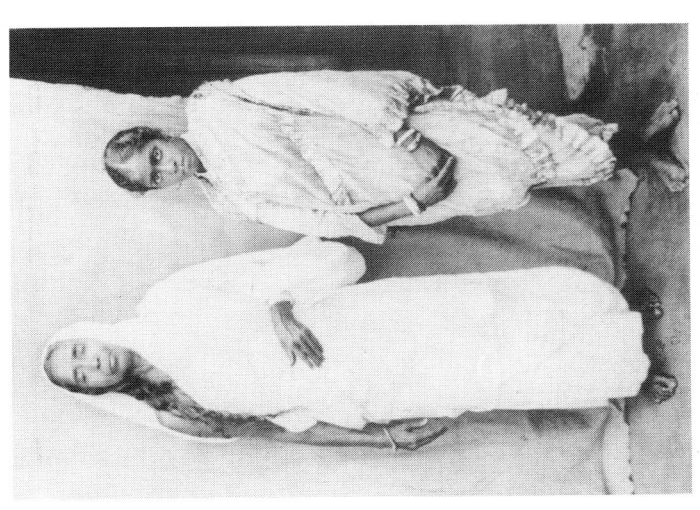

ಌ With Radhu, 1918 ಌ

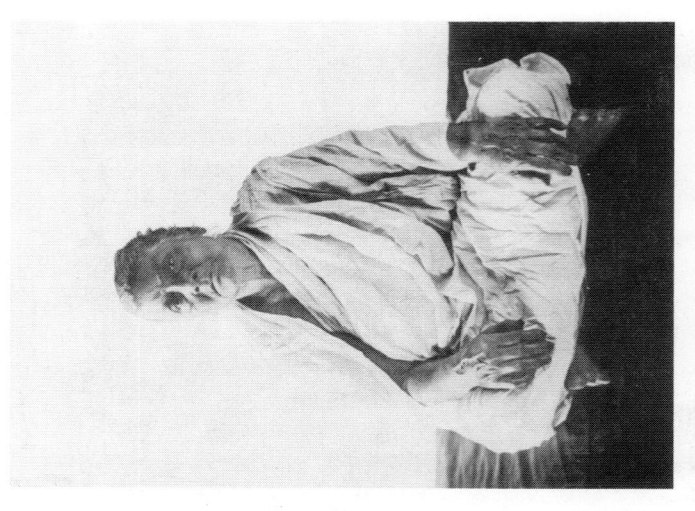

ॐ Yoginma ॐ

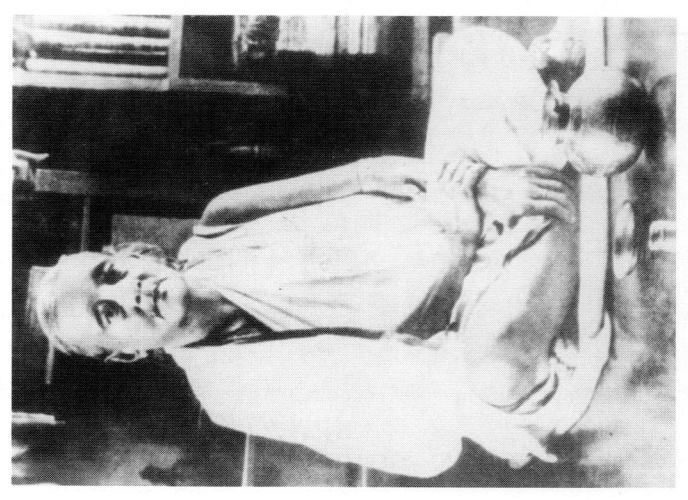

ॐ Golapma ॐ

which he has dedicated to the Holy Mother with the noble and significant words: 'By whose gracious look the author has been able to realize the revelation of Divine Motherhood in every female form,—to her lotus feet this work is dedicated in all humility and devotion.'

In addition to these Sannyasin disciples of Sri Ramakrishna, the great women disciples of the Master also formed the lifelong companions of the Holy Mother. There were several of them—Golap-Ma, Yogin-Ma, Lakshmi Devi and Gauri-Ma being the most important. All of them except the last were widows and they all lived a holy life of contemplation and service.

Of these, Golap-Ma was the closest to the Holy Mother, and acted also as something of a *gendarme* to her in her later days. She was a widow belonging to a poor but artistocratic Brahmin family. She took shelter at the feet of the Master when she was stricken with grief owing to the death of her only daughter who had been married into a rich family. Ever since, she was intimate with the Holy Mother, and had constantly stayed with her except for brief periods, safeguarding her interests in all matters and rendering devoted and loving service to her in her daily life. Referring to her, the Master had said to the Holy Mother, 'Take care of this Brahmin woman. She will stay with you all along.' True to this, she followed the Holy Mother like a shadow for full thirty-six years after the Master's passing away. As we have seen, she was with the Holy Mother during most of her pilgrimages and often formed one of her escort party when she went to visit any place. Whenever the Mother was in Calcutta,

Golap-Ma invariably stayed with her, looked after the internal management of her household, and often protected her from the importunities of indiscreet devotees. As the Holy Mother did not generally speak directly with men devotees, it was Golap-Ma who often conveyed the Mother's blessings to them or interpreted what she said in very low tones by way of reply to their questions. She helped the Mother to get in and out of vehicles, and whenever the Mother had to go on foot she would walk only behind Golap-Ma. When she went on a visit to any devotee's house, she would invariably take Golap-Ma with her, saying, 'Unless she goes, how can I? I feel bold in her company.' Her attitude towards Golap-Ma was that of a young daughter.

Golap-Ma was also a woman of great spiritual attainments. She used to spend several hours in the morning and evening in meditation. The Holy Mother always spoke highly of the purity of her mind, and considered her as having attained perfection in Japa. She was free from any exaggerated feminine shyness and therefore eminently fit to play the part of an intermediary between the Holy Mother and the devotees. Being very outspoken by nature, she would speak the plain truth to anybody's face. As a result, though she looked upon the Holy Mother with great reverence, she would not hesitate to take even her to task as a mother would her daughter. The Mother often corrected her, telling her that in the name of truth she was losing sensitiveness to others' feelings, and that sometimes it would be no sin not to speak an unpleasant truth.

Her Later Life

But everyone knew that in spite of her curt speech and impulsive nature, Golap-Ma had a very sound and loving heart. Indeed, her spirit of service was wonderful. When she found dirt anywhere on the bathing ghat, she would remove it with rags and wash the place with water. Once at Vrindaban she found that somebody's child had dirtied the precincts of a temple. As she found no one coming forward to clean the spot, she did the work herself, whereupon some of the assembled devotees began to say that it must have been done by her child. They were, however, silenced by others who pointed out the truth.

She used to receive a small allowance from her daughter's son, half of which she would give to the Udbodhan Office for her own maintenance, and utilize the remaining half in helping indigent people. She used to induce some of the Mother's doctor devotees to visit the homes of poor patients free of charge. Her daily life at the Udbodhan Office was one of tireless service. She supervised all the departments of the household, distributed Prasada among the devotees, and in various ways served the monks like a mother. She passed away in December 1924, about four years after the Holy Mother's Mahasamadhi.

Yogin-Ma (Yogendra Mohini Biswas) was another intimate companion of the Holy Mother. She, as also Golap-Ma, had spent so much time in her company from early days that the Holy Mother used to say, 'Yogin and Golap know all about every phase of my life.' Yogin-Ma was the most impressive among the Mother's companions and was highly spiritual too.

Sri Ramakrishna used to speak of her, 'Among women, Yogin is the Jnani;' and also 'She is not an ordinary flower bud that opens in a short time. She is a thousand-petalled lotus which will open only in course of time.' Her later life fully corroborated this estimate. While she was in Vrindaban with the Holy Mother, she often experienced Samadhi. One day she was found in that state at the temple of Lala Babu and could not be roused from it even when the priest was about to close the temple at night. Later, speaking about her experience, she said, 'In that state I felt that the world did not exist.' Referring to an experience of another period of her life, she said, 'I passed through a stage in which I saw my Ishtam (Chosen Deity) in all objects around. This lasted for three days.'

She was the wife of a rich Zamindar, but owing to certain unhappy domestic circumstances she generally lived in her paternal home from her early days. She was taken to the Master by Balaram Bose, and since then became the most confidential friend of the Holy Mother, whose equal she was in age. In her days at Dakshineswar the Holy Mother used to have her hair braided by Yogin-Ma, and so much did she like her braiding that she would not disturb it even at the time of bathing, until Yogin-Ma visited her a week after. We have already seen how she accompanied the Holy Mother during many of her pilgrimages. After the Holy Mother began to live in Calcutta, she would contribute her share in the management and unkeep of her household. She stayed in her own house at Baghbazar, where she had to look after her old mother and her grandchildren.

But she would visit the Holy Mother in the morning, dress vegetables for the day's cooking, then return home, cook for her old mother, and again go to the Holy Mother and serve her in all possible ways till night.

Though Yogin-Ma continued to stay in her home, she had performed the Purnabhisheka of the Tantras, as well as the Viraja Homa of the Vedas, both indicative of one's having renounced the worldly life. Every day, after a bath in the Ganges, she spent a couple of hours at the bathing ghat of the holy river, doing Japa with perfect absorption, irrespective of the inclemencies of weather. She was well versed in ceremonial worship, but to this she added a temperament full of ecstatic devotion. She was never seen to waste her time, all her leisure being devoted to the study of the Gita, the Bhagavata, the Chaitanya Charitamrita, and books on the Master. Her memory was keen, and she could narrate the Puranic stories with great accuracy and repeat verbatim passages from the Chaitanya Charitamrita. She passed away at the age of seventy-three, in 1924, the same year as Golap-Ma did.

Still another woman disciple of the Master who lived in close association with the Holy Mother, was Gauri-Ma. Besides being deeply spiritual, she possessed great learning, intrepidity and organizing power. She had felt the call of the higher life from her very girlhood and had therefore resisted all the attempts of her relatives to get her married. Having come into contact with Sri Ramakrishna early in life, she renounced hearth and home and is reported to have performed austerities in the Himalayas as a Sannyasini. After 1882 she stayed mostly at the Nahabat with the Holy Mother, serving her and the Master to the best of her capacity. Sri Ramakrishna, who had a full appreciation of her capacities, often sent her to disseminate religious ideas among women, and commissioned her to devotee her life to the uplift of women. So, after the Master's passing, she spent some years in hard austerities at Brindavan, and then started an educational institution for girls, which she named Sri Saradeswari Ashrama and School, as a token of her reverence for the Holy Mother. This institution, at present situated at 26, Maharani Hemanta Kumari Street, Calcutta, is one of the noted women's educational institutions in that city. Besides imparting general education to girls, it gives them a sound home training based on the great Hindu ideals of purity, service and devotion. It is run by a band of capable women who have dedicated their lives to asceticism and service under the inspiring influence of Gauri-Ma.

The relationship between Gauri-Ma and the Holy Mother was characterized by deep love and regard for each other. Once Gauri-Ma expressed her unbounded reverence for the Holy Mother in the following terms: 'Sri Sarada Devi was not only the Master's partner in his life-work but also the object wherein he worshipped the Cosmic Mother. The worship of one's own wife as the Divine Mother is indeed a phenomenon which no other age had witnessed... People have not yet been able to know the Holy Mother. A full appreciation of the significance of her life is bound to have a liberalizing influence upon the whole world.'

Her Later Life

Her deep regard for the Holy Mother found expression once on the occasion of the Durga Puja. She was reading the Chandi (Saptasati) in the presence of the Holy Mother on all the days of the worship. On the final day she worshipped the Mother with a hundred and eight crimson lotuses and said, 'Mother, having read the Chandi (the book on the Divine Mother) in the living presence of Chandi (the Divine Mother) Herself, I complete today my vow of the study of this great book. Hereafter the study of it during the Durga Puja will not be compulsory for me, but will be determined by your will.'

The Holy Mother on her part loved Gauri-Ma like a daughter, and the deep reverence that the latter had for her was not therefore without frequent exchange of fun between them. She used to call her endearingly as Gaurdasi. There were occasions when the Holy Mother nursed Gauri-Ma all through night in her illness. Though she herself was not learned in the Scriptures, the Holy Mother admired Gauri-Ma's erudition and many-sided talents. Once she remarked, 'A great soul is always a rarity, having hardly any parallel. Gaurdasi is one such rare soul.' Again, during her visit to Madras, when she was requested by the ladies there to deliver a speech, she said, 'I cannot deliver public speeches. Had Gaurdasi come with me, she would have delivered one.'

In all her public activities Gauri-Ma had the hearty approval and encouragement of the Holy Mother. She started her educational institution with the Holy Mother's blessings, and the latter often visited it and expressed her warm approval of the lines on which it was run. After the starting of the Ashrama and School, Gauri-Ma could not live with the Holy Mother as before, since she had to attend to the work connected with it. Yet she visited her frequently and brought many of her students and devotees to her for initiation.[6]

The Holy Mother's close association with these women companions, some of whom were so unlike her in habits and disposition, brings us to the question as to what her ideal of womanhood was. For we have seen how she ever retained the temperament of a bashful maiden, kept herself aloof from all public activities, did not appear before men without a veil, and would not even talk directly to them, barring a select few. Yet how could she approve of a Gauri-Ma doing just the opposite of it? Not only that, there were several other women who also took part in public activities with her approval. She blessed Sister Nivedita in her great efforts for the education of women. She encouraged Sister Sudhira to continue Nivedita's work and even allowed her to finance her boarding home for girls by undertaking tuition in families. She permitted a girl disciple of hers to study midwifery on the ground that she would thus be useful to many, although conservative women like Golap-Ma objected to the idea of a high-caste Hindu girl working in a hospital, however noble the motives behind might be. How are all these facts to be reconciled with her own habits of life, so contrary to them in every respect?

Then again the Holy Mother herself was not educated. She was married early in life. When she is spoken of as 'the last word of Sri Ramakrishna on the

Her Later Life

ideal of Indian womanhood,' does it mean that Indian women should follow her in these respects also? These are questions that naturally suggest themselves to a student of the Holy Mother's life.

The difficulty that one feels in this respect can be solved if one clarifies one's idea as to what constitutes the essence of the feminine ideal. It is an undeniable fact that women's habits and mode of living, their upbringing and the part played by them in social life, have varied from country to country and from time to time. But in this world, even change is a relative phenomenon; it is felt only in relation to something that is comparatively stationary. Thus, behind the great variations in the pattern of womanhood, one can discover an essential unchanging principle that is uniquely feminine and quite distinct from every phase of the masculine ideal of character. We may describe this distinctively feminine principle as the Mother Ideal. It is a cosmic principle which expresses itself concretely at our physical level through women in their capacity as mothers—a capacity that forms the special privilege of woman, in both the physiological and the psychological senses.

It may be questioned why the feminine principle should be identified with motherhood. Why should it not be equated with wifehood, which after all precedes motherhood and also constitutes a special function of woman? The answer is that a woman is a wife, or rather a successful wife, to the extent that she is a mother. The biological function of sex is not the essence of wifehood. In the life of the average individual, sex may be an indispensable part of one's role as wife, but the Holy

Mother's example has at least shown us that a great woman can be a successful wife even if the whole of the biological value of sex is eliminated from her life. Then again, a woman in her purely sexual role is outside the pale of wifehood—nay, she then eschews every one of those sacred functions, responsibilities and privileges that we always associate with wifehood. Thus the essence of wifehood lies in a 'more' than mere sex life, and if we investigate what that 'more' is, we shall find that it lies in motherhood.

For one thing, the position of a woman as wife depends on the home and home life, and whenever these disappear, wifehood too is bound to disappear. A home is an institution in which a man, his wife, his children and other dependants share a common life, held together by a cementing force—that force being the influence of the wife over all the other members. Now a wife is able to exercise this influence only to the extent that she embodies in herself the principle of motherhood—the quality by which a woman is able to love disinterestedly, have infinite patience and forgiveness in dealing with the failings of others, and serve others heart and soul without any thought of return. No doubt she reveals these qualities in the first instance in relation to her own offspring, but unless she expresses this unique side of her nature in her dealings with her husband and the other members of the family—of course with modifications suited to the needs of different forms of relationship—she will not be fulfilling her position as the wife, the mistress of the family. In any society where, for some reason or other, women lack this precious quality, the art of wifehood is forgotten and, as a consequence, homes break up and family life becomes an impossibility; or even if it continues nominally owing to the conservatism of law, it loses all its sanctity and fails to breed those great racial virtues of which it is the custodian. Such a state of affairs always marks the decline of a culture.

It is therefore appropriate to characterize the feminine ideal as the principle of motherhood. It forms the central core in woman, whose integrity has to be preserved in the midst of all her changing modes of life, if she is not to lose her soul in the pursuit of aggressive masculine standards. She may be a mere housewife, or become a fair-minded or business-minded woman; she may remain behind the purdah, or take part in public life; she may put on the skirt, or wear the sari; she may live a married life, or prefer to remain single. All these varying modes and avocations of life are but the cultural garb of womanhood, their differences being dictated by the changing social needs. She does no violence to her nature by following them, provided she remains true to the ideal of motherhood, the eternal feminine principle, and tries to express the love, the forgiveness and the spirit of service characterizing it, in all the spheres of her activity, whatever they may be.

In the light of this explanation the Holy Mother's conduct in encouraging several of her women companions and disciples to follow ways of living quite different from her own, becomes understandable. In fact she liked to see that Indian women were married a little later in life than was often the case, that they were better educated, that they developed qualities of leadership and self-reliance, and that they were not forced into the married state if some of them preferred to live a life of continence and service in a wider circle than the family. But whatever their mode of life, she wanted them always to remain true to the eternal feminine nature in them—the principle of motherhood—, and thus prevent human culture from becoming exclusively preoccupied with masculine standards. Strength and dynamism have to be moderated by sensitiveness, sympathy and self-abnegation.

Her own life was meant to be an example of the pure feminine type. There are many examples of great women from whom one may seek guidance in the lesser accomplishments of womanhood that change with time and country. But one may turn the pages of the world's history and yet not come across another instance like the Holy Mother in embodying the ideal of motherhood in all its purity. She has sometimes been spoken of as Sri Ramakrishna's last word on Indian womanhood. It will be better to amend it as 'his last word on womanhood of all times and countries.' For wife, nun and mother in one, she stands as the fulfilment of the idea of a Madonna—not the hazy figure of a distant time and place, like the mother of Christ depicted in the Christian scriptures, but a personality in flesh and blood, boldly imprinted on the canvas of recent history and having a spiritual content that is not dependent on the pious imagination of the faithful. In the light of this idea one can understand the meaning of the Holy Mother's significant words, that the Master left her on this earth to reveal the Motherhood of God. ❑

1. Abhay Charan, the youngest of the Holy Mother's brothers, was staying at Calcutta along with his two brothers Prasanna and Varada, who were earning their livelihood in that city through priestly work. After passing the entrance examination, Abhay studied medicine at the Campbell Medical School. He had finished the course and was waiting for the results of his final examination, when he succumbed to an attack of cholera in August 1899. The shocking effect of this lingered on the Mother's mind, and once it took a curious expression when she blessed her little nephews thus: 'May these live long, even though they may not be educated.' When their mother, her sister-in-law, protested against this way of blessing, she replied: 'Yes, dear, yes! What do you know! I brought up Abhay, and he is gone!'

2. We may mention here an incident that reveals the depth of the Holy Mother's affection for Swami Yogananda. The Swami had once presented her with a quilt which became worn out after some years. So she at first made arrangements to get it stuffed with new cotton but afterwards desisted from the course because she thought that it would change beyond all recognition the thing presented by her beloved Yogen. She had the habit of preserving even trifling presents as mementos of loved ones.

3. Whenever the Holy Mother lived in Calcutta at the Udbodhan Office, Swami Saradananda met all her expenses. At Jayrambati, she herself met the expenses of her household, although Swami Saradananda used to send her remittances now and then when she was in need. Her income consisted of the gifts made by disciples at the time of initiation, and of the small contributions made by her intimate devotees. Most of her disciples being students and middle class men, their contribution was neither large nor very steady, so much so that when Mrs. Ole Bull, a great American devotee of Swami Vivekananda, began to send her a regular donation of twenty-five rupees a month, she felt it as a substantial addition to her financial resources. In later days, whenever she stayed at Jayrambati, she had to spend nothing less than one hundred rupees a month. As a rule very little of this amount was spent on herself personally. It was used mainly for the entertainment of devotee-visitors, whose number came to ten or fifteen at times, for the maintenance of her

dependants like Radhu and her mother, and for helping her indigent relatives and co-villagers. Especially in her last years, her expenses increased very much owing to the protracted illness of Radhu.

4. There are some striking instances of his devotion to the Mother, which more than rival certain Pauranika accounts of devotion to Guru and God. Once when the Holy Mother was travelling at night a part of the distance to Jayrambati in a bullock bandy in the rainy season, the party came across breaches on the road caused by flood waters. If the bullock bandy were to pass through one of these big breaches, it would have caused a violent jolt and disturbed the Mother's sleep. So Swami Trigunatita, who was walking in front, stretched himself in the breach and asked the cartman to drive over to prevent the jolt. The Holy Mother, who was awake, saw the situation and at once interfered and stopped the fool-hardy venture, reproving the Swami for his rashness. Another instance of such reckless devotion on his part took place when Golap-Ma asked him to get the hottest chillies available in the market for the Mother. It seems the Swami went up to a distance of three miles tasting samples of chillies, so that his tongue became horribly irritated and swollen by the time he made the selection.

5. He spent his days in a front room of this house as the 'Mother's gate-keeper.'

6. There were also several others among the Master's women devotees who moved closely with the Holy Mother. Important among them was Lakshmi-Didi (Sister Lakshmi), the niece of Sri Ramakrishna, whose name has been frequently mentioned in this narrative. She was a virgin widow, junior to the Holy Mother in age. She used to stay with her for long periods in the Nahabat in her Dakshineswar days, sharing her work and undergoing spiritual practices with her. In later days, after the Holy Mother began to live in Calcutta, she mostly stayed with her relatives at Dakshineswar or at her village or in places of pilgrimage. She was a talented conversationalist and could hold her devotees spell-bound by her thrilling narration of the incidents of Sri Ramakrishna's life and her realistic imitation of his manners and speech. She could also sing devotional songs and perform devotional dances with great charm, and in later days she often used to pass into ecstasy while doing so. She was noted for her prodigious memory and her mastery of Indian mythology. In the last period of her life she gave initiation to many disciples. She passed away at Puri where she spent most of her time towards the end of her life.

Gopaler-Ma ('mother of Gopala') was another ascetic woman who was closely associated with the Holy Mother. She was a child-widow and senior to the Holy Mother by many years. She worshipped Gopala or child Krishna as her chosen Deity and, as we learn from *The Life of*

Her Later Life

Sri Ramakrishna, had attained great realizations. She looked upon the Master as her 'child Gopala' and therefore considered herself his mother. For this reason she treated the Holy Mother as her daughter-in-law. She used to live at Kamarhati, a few miles from Calcutta, and stayed for a few days with the Holy Mother whenever she visited Dakshineswar. After the Holy Mother settled down in Calcutta, she frequently visited her. In her last days she was taken care of by Sister Nivedita.

The Holy Mother was on intimate terms not only with these devoted ladies, but also with the wives of several of Sri Ramakrishna's great householder disciples like Balaram Bose, Mahendra Nath Gupta and others.

18. HER MESSAGE

EVERY GREAT PERSONAGE delivers his message partly through his life and partly through his teachings. No doubt they are complementary, but it seems that in certain spiritual types the message delivered in terms of life is more significant than the message conveyed through words. The Holy Mother belongs to this category.

This account of her life, describes at length what she teaches man by her life, and the companion volume of the *Gospel of the Holy Mother* contains the teachings she conveyed through her words. Here only a bare analysis of her message is given with a view to drawing one's attention to its essential contents.

Any great spiritual movement and the personalities inaugurating it have two sets of teaching, interdependent, no doubt, yet each having its distinctiveness. One is the cult side of the teaching and the other the cultural or philosophical side of it. The first is centred in Personalities and the second in principles. The cult side of the teaching consists of the beliefs and devotional attitudes concerning the personality from whom the movement started, while the cultural aspect is formed of the philosophical and theological teachings of these personalities. Thus the cultural side of Sri Krishna's message is contained in the philosophy of non-attached activity preached in the Gita, and the cult side in the specific theory of devotion centring on him. In the case of the Buddha, the former lies in the four Noble Truths and the Eightfold Path, and the latter in the theory of Buddhahood, which developed into the Buddhology of the Mahayana system. The cultural aspect of Christ's message is embodied in the Sermon on the Mount, and the cult aspect in the doctrine of his Sonship. In the teachings of Mohammed, the cultural side is represented by his teaching on the unity of God, and the cult side by his claim to Prophethood.

Now both cult and culture are equally important for a religious movement, for its health and vitality depend on maintaining the balance between these two aspects of its spiritual content. The cult is the heart of a religious movement, and the culture the framework of bones and muscles constituting its body. The cult, like the heart of an organism, is the unseen source of vigour in a religious movement. On the other hand, culture, like the body of a creature, is the form through which this vigour becomes expressive, attractive and significant Without the cultural aspect, cult becomes mere sentimentalism or fanaticism—in the former case, bearing no significance to the life around, and in the later, becoming a positive menace to society. So also without the cult and the devotional spirit generated by it, mere culture degenerates into feeble intellectualism or vapid cosmopolitanism, devoid of that dynamism and spirit of self-sacrifice so essential for making any religious movement expressive and significant.

Even with regard to the spiritual movement inaugurated by Sri Ramakrishna, this twofold division into cult and culture holds good. The cult side of the teaching may briefly be formulated thus: (a) Sri Ramakrishna is a divine incarnation who embodies in himself the spiritual consciousness of the past incarnations and of all expressions of the Deity. (b) He is a Living Presence whom a devotee can 'contact' through love and discipline. (c) His life and personality have opened a new way of salvation, for by personal devotion and service to him one becomes a participant in the spiritual consciousness he had created, and this expedites one's spiritual evolution just as a river hurries to its destination an object that has entrusted itself to its current.

The culture side of it is embodied in the great ideals exemplified in the life of Sri Ramakrishna and his apostles, in the teachings of the Master recorded by his disciples, and in the Neo-Vedanta or science of religion preached by Swami Vivekananda, reconciling the varied aspects of the spiritual heritage that has come down through the different religions of the world.

To get the right perspective of the message of the Holy Mother, it has to be viewed in the light of this analysis. The message of every one of the great disciples of Sri Ramakrishna represents both the cult and the culture aspects of the movement, but the proportion may differ. Thus Swami Vivekananda is the most

Her message

illustrious representative of the culture aspect, his lifework and discourses being the most important factors that have made the life and teachings of Sri Ramakrishna significant to the generality of men who are not his professed followers. The Swami was an ardent believer in the cult too, but his conviction in this respect did not find expression in his preachings. The Holy Mother, on the other hand, is the greatest representative of the cult side of the movement. In making this statement, it is not implied that she made no contribution to the cultural side. In fact she has made very valuable contributions to it, as will be evident from what follows. But the distinctiveness and originality of her message consist in that she was the first person to exemplify the principles of the cult which has given the Ramakrishna Movement the vitality it possesses. In this sense she may truly be described as the Sakti (Power) behind the Movement.

Her contribution to the cult may briefly be stated as follows: (1) The central idea that forms the motive force behind the Ramakrishna Movement is the notion that an aspirant's spiritual potentialities are unfolded by service of Sri Ramakrishna through dedicated work done in his name and for the advancement of his mission on earth. Although it was only in later days that this service took an organizational shape, the inception of the idea goes back to the lifetime of the Master when his immediate disciples served him in flesh and blood. Of them all, the Holy Mother is the pioneer and the best exemplar of this new form of spiritual practice. (2) All through her life she bore witness to the fact that the

Master is a Living Presence. The way in which she made her daily offerings and the manner in which she had vivid visions of him in all critical situations are the assurances we get from her life in regard to this important aspect of the cult.

Thus it is no exaggeration to say that the cult associated with Sri Ramakrishna is based less on the experiences of her life than on the spiritual power manifested in a unique manner in her person.

Next comes the cultural aspect of her message. It is an aspect in which even those who do not care for the cult will be interested. Her teachings in this respect are to be gleaned more from her actions and behaviour in life than from any formal discourses or lectures. She was born in humble circumstances and had no schooling of any kind. She was therefore neither an intellectual nor an exponent of any system of philosophy. But her life was rooted in a cultural soil, the quality of which she exhibited as a glorious character and as steadfast devotion to certain ideals. In her life more than in the life of any of the Master's disciples, or even of the Master himself, we find an illustration of the ideal of living *in* the world but yet being not *of* it. The most noted of the Master's disciples were monks and though they concerned themselves with preaching, philanthropic activities and administrative work, they all lived outside the family. Even the Master, though married, had nothing to do with the family, except for the very pure and tender relationship he had with the Holy Mother. But in the Holy Mother we find the unique example of one who lived in the circle of her relatives and bore the worries of such a life to the fullest extent, but at the same time kept intact her spirit of renunciation, discrimination and devotion.

The uniqueness of her life, however, consists in that she was wife, nun and mother at the same time. These three functions in life may at first look conflicting, but the Holy Mother harmonized them in her life. She was wedded to Sri Ramakrishna at the age of five, and till the end of the Master's life she kept company with him and served him to the best of her ability like any Hindu wife. But a woman who does only this and keeps aloof from the intellectual and spiritual life of her husband, either due to deficiencies of endowment or differences of temperament, cannot be a companion to him in a true sense. How the Holy Mother was a flawless pattern of wifehood in this respect also, how she could easily grasp and fully participate in the spiritual ideals of her husband, and how she made herself fit to continue his work of spiritual ministry after his death— are aspects of her life that have been dealt with at length in these pages. If to be a companion in life to her husband is the fundamental duty of a wife, the Holy Mother has set the highest example of it, and that at a level where such companionship means also the pursuit of lofty spiritual ideals. Being the wife of a spiritual teacher who remained a Brahmachari (celibate) for life and insisted on celibacy as an essential discipline of spiritual life, she remained a nun in spite of her married condition. As such she had no children of the body, but she had such a large number of devotees and disciples, to whom she was a mother and much more, and in relation to them she displayed all the love and sweetness which a woman reveals when she receives fulfilment as a mother. In this respect the Holy Mother is a unique figure in the world's history. There have been great wives, great mothers and great nuns, but few, if any, who have been all these at the same time. She, therefore, reveals a new possibility in the field of womanly character.

It is this aspect of the Holy Mother that all have to remember when she is spoken of as the last word of Sri Ramakrishna on the ideal of womanhood. To follow in her footsteps a woman need not get married at the age of five, or observe purdah, or remain illiterate for life. These features are the mere accidents of her life, not the essentials of the ideal she represented. But a woman who proposes to follow her must necessarily be a real companion, a real participant, in the intellectual and spiritual life of her husband, have a maternal tenderness in her relation with all, and be austere and godly in her life. The Holy Mother demonstrates that wifely devotion is possible without the attraction of sex, that maternal love can be manifested without oneself bearing children, and that the highest godliness can be cultivated even in the midst of the common avocations of life. Especially today, when changed social conditions are forcing many women out of their traditional role as housewives and are approximating them to masculine standards, the Holy Mother reminds them that even in so doing, woman need not lose her soul but can express her latent possibilities in a wider relationship.

Her message

In her conversation with disciples she has left behind a valuable body of instructions, emphasizing certain aspects of the cultural side of the movement. *The Gospel of the Holy Mother* sets them forth in detail. Here only a brief summary of their salient features is given.

In her teachings she presupposed all the important doctrines of the Vedanta, but never entered into the subtleties of metaphysics or the theoretical exposition of any particular philosophical doctrine. She admitted that in the fullness of one's spiritual evolution, one reached a state in which all manifested phenomena were realized as transitory and even the idea of God got expanded. 'In course of time,' she once said, 'one does not feel even the existence of God as a separate entity. After attaining Jnana (wisdom), one sees that gods and deities are all Maya. Everything comes into existence in time and also disappears in time....'

While thus admitting the truth of the non-dualistic goal, she never compromised on the question of the absolute supremacy of the path of devotion in all spiritual striving. Thus when a disciple once spoke to her complacently about the ultimate unreality of God, creation and the rest, she said reply, 'Narendra once said to me, "Mother, the knowledge that explains away the lotus feet of the Guru is nothing but ignorance. What is the validity of knowledge if it proves that the Guru is nought?" Give up this dry discussion, this hodge-podge of philosophy. Who has been able to know God by reasoning? Even sages like Suka and Vyasa are at best like big ants trying to carry away a few grains of sugar from a large heap.'

From statements such as these, it would seem that she did not hold dogmatically to any metaphysical position. She does not deny the non-dual state of consciousness, but does not highlight it. If there is a state of non-duality that obliterates the distinction between Jiva and Isvara, it is one that dawns naturally through the cultivation of devotion and self-surrender, and the consequent bestowal of His grace on the Jiva. The sublation of the Guru (ie God) through ratiocination is both impossible and illegitimate. God, the Satchidananda, is the highest spiritual ideal that man can have, and the duty of man therefore consists in adoring, loving and serving Him. So the path of devotion formed the principal subject of her teaching. She always impressed on aspirants the need of looking upon God as one's 'own' and of surrendering oneself unconditionally to Him. For spiritual illumination ultimately depends on His grace alone, and all spiritual practices, which men generally perform for attaining Him, are at best only contributive factors. For this reason she often spoke of God as possessing the nature of a child. A child might not give a thing to a person who asked for it a hundred times, whereas it might give it away to another man even at the first request. In the same way the grace of God is not conditioned by anything.

She did not, however, mean thereby to minimize the importance of self-effort. 'Everything, no doubt, happens only by the will of God,' she used to say. 'Yet man must work, because God expresses His will through the actions of man. Again, all the facilities that one gets in life are determined by one's past actions and, besides, by one's present actions one can counteract one's past actions.' What she sought to impress on the devotees was that they should neither overestimate nor underestimate the value of spiritual practices. It is wrong if one thought that just as goods could be purchased from the market for a price, God could be attained by the power of one's spiritual practices like Japa and meditation. For ultimately it is the result of divine grace alone. If, however, there is any condition in grace, it is pure devotion. So she said, 'Neither Mantra nor scripture is of any avail. Pure loving devotion alone can win everything.'

But this kind of devotion, according to her, is the most difficult thing to attain. For it cannot be had so long as there is the slightest trace of worldly desire in the mind. Only Isvarakotis (aspirants born with divine tendency) possess it in abundance, and others attain to it to the extent they free themselves from all worldly desires. For this reason, she once said, God might give salvation to anyone, but He seldom confers devotion on men.

Spiritual practices, according to her, are useful in bestowing this purity of mind so necessary for the dawn of devotion. They cut asunder the ties of past Karma and help to subdue the power of the senses. As the wind scatters the clouds, the Name of God destroys worldliness. And again, just as by handling flowers or pieces of sandal-wood one's palms catch the fragrance of those objects, so divine contemplation helps one to mould one's mind in His image.

Hence, while maintaining the importance of grace, she always insisted on the value of regular and persistent spiritual practices. 'Don't relax practice,' she used to say, 'simply because you do not get His vision. Does an angler catch a big carp every day the moment he sits with the rod? He has to wait and wait, and many a time he is disappointed.'

She seemed to have attached special importance to spiritual experiences that came as a result of strenuous practice. 'God-realization,' she said, 'can be had at any time by the grace of God, but there is a difference between it and what comes in the fullness of time, as there is a difference between mangoes that ripen in the proper season and those that ripen in the month of Jyaishta (May-June). The latter are not very sweet.' She also insisted that the normal course of spiritual progress was gradual. Perhaps one had practised Japa and austerities in one life; in the next life one's spiritual mood deepened thereby; and in the life following, still more and so on.

Among spiritual disciplines, she stressed Japa as the most important. According to her, initiation with the Mantra purifies the body. God, she said, has given fingers in order that they might be blessed by counting Japa. An athlete was in the habit of carrying a calf in his arms from its very birth. He did it every day and as a consequence he gradually developed the strength necessary to carry it without effort even after it had become a full-grown animal. Exactly similar, she used to say, is the nature of the spiritual progress one makes, gradually and unobserved, through the practice of Japa. By continually making Japa thousands of times, one's mind automatically gets steadied and absorbed in meditation and one's Kundalini (spiritual power) is ultimately roused. When a pure mind performs Japa, the Holy Word bubbles itself up spontaneously from within without any effort on its part. One who reaches this state attains success in Japa.

Along with the practice of Japa and meditation, she advocated the importance of healthy altruistic works. For, men ordinarily cannot do spiritual practices all the twenty-four hours of the day. So work performed with a spiritual motive is the best thing to fill up the gap. Without that there is even positive danger: for, an idle mind is proverbially the devil's workshop. So she favoured the type of altruistic activities undertaken by the monks of the Ramakrishna Order.

She always advised spiritual atpirants to be patient in times of difficulties and troubles. For misery, she said, is the symbol of God's compassion. Instead of getting worried, and aspirant should pray to the Divine with tears in his eyes when he wants illumination, or finds himself faced with doubts and difficulties. She impressed on all aspirants, whether householder or Sannyasin, the need of being continent—if they were really serious about their spiritual life. For to have non-attachment to the body and its pleasure is the *sine qua non* of spiritual life. 'Today the human body is, tomorrow it is not; and even its short span of life is beset with pain and misery'—discriminating thus, one should cultivate a spirit of dispassion and renunciation, and then the true love of God dawns in one's mind. She put all her ideas on spiritual life in a clinching form when she said, 'He who is able to renounce all for His sake is a living god. Even the decrees of fate are cancelled if one takes refuge in God. Fate strikes off with her own hand what she has written about such a person. What does one obtain by realizing God? Does he develop a pair of horns? No. He gains discrimination between the real and the unreal, gets spiritual consciousness, and passes beyond life and death.' ❏

19. THE MAHA SAMADHI

IT REMAINS NOW to record the incidents connected with the passing away of the Holy Mother. In January 1919 she went to her native place, chiefly in the interests of Radhu, who was expecting a child. Instead of proceeding straight to Jayrambati she halted on the way at the Jagadamba Ashrama at Koalpara situated some ten miles away from Jayrambati. Though the halt was planned originally only for rest on the way, the Mother decided to stay there for several days, as Radhu liked the wooded scenery and the rural quietness of the place very much and insisted on prologing her stay there—an idea with which uncle Kali and other elders also were in agreement. So the Mother camped there till the last week of July. The period of her stay there was full of anxiety for the Holy Mother on account of Radhu's poor health, augmented by the tribulations of expectancy. Radhu was in a completely neurasthenic condition. She was extremely weak, listless and irritable. She could not stand any sound—loud speech, a crow's cry, or clang of metallic vessels. It set her heart beating fast and irritated her in the extreme. She was always having burning sensation in body and head. To add to the anxiety, the story of a wild bear appearing in the neighbourhood and tearing up the village watchman was circulated. As the Ashrama was surrounded by thickets, the bear could appear anywhere there—so the people thought. Also, an insane man intruded into the place at night, spreading consternation among the women but the Mother pacified him with kind words and some food.

Amidst all this, well-wishers were not wanting to suggest occult cures for Radhu, on whom medicines seemed to have little effect. One was Nalini Devi's suggestion to get the 'bangle' of the 'Mad Kali' of Troll, a place seventeen miles away, and make Radhu wear it. Instances of its curative effect were cited. The bangle was brought one evening, hung on a tree for the night as it should not be placed on floor, and Radhu made to wear it the next day. But it had no effect on Radhu's implacable neurasthenia. Next came the compelling demand of Radhu's own mother, who was very angry at her being brought away from Calcutta, that application of ice on her head was the one remedy called for. Ice was procured with difficulty, and an ice cap applied. Uncle Kali, on seeing this, ridiculed this acceptance of a mad woman's prescription. His own experience of men and their ailments convinced him that Radhu's was not a physical ailment but a case of possession by some demigod or ghost, who could surely be exorcized by a certain expert Tantrika sorcerer of Sushnegede. The Tantrika was approached, invited and received with all ceremony. He was given a full account of Radhu's conditions. He was quick in understanding all details

The Maha Samadhi

and equally quick to give his prescription. But that prescription was the despair of the Mother and a breath-taking surprise for the generality of men, probably with the exception of uncle Kali whose eyes must have become wide open in triumphant appreciation. The prescription was this: The oil and liver of a Rohita fish weighing more than forty pounds were to be boiled in oil extracted from gingili seed in a village oil press. With that was to be cooked iron, several scented drugs, the dung of a bull etc. got from inaccessible places. The ointment made with this strange combination was to be rubbed over Radhu's body, and also an amulet prescribed by him to be tied on her. Nobody, however, had the daring or resourcefulness to apply this remedy and test its potency. One more occult remedy, suggested by a chanda (a spirit) through a medium in a seance was tried, but with no result. At last a person with much better sense suggested that a doctor should be called in. The Mother, tired of all remedies, said in a spirit of resignation: 'Are not the bitches of the country-side and vixen of the forest delivered of their litter?' Indeed, thanks to the foresight of Swami Saradananda, a doctor and a midwife were despatched from Calcutta before Radhu reached term. But fortunately Radhu had a normal delivery of a male infant on May 9th, to the great relief, at least for the time being, of the Mother and all the others concerned. The relief that the Mother got from it was, however, considerably neutralized by the death of Maku's child, Neda, who was a pet of hers.

The Mother proceeded from Koalpara to Jayrambati only towards the third week of July 1919, and continued to stay there till 24 February 1920, when she left for Calcutta, bidding adieu to her birth place for the last time. The last months of her stay at Jayrambati were full of trials for her. Even after her delivery Radhu's mental condition did not improve. Not only did she worry the Mother by her eccentricities, but aggressively persecuted her by her impudence and occasional violence. Examples of such situations will be seen in chapter eight. The Mother's health was fast declining during these months; it broke down under a kind of intermittent fever, which was first noticed soon after a very tiring celebration of her 66th birthday on 13 December 1919. Without realizing the seriousness of it, local treatment was at first tried, but the fever continued intermittently, resulting in complete prostration. In the end, at the instance of Swami Saradananda, arrangements were made for her to start for Calcutta on 24th February along with Radhu, Radhu's mother, Maku, Nalini and others.

Very touching scenes were witnessed at what the Mother must have felt to be her last leave-taking of her native village. All the villagers gathered, and with tears in their eyes requested her again and again that she should not forget them, but return soon into their midst. The Mother made salutation to Simhavahini and other deities of the village, naming them one after another. She would not get into a palanquin out of her regard for the village deities, but insisted on walking up to the limits of the village. Then she turned round and did obeisance to the village of her birth and got into the palanquin. Her brother Prasanna's wife ceremonially

The Maha Samadhi

washed her feet, and made offering of water, betel and sweets as to a deity before the two palanquins moved away on the shoulders of the fleet-footed bearers. Late in the night they reached Koalpara where they rested for the night. While starting from there in the morning, the Mother gave Brahmachari Yogen a walking stick, a property of uncle Prasanna, to be returned to him along with a mosquito curtain, adding significantly, 'My son, there is Sarat (Swami Saradananda) to look after you all.' Travelling from Koalpara via Kotulpur they reached Vishnupur only at 2 p.m., rather late, because of a halt on the way for refreshments and some purchases from wayside shops. At Vishnupur the party rested for that night and the next day at the house of the devotee Sureshwar Sen, and then proceeded to Calcutta by train, reaching there at 9 p.m. on 27th of February. When she got down from the train, Yogin-Ma and Golap-Ma, who were waiting on the railway platform to receive her, were shocked to see her emaciated body, and exclaimed in consternation to the disciple accompanying, 'Oh, in what a pitiable condition you have brought the Mother to us! Why, she is black as soot! You have brought here a skeleton covered with skin.'

She arrived in Calcutta on 27 February 1920, and for the next five months she suffered from this malignant fever. Immediately after her arrival, she was placed under the treatment of the reputed Ayurvedic physician, Kaviraj Shyamadas Vachaspati. The treatment at first gave her some relief. But the medicine given was so bitter that the unpleasant taste persisted even at mealtime, so much so that she could not take her food with relish. Since the physician could not prescribe any alternative medicine, allopathic treatment was next tried. Dr. Nilratan Sirkar, the renowned doctor of Calcutta, was called in, and he diagnosed the disease as Kala-azar, a kind of malignant tropical fever resembling malaria, for which there was no effective treatment in those days. Under his instruction, Dr. Pradhan Bose treated the Holy Mother for two months, but with little result. So the Ayurvedic treatment was again tried.

The fever, in its early stages, used to appear in the evening and subside at night. In the second stage it appeared in the morning and evening, and in the last stage it continued without intermission, the temperature sometimes going up to 103 degrees. She also began to suffer from an intense burning sensation all over the body, to get a little relief from which she often used to clasp Yogin-Ma. She had constantly to be fanned and ice had to be applied to her palms to give her some relief.

Her diet during illness consisted generally of rice, milk and vegetables prepared according to medical directions, supplemented with fruits. The Ayurvedic physician had directed that, as she was anaemic, she should be given anything she liked to eat, because it might perhaps get digested and help to revive her failing strength. One day, as the girl disciple Sarala, who nursed her in her last illness, brought the plate of food for her, Dr. J.N. Kanjilal, a homeopathic physician and a close disciple of the Mother, came into the room. He thought that the food was too much and flew into a rage at the disciple. He said that she knew nothing of nursing, that she was killing the Mother through overfeeding, and declared that he would bring two trained nurses to replace her in the service of the Mother. The disciple was very much mortified, but when Dr. Kanjilal left the room, the Holy Mother consoled her saying that the doctor's behaviour was quite unjustified, and that under no circumstances would she allow herself to be nursed by 'those booted women' (meaning hospital nurses). After this incident even the little appetite she had for food disappeared.

During this protracted illness, her nature became like that of a little girl. Often she would say that she wanted to go to the Ganges, of which she was very fond all through life, and would refuse to eat any food until someone agreed to take her. Once late at night the attending disciple, Sarala, was trying to feed her. But the Mother, like a child, said, 'No, I won't eat. You always ask me to eat and apply that 'stick' (meaning the thermometer) under the arm.' At this the disciple said that she would call Swami Saradananda, for generally she would take food when his name was mentioned. But this time she refused to eat and said, 'Call him, I won't eat from your hand.' The Swami therefore came upstairs at once. All were astonished to notice the great change in her behaviour towards him on this occasion. Generally she appeared before him only veiled and talked to him through an intermediary. But this time she beckoned him to sit by her side, touched him endearingly on the chin by way of kissing, and taking his two hands into hers, said complainingly, 'My child, how they annoy me! They are always saying, "Eat, eat", and they know only one thing—how to put the 'stick' under my arm. You tell her (the disciple) not to annoy me any more.' The Swami consoled her, saying that she would not do so thereafter, and asked her whether she would like to take something. She agreed, but as soon as he asked the disciple to bring some food, she added, 'No, you feed me. I won't eat from her hand.' After putting a little milk into her mouth, the swami said, 'Mother, rest a while and then eat.' Hearing these words, she said with delight, 'See, how nicely he speaks! He said, "Mother, rest a while and eat." Can't these people speak like that? They have given so much trouble to my child at this late hour of the night. Go, my son, and rest now. Ah! how much he has suffered for me!'

Even when illness and physical suffering had reduced her to the last extremity, her great quality of motherliness persisted. She would never forget to make kind enquiries about people's health, or to arrange to feed her disciples who had to go out on errands. When doctors came, she was very particular about giving them fruits and sweets. If any disciple fanned her, she would ask the fanning to be stopped after a short time, saying that it would pain the hand and that she would not be able to sleep, thinking of it. Ramani, a woman of Jayrambati, came with some green palm fruits sent by a disciple and went back with some articles. The Holy Mother could not see her or receive her properly, because she was unconscious owing to high fever. She was very sorry for this and sent her apologies to the woman. Her nephew Ramlal and niece Lakshmi Devi

The Maha Samadhi

came to see her in her sickbed. When they left, she forgot to give any present to Lakshmi Devi, as she was required to do by custom. On remembering this omission her sense of courtesy would not allow her any peace, until she sent a fine cloth and some money to Lakshmi Devi through a messenger.

About a month before the Mother's passing away, she surprised all by asking the Master's picture to be removed from her room to an adjoining one. When asked for the reason, she said that thereafter she would not be able to go to the bath-room, and that under the circumstances she did not like her room to continue to be the shrine as well. She also asked her own bed to be made on the floor, owing probably to the popular notion that one should pass away only lying on the floor.

Even in this state of her health, she would take anything only after offering it to the Master. When external offering became impossible, she would make the offering mentally. All through her protracted illness, the one theme she used to harp on was resignation to the will of the Master. If anyone asked her as to when she would recover, she would say that it depended on the Master's will. One day she was speaking to Gauri-Ma of the happy and inspiring days she had spent at Dakshineswar in Sri Ramakrishna's company. Gauri-Ma replied that even after the Master's passing away she lived happily in worship and meditation, and that it was only after her assuming the responsibility of Radhu that those days came to an end.

This brings us to that remarkable episode in the last days of the Holy Mother's life, namely, the way in which she broke that golden chain of attachment to Radhu, by means of which she had tied herself to the world all these years. A few days before her passing away, she ceased to make any enquiries about Radhu. This was quite unlike her usual habit, for ordinarily Radhu was the constant preoccupation of her mind. One day she said to Radhu, 'Go to Jayrambati at once. Don't stay here any longer.' The disciple, Sarala, who was standing by, intervened and said to the Mother, 'Why do you say so? You will not be able to live without Radhu.' 'Certainly I can,' said the Mother. 'I have withdrawn my mind from her.' The disciple reported this to Yogin-Ma and Swami Saradananda. Yogin-Ma at once went to the Holy Mother and asked her, 'Mother, why do you want Radhu to go away?' At this the Mother said, 'Yogin, henceforth she will have to live at Jayrambati. You send her there. I have taken my mind away from her. I do not want her any more.' Yogin-Ma replied, 'Don't say so, Mother. If you have taken your mind away from Radhu, then how shall we live?' But to these pleadings of Yogin-Ma the Mother's answer was, 'Yogin, I have cut off my ties of attachment from her. No more of this.' Yogin-Ma reported the whole thing to Swami Saradananda, who thereupon remarked, 'Well, it means that we shall not be able to keep the Mother among us any longer. There is no hope of her life, as she has withdrawn her mind from Radhu.' And addressing Sarala, he added, 'You spend a great deal of time with the Mother, nursing her. Try your utmost to divert her mind again to Radhu.' The disciple attempted to do so in many ways, but could not succeed. Her vain efforts in

The Maha Samadhi

this direction were put an end to when the Holy Mother said to her one day very emphatically, 'The mind that has been withdrawn will no more settle there. Remember this.'

Nalini Devi, her niece, was very apprehensive of approaching the Mother, noticing her irritation at the sight of all her close relatives. She was shedding tears in silence, and remarked, 'If our presence is so galling to aunt, it is better we clear away. But what will people say?—The Mother is so badly ill, and these people, her nearest kith and kin, have deserted her at this critical time!' So Swami Saradananda interfered on their behalf and pleaded with the Mother: 'It will be very painful for them to leave you when you are so ill. They will go after you are somewhat better.' But the Mother persisted, expressing her firm resolve, 'Well, it is better they are sent away now itself. In any case, see that they do not come anywhere near me. I do not like to see even their shadow.'

And she proved the truth of her statement one day when she was put to the test by a very moving incident. One noon Radhu's little child came crawling from the side of her mother who was sleeping in the adjacent room, and tried to reach the Holy Mother's body. At this she said to the child, 'I have given up attachment to you altogether. Go away, you cannot entangle me any more.' And addressing a disciple who was standing by, she said, 'Take this baby away. I don't care for it any more.'

In Chapter 8 the significance of Radhu coming into the Mother's life was explained. So long as the Great

Master was alive, his service was the pivot on which the Mother's life revolved. After his passing, there was no anchor to hold the ship of her spirit to the sea-shore of our earthly dimension. With the anchor cut off, it would have drifted into the high seas of Brahmic Consciousness and be lost for the world. But the Great Master's mission had to be fulfilled. She was one of the major instruments for its fulfilment. Her body and mind had therefore to be preserved and held at the level of earth consciousness. An attachment of a purely worldly type was required for it, and the great Providence that designed the grand plan of the Master's life and mission achieved this by tying her with the secure chain of affection and attachment for Radhu and her like, until she had played her part and was free to shuffle off the mortal coil.

She was now fast sinking. When all medical treatment had failed, occult remedies were tried but to no purpose. Gradually, owing to anaemia, the legs began to swell. She could not even get up from the bed. Five days before her passing away, a lady devotee known as 'mother of Annapurna' came to see her. As no one was then allowed to enter the Holy Mother's room, she sat at the doorway. The Mother caught sight of her and beckoned to her to come near. She bowed down and sobbed out, 'Mother, what will happen to us hereafter?' The Mother consoled her in a low, almost inaudible voice, 'Why do you fear? You have seen the Master.' After a pause she added, 'But I tell you one thing—if you want peace of mind, do not find fault with others. Rather see your own faults. Learn to make the whole world your own. No one is a stranger, my child; this whole world is your own!' Perhaps this embodies her last message to the world also.

During her last three days she spoke practically nothing, partly owing to physical weakness and partly owing to the deep introspective mood that was now upon her. When anyone went and talked to her, she expressed annoyance. Once Gauri-Ma went to her bedside and announced herself several times, but the Mother only asked why she was thus disturbing her. In those last days she once called Swami Saradananda to her side and said, 'Sarat, I am going. Yogin, Golap and the rest are here. You look after them.' This was her last complete utterance. The day before her end, she called the Swami again and tried to say something, but could not speak more than one or two words.

Towards the close there was hard breathing for some time. Just before her passing away, her face and body became very dark and shrivelled, but to the astonishment of those who stood by her, a great change took place immediately after life was extinct. Her shrivelled form was seen to relax, and her face swelled up and assumed a radiant hue. To a disciple who stood by, her countenance seemed to resemble the face of the image of the Goddess Durga used in worship—mellow and golden in colour, with the expression of calmness and serenity writ large on it. This expression lingered in her face for some length of time.

She entered into Mahasamadhi at 1.30 a.m. on 20th July 1920. In the morning arrangements were made to take the body in procession to the Belur Math for cremation. According to her oft-repeated desire, the body was bathed in the Ganges and was carried in a bier decorated with flowers, on the shoulders of pious devotees. Some of the prominent disciples of Sri Ramakrishna, like Swami Saradananda, Swami Shivananda and Master Mahasaya, accompanied by several respectable persons of the city, followed the procession, which at times swelled to thousands. By about 2 p.m. the body was consigned to the flames at a spot near the Ganges, within the Belur Math compound.

Today, beside the vivid impressions of her in the minds of devoted disciples, there are three shrines that specially commemorate her life and doings. In the Belur Math there is a beautiful small temple facing the Ganges, built on the spot where her body was cremated. In the shrine of the Udbodhan Office, her portrait is kept facing that of the Master, just as she used to face it in her lifetime. And lastly, at the village of Jayrambati, in the compound where she was born, the devotion of Swami Saradananda has erected a temple[1] in her memory, with a monastery attached to it. In that shrine is installed a life-size oil painting of hers, and in the solemn stillness and holy atmosphere of that sanctuary, seated before the Mother's portrait—bearing a mild and meek, yet serene and dignified expression—one still gets a brooding sense of the Mother-Heart that was embodied as Sarada Devi, the Holy Mother. ❏

---

1. The reference here is to the old temple which existed in 1940 when the first edition of this book was published. Since then a beautiful and well-designed temple has been built at Jayrambati on the occasion of the Holy Mother's Birth Centenary celebrated in 1954.

20. THE HOLY MOTHER AS A REVELATION OF THE MOTHERHOOD OF GOD

THE IMPERFECT ACCOUNT of the life and message of the Holy Mother may perhaps gain some measure of completion by the addition of the following explanation of what she means to mankind in the context of the comprehensive revelation of Divinity which we get in the life and teachings of Sri Ramakrishna. The Holy Mother herself declared that the Master left her on earth to reveal the Motherhood of God. Without a proper understanding of the significance of this statement, the personality of the Holy Mother would look enigmatic to a critical student.

To an ordinary Hindu, brought up in the theological conceptions of the prevailing cults like Vaishnavism, Saivism, and Saktaism, the Deity and His incarnations are always associated with a Female (Mother) element. Thus Vishnu and Lakshmi, Siva and Parvati, Rama and Sita, Krishna and Radha are distinct divinities forming the Male and the Female counterparts in the highly anthropomorphized conceptions obtaining in these cults. Anthropomorphism has gone to the furthest limit by conceiving each of these Deities as forming a regular family group consisting of a father, mother, children, servants, heavenly abodes and all kinds of special paraphernalia characteristic of each group. By describing Sri Sarada Devi as a revelation of the Motherhood of God, are we to look upon her merely as an addition to this already long list of Mother-Goddesses?

A naive Hindu mind, devoted to the cult centering on Sri Ramakrishna, may not see more meaning than this in the statement and may feel satisfied that a votary pays the highest compliment to Sri Sarada Devi by recognising her as an incarnation of Lakshmi or Parvati. But the world culture today requires a theology spelt in more universally understandable terms than what is known to the language of Hindu mythology. Besides, anthropomorphism has its limitations. A liberal mind may accept its validity as an aid to human thought in its development towards higher stages of abstract thinking and subtle perception, but anthropomorphism as an end in itself and as unrelated to more universally understandable implications, has very little to commend itself in the modern cultural milieu.

The message of Sri Ramakrishna and Sri Sarada Devi is universal in its significance and should not be allowed to fall into narrow theological ruts. They convey the spirit of that universal philosophy of religion known today as the Vedanta, and accordingly even features that look merely personal in them are expressions of universal principles. In such a context, a striking statement as the one under consideration, that the Master left the Holy Mother in the world to reveal

A revelation of the motherhood of God

the Motherhood of God, must have far more universally acceptable and meaningful implications than what any mythological interpretation would yield.

The key to the interpretation of the Holy Mother's message in this respect is to be found in the following words of advice she gave to a devotee five days before her passing, which have been described in the last chapter of this book as her final message to mankind. 'If you want peace,' she said, 'do not see the faults of others. Rather see your own faults. Learn to make the whole world your own. No one is a stranger, my child. This whole world is your own.' These words are much more than a mere homily. They are an expression of her own innate nature and a summary of the tenor of her whole life. What is more, it is the point at which we get a gleam of her Divine nature bursting through the thick veil of her humanity. We are here face to face with God's Motherhood.

In the first place we have to be clear about what we mean by calling God as Mother. It is not primarily to show a distinction of sex in Divinity, although as pointed out already, anthropomorphism tends to distinguish between 'mother' God and 'father' God. In the philosophic conception of Sakti, which forms the background of the Mother Cult, Sakti is the dynamic aspect of the Absolute while in the Cult itself this dynamic principle is anthropomorphized as the Consort of the Absolute who is Himself pictured as male (Siva). Much of what goes under occult psychism (Siddhi) and esoteric sex-ritualism (Vamachara), which form the characteristic features of medieval Sakti cult, is the direct legacy of this bipolar notion of the Deity. It is one of the great contributions of Sri Ramakrishna to Indian religious tradition that his spiritual experience has identified the Sakti not as a mere female counterpart of the Absolute, but as the Absolute Himself personalised—the Saguna Brahman of the Vedanta, who is the origin, the support and the end of the manifold universe. The Saguna Brahman is, in a devotional sense, Father or Mother, and, for the matter of that, can be invoked in any other loving relationship as Master, Friend, Lover, Teacher and so on. But the Master described the Saguna Brahman specially by the epithet 'Mother', and conceived and invoked Him as the Mother of all beings. In doing so, it must be clearly understood that he did not have in mind the contrast between masculinity and femininity or the bipolarity of a male and female element in the Deity as in orthodox Sakta theologies, although he often used the current phraseology of the Sakta schools. In other words, when God is called Mother, the implication is not so much to give us a Female Deity as to remind us that in His function of redemption (Anugraha), Motherhood is the most adequate of all humanly understandable concepts to describe His unconditioned love for those who seek shelter in Him, abandoning all other support.

Human experience vouches for the fact that the mother's love is unconditioned by any consideration of merit or demerit, excellence or lack of it in respect of another related as off-spring. The capacity to do so is the uniqueness of the mother's heart. Hence Acharya Sankara has, in a well known hymn to the Divine

A revelation of the motherhood of God

Mother, appealed to Her for Her grace in spite of all his shortcomings, on the ground that 'a perverse son there can be, but never a bad mother.' As a matter of fact a weak child is specially the pet of the mother, eliciting from her even a differential treatment denied to those who are meritorious and strong enough to stand on their own feet.

In grasping the nature of the Deity, anthropomorphism rises to its noblest achievement when it helps us discover that this unique feature of human psychology is a clue to the understanding of the Supreme Being as the Redeemer (Anugraha Sakti). The merits and demerits, the wisdom and ignorance, the strength and weakness of the little self-conscious individual ego (Jiva) loses all their quantitative or even qualitative significance before the Infinite Power and Excellence of the Supreme Divine. A grain of sand and a hillock both become equally small in the unfathomed depths of the mighty Pacific Ocean in spite of the differences that the human scale of observation finds in them. The Jiva (the individual spiritual seeker) needs have only one excellence, and that is to recognise that, like a mother, God as Redeemer is all love, before the blazing splendour of which all considerations of merit and demerit become insubstantial and irrelevant, provided the devotee recognises in Him his eternal Mother and puts himself entirely and unconditionally under the mercy and protection of that Mother love. It is this truth that is revealed in the Bhagavad Gita verse: 'I am equal to all, none being specially inimical or dear to Me. But He who surrenders with all devotion and depends on Me entirely, he lives in Me and I in him.' In other words God the Redeemer, who is the same as God the Mother, sees not the merit or demerit of a seeker, but His love and protection are open to all who seek it in absolute trust and self-surrender.

When the Holy Mother is spoken of as a revelation of Divine Motherhood, it is better to understand the statement in this psychological sense than in the usual theological way that she was some goddess like Lakshmi or Durga appearing on earth. A reader of the foregoing pages would have noted how she was incapable of seeing evil in any one and how it was the constant complaint of Golap-Ma that whoever went to her calling her 'Mother', got kind response from her without any consideration of his nature or attainments. Defect and shortcomings, however grievous, and merits, however significant from the worldly point of view, did not obstruct or regulate the even flow of the current of her universal benevolence, even as a mother's love for her children is not affected by considerations of their merit or demerit. Devotees who went to her for initiation were accepted by her irrespective of all questions of their fitness.

Her conduct in this respect may at times look as born of indifference to quality. But a close acquaintance with her nature will show that the reason was quite different. She was the Mother of men and not their judge. For, to judge is human, but to love, forgetting all shortcomings, is Divine. In the Chapter entitled 'Her Spiritual Ministry' a detailed account has been given of how all who sought her blessings obtained it, though it

A revelation of the motherhood of God

meant suffering to her. The holy essence in her was highly sensitive to the repulsive aura of sinful people, which, to put it in her own words, she felt like 'the sting of a wasp.' An enlightened teacher takes upon himself the sins of disciples whose spiritual responsibility he assumes by initiation. Conscious of this, Swami Brahmananda, direct disciple of the Master and Head of the monastic Order whose duty it was to give initiation, felt highly dismayed when so many unworthy men went for spiritual initiation. The Swami often directed such persons to the Holy Mother. Swami Premananda remarked once that they were sending to the Holy Mother the poison that they could not swallow. And she did swallow all that poison, which was enough to kill others, but which in her case became her brightest decoration even as in the Great God Siva, whom Hindu mythology describes as having swallowed the virulent poison that threatened the very existence of the world and sent a shudder of horror through all the gods, but which remained only to get transformed in the Great's God's throat into a distinguishing blue mark of embellishment.

In fact she was very conscious of the fact that the Master and herself who was a part and parcel of his Divine manifestation, came to suffer vicariously for the sins of those who took shelter in them. It has already been narrated how, when a disciple hesitated to touch her feet thinking that it would cause her suffering, she remarked: 'No, my child, we are born for this purpose. If we do not accept others' sins and sorrows and do not assimilate these, who else will do so? Who else will bear the responsibilities of the sinners and the afflicted?' When, during her last illness, some one remarked that her physical sufferings were due to unholy contacts and that after her recovery, she should be completely protected from these, she remarked 'Why do you say so? Do you think that the Master only came to take Rasagollas (a delicious sweet)?' She meant that the purpose of the Master's and her lives was not to attain anything for themselves, but to sacrifice themselves for the enlightenment and salvation of others.

No narrow love, however noble from practical worldly considerations, could enter into her heart and obstruct her dominant sense of universal benevolence. Patriotism, for example, is unquestionably an ennobling sentiment for all men ordinarily, but not for the Holy Mother. Her reaction to the idea of boycott of foreign cloth is a remarkable example of this. A disciple was asked to purchase a particular kind of cloth to be given as a present. It was to be of British make and not of Indian. The disciple was deeply imbued with the prevailing sentiment against foreign cloth, the boycott of which was preached as a primary act of partiotism by the national leaders of India at that time. So he objected to the Mother that this particular brand of cloth was made by the British, who were the oppressors and therefore the enemies of India. But the Mother's quick reply was: 'No, I cannot be as narrow as that. They too are my children.' But, in order to respect the disciple's sentiment, she exempted him from the work and asked some one else to purchase the cloth. The incident is

A revelation of the motherhood of God

thrilling to contemplate. It must be remembered that she was an absolutely old-world lady who knew nothing of modern political ideologies or international relations. The attitude she evinced in this instance was therefore neither tutored nor assumed. It was the spontaneous expression of her innate nature. Poised in the sense of Motherhood, she could stand above all humanity, whether of the East or the West, Indian or foreign, righteous or erring, and view it all alike in an attitude of universal love that broke all barriers between man and man.

Another remarkable example of her same-sightedness, which set at naught all our usual human standards of excellence, is seen in the incident connected with the labourer Amjad described in detail in an earlier chapter. This Amjad, a Muslim labourer, along with others, was engaged for some construction work at her Jayrambati house. Amjad became familiar with the Mother and even began to bring offerings to the shrine. At the close of the work, the Mother invited him for a parting feast. Her niece Nalini, owing to narrow caste prejudice, disliked the Muslim being fed in the verandah, and much more, being served food personally. She was therefore throwing articles of food into his plate from a distance, when the Holy Mother, unable to bear this shocking exhibition of caste prejudice, herself took the serving vessels and began serving him with great affection. After the man finished eating his food, she herself cleaned the place, at which Nalini, shocked at her aunt's revolutionary heterodoxy, burst out into a wild exclamation. Deprecating her attitude of mind, the

Mother retorted: 'Do you know that this Amjad is as much my son as Sarat is?'

The implications of this assertion are staggering. Amjad was an uncultured Muslim labourer belonging to a gang which, the villagers suspected, was given to robbery and house-breaking at night, while Sarat, alias Swami Saradananda, was a direct disciple of Sri Ramakrishna, a holy and learned monk respected by vast numbers of men of light and learning as a great spiritual luminary. He was, besides, the care-taker of the Holy Mother and the Secretary of the Ramakrishna Math and Mission. To equate them both in the claim of sonship to her, and behave towards them in that spirit, is possible only for those who are of the essence of God, the Father and Mother of all beings. No doubt, there are men aspiring for leadership and a place in history, who are prepared to make similar claims for universality of outlook in their platform speeches and autobiographies, if these would be blazed forth by the world publicity media. But as far as the above expressions of the Holy Mother's sentiments were concerned, there was none by her side to hear and publicize it besides the obscure person of an uneducated Nalini, and had it not been for the fact that it was recorded by a disciple in a diary, this revealing incident would not have even been known to the world at large after decades of its occurrence. It was therefore really a spontaneous revelation of her nature without any affectation in it. Universal benevolence had obliterated in her all distinctions of high and low, deserving and undeserving, through the comprehension of all in the relation of sonship. In the divine mode of valuation, with Infinity as the unit, scales cease to tilt in favour of narrow values recognised by the world. Saint and sinner are alike in the utter holiness and love that is God. To abide in Him purifies even the worst.

It is in such little incidents of her life like the Amjad episode and the boycott of foreign cloth, in her constitutional incapacity to see the faults and bad sides of others, in her readiness to bless all alike irrespective of their merits and demerits—that we get a glimpse of God's Motherhood as also a living commentary on the great but enigmatic verse of the Bhagavad Gita: 'I am evenly disposed to all, being neither friendly nor inimical to any one. He who resigns himself to Me, he dwells in Me and I in him.'

Generally we are nowadays prone to consider only cataclysmic events and doings of powerful dictators, military men and political leaders as of importance in human history. Nothing is more symptomatic of our colossal ignorance of the trends of human evolution. These striking events of the day pass away like storms, their memories getting submerged and forgotten in the fathomless depths of time. Only historians remember them. On the other hand the little actions of the great Saviours like Krishna, Buddha and Christ, though seemingly of little significance in their own time, have continued to stimulate the thoughts of an ever-expanding circle of men. The reason for this is that men have their egoes poised in the Supreme Being and therefore their thoughts and actions are charged with the power, which is of God. The Holy Mother's life and doings form an instance of the same kind. Her action and words have transcended the obscurity of their domestic context and have entered into the thought of vast numbers of devotees, because they are suffused with the aroma of the redeeming love of her Divine Motherhood. In the countless procession of the members of the human species on this planet of ours, the Holy Mother stands out as a unique example of one whose utter innocence could melt even the hardest of hearts, who never looked at the faults of others, whose love never made a distinction between the deserving and the undeserving, in whose eyes the saint and the sinner were alike precious as her children, whose wide heart embraced all humanity in the sense of sonship, and who considered it a privilege to labour and to suffer for even the least of them. If we cannot see here the face of the all-loving Universal Mother, of God the Redeemer, where else can we? Only we should have the sensitiveness to recognise that the subtle potency of love transcends the obtrusive displays of power.

It is significant in this context to note what she replied to a disciple who, being enchanted by her personality, enquired of her, 'Mother, after seeing you, how will people respect all the goddesses?' Her significant reply was, 'Why not? They are all my parts.' To one who knows the character of the Holy Mother, so full of innocence and humility, this is no boastful speech. It is a revelation of her innate nature—of the Divine Motherhood of which she was an embodiment.

It may be fitting to conclude this topic with a hymn by Swami Abhedananda, a great disciple of

A revelation of the motherhood of God

Sri Ramakrishna, addressed to the Universal Divine Mother revealed through Sri Sarada Devi:

> ध्यायेद्‌हृत्कमलमध्ये हेमवर्णां सुखासनाम् ।
> आलुलायितकेशार्धवक्षःस्थलाभिमण्डिताम् ॥
>
> श्वेतवस्त्रावृतार्धाङ्गां हेमालङ्कारभूषिताम् ।
> स्वक्रोडन्यस्त-हस्ताब्ज द्विभुजां स्थिरलोचनाम् ॥
>
> प्रसन्नवदनां जीवदुःखगलितचेतसाम् ।
> शुभ्रज्योतिर्मयीं देवीं वरदां सर्वमङ्गलाम् ॥
>
> रामकृष्णगतप्राणां तन्नामश्रवणप्रियाम् ।
> तद्भावरञ्जिताकारां विश्वमातृस्वरूपिणीम् ॥
>
> स्नेहमयीं शिवां शान्तां भक्तिमुक्तिप्रदायिनीम् ।
> सर्वजीवत्राणकर्त्रीं सारदां ज्ञानदायिनीम् ॥

Let us meditate in the lotus of the heart
    on Mother Sarada—
Of golden hue;
Seated cross-legged;
Half of her dishevelled hair flowing down the chest;
Wrapped in white cloth;
Wearing golden bracelets;
With two palms crossed and resting in the lap;
Of steady gaze;
With visage beaming with grace;
And heart melting at the sorrows of living beings;
Radiant light of purity;
The bounteous;
Come for the good of all;

With life centred in Ramakrishna and mind
  ever delighting in his thought;
Veritably an embodiment of his ideas;
Manifestation of Universal Motherhood;
Overflowing with universal benevolence,
  goodness and peace;
Bestower of devotion and salvation;
Redeemer of all Jivas;
Giver of Divine Knowledge. ❑

APPENDICES

1. CHRONOLOGY

1. Birth: 22nd December, 1853.

2. Marriage and first visit to Kamarpukur, May 1859.

3. First visit to Dakshineswar: March 1872.

4. Serving Sri Ramakrishna at Dakshineswar, with intervals of visits to Kamarpukur and Jayrambati: March 1872 to September 1885.

5. Shodasi Puja: New Moon night of 25th May, 1873, according to *Lila Prasanga;* New Moon night of 5th June, 1872, according to *Mayer Katha* Vol.II.

6. First return from Dakshineswar to Jayrambati: October 1873.

7. Death of Ramachandra Mukherjee, the Holy Mother's father: 26th April, 1874.

8. Severe attack of dysentery and awakening of Simhavahini: September, 1875.

9. The incident connected with the 'dacoit father.' Probably at the time of the third visit to Dakshineswar in 1877.

10. Serving Sri Ramakrishna at Syampukur and Cossipore: September 1885 to August 1886.

11. Mahasamadhi of Sri Ramakrishna: 16th August, 1886.

12. First pilgrimage to Brindavan: 30th August, 1886.
13. Visit to Kamarpukur after returning from Brindavan: August 1887.
14. Return to Calcutta: 1888.
15. Her spiritual ministry, her time being divided between Calcutta and Jayrambati: 1888-1920.
16. Performance of Panchatapa: 1893.
17. First visit to Belur Math: 12th November, 1898.
18. Mahasamadhi of Swami Yogananda: 28th March, 1899.
19. Passing away of Abhay Charan, the youngest brother of the Holy Mother: 2nd August, 1899.
20. Birth of Radhu or Radharani, and beginning of domestic entanglements: February 1900.
21. Passing away of Syamasundari Devi: January 1906.
22. Attending Durga Puja at the house of Girish Ghosh: 1907.
23. Opening of the Udbodhan Office, the Holy Mother's Calcutta residence: 23rd May, 1909.
24. Pilgrimage to Rameswaram: 1911.
25. Third visit to Banaras: 5th November, 1912.
26. Beginnings of her last illness: December 1919.
27. Mahasamadhi at 1-30 a.m. on 20th July, 1920.

2. THE HOROSCOPE OF THE HOLY MOTHER

The following is the horoscope of the Holy Mother as cast by Sjt. Narayana Chandra Jyotirbhushana:

	1	2	3
12		Saturn Rahu	Ascendant or *Lagnam*
11			4
10	Venus		Mars Moon / 5
	Jupiter Sun	Mercury Ketu	6
9	8	7	

THE NAMES OF THE PLANETS WITH SANSKRIT EQUIVALENTS

Saturn=Sani
Rahu=Rahu
Mars=Kuja
Moon=Chandra

Mercury=Budha
Ketu=Ketu
Jupiter=Guru
Sun=Surya

Venus=Sukra

THE SIGNS OF THE ZODIAC

1. Aries
2. Taurus
3. Gemini
4. Cancer
5. Leo
6. Virgo
7. Libra
8. Scorpio
9. Sagittarius
10. Capricornus
11. Aquarius
12. Pisces

3. Bibliography

Books in Bengali:

1. *Sri Sri Ramakrishna-lilaprasanga:* By Swami Saradananda. In five parts. Published by the Udbodhan Office, Calcutta.

This is the most authoritative biography of Sri Ramakrishna. It gives much valuable information on the Holy Mother's association with Sri Ramakrishna. Its English translation, *Sri Ramakrishna, the Great Master,* has been published by Sri Ramakrishna Math, Madras.

2. *Sri Sri Mayer Katha:* Being the conversations of the Holy Mother as recorded in the diaries of several disciples. In two volumes. Published by the Udbodhan Office, Calcutta. Its English translation is available in a single volume, *The Gospel of the Holy Mother,* published by Sri Ramakrishna Math, Madras.

Besides giving the Holy Mother's teachings, these conversations give much valuable biographical material in her own words.

3. *Sri Sri Sarada Devi:* By Brahmachari Akshaya-chaitanya. First Edition. Published by Bhattacharya and Sons Ltd., 19, Shyamacharan Dey Street, Calcutta.

This book of 313 pages has the distinction of being the first complete biography of the Holy Mother to appear in any language. It has chronicled a large body of biographical facts and worked out the chronology of the whole life. But it is lacking in sense of discrimination and fails to distinguish between the essential and the non-essential as seen from a free use of facts gathered even from doubtful authorities.

4. *Sri Sri Mayer Jivankatha*: Published in the Bengali weekly Desh, Vol. V, (1938), Calcutta.

This anonymous serial appeared in about fifteen issues of the Weekly during the year 1938. Though the writer's name is not published, he seems to have had access to many first-rate authorities and cites the evidence of the Holy Mother's intimate companions like Yogin-Ma and others. The writer seems also to have moved closely with the Holy Mother. Though it is not a complete or systematic biography, it sheds much light on periods of her life, especially on her life at Kamarpukur after Sri Ramakrishna's Mahasamadhi, of which little was known before.

Books in English:

There were no original or comprehensive writings in English on the Holy Mother when this book was first published in the year 1940. *The Life of Sri Ramakrishna*, published by the Advaita Ashrama, Calcutta, gives the substance of Swami Saradananda's account contained in the *Lilaprasanga*. In Sister Nivedita's *The Master as I saw Him* and in Sister Devamata's *Sri Ramakrishna and His Disciples and Days in an Indian Monastery*, one gets glimpses of the Holy Mothers's personality as it appeared to the two Western Sisters in their close association with her.

In the third edition of this book, we have incorporated some more interesting and revealing information about the Mother's life, taken from the Centenary Memorial Volume entitled *Holy Mother Sri Sarada Devi*, by Swami Gambhirananda. This well-documented biography was originally written in Bengali as a Holy Mother Centenary Publication and soon after rendered into English by the author himself and published by Sri Ramakrishna Math, Madras, in 1955.

INDEX AND GLOSSARY

ABHAYA CHARAN: the fourth brother of the Holy Mother, he was the husband of Surabala and the father of Radhu, 89, 98, 129, 134, 259, 285.

Abhedananda, Swami: a Sannyasin disciple of Sri Ramakrishna, also known by this premonastic name, Kali, 108, 326.

Adbhutananda, Swami: a Sannyasin disciple of Sri Ramakrishna, also known by the premonastic name of Latu, 75, 85, 108, 271.

Advaita: Philosophy of non-dualism, its chief exponent being Sankaracharya.

Advaitananda, Swami: a Sannyasin disciple of Sri Ramakrishna, also known by the premonasitc name of Gopal senior, 66, 245.

Akshay: a nephew of Sri Ramakrishna, 35.

Akshay Kumar Sen: a lay disciple of Sri Ramakrishna and the author of a poetical biography of the Master in Bengali, called Sri Sri Ramakrishna Punthi, 204.

Altekar: the author of the book Woman in Hindu Civilization, 28.

Amjad: a Muslim labourer, 206–7, 323.

Amodar: a river in Jayrambati, 11.

Amrul: a kind of green, supposed to be beneficial in dysentery, 99.

Analogy: of Crabs 194, moon 55.

Annapurna: the image of the Divine Mother in the temple of Viswanath at Banaras, 253, 255.

Anthropomorphism: Thinking of God in human terms, 319.

Anugraha: Redemption, 319.

Arambag: a place on the way from Calcutta to Jayrambati, 95.

Aratrika: vesper service in a Hindu temple, the chief feature of which is the waving of lighted wicks and incense before the image, 150.

Ashrama: any centre of service, study or meditation; a retreat; a monastery.

Atman: the Divinity in its individualized state as the soul.

Ayodhya: a place of pilgrimage in North India, reputed to be the birth-place of Sri Rama, 108.

Ayurveda: the old traditional system of Indian medicine which is still widely practised, 305.

BABURAM: see 'Premananda.'

Balaram Bose: a householder disciple of Sri Ramakrishna, 106, 248.

Banaras: the holiest of all places of pilgrimage for Hindus, situated in the Uttar Pradesh of India and noted for the temple of Viswanath. Holy Mother at, 108, 247, 253.

Banerji: a Brahmanical family name special to Bengal, 12.

Barada Prasad: the third brother of the Holy Mother 89, 129.

Belur Math: the head monastery of the Ramakrishna Order near Calcutta, Durga Puja there, 264.

Index and glossary

Bhagavad Gita: a great Hindu scripture noted for its universal teachings. See 'Gita'.

Bhagavata Purana: a Vaishnavite scripture dealing with the traditions and philosophy of Bhakti or love of God.

Bhakta: a follower of the Path of Bhakti or devotion; a devotee.

Bhakti: devotion; love of God. See 'Holy Mother, her teachings on devotion.'

Bharata: a famous king of ancient India from whom the land derived the name of Bharatavarsha, 154.

Bhaskarananda, Swami: a reputed Sannyasin of Banaras, 109.

Bilva: a kind of fragrant leaf used in worship and specially sacred to Siva, 210.

Bodh Gaya: a place in the U.P. where Gautama, the Buddha, attained illumination. The Holy Mother's prayer there for the consolidation of the monastic Order, 245.

Brahma: Brahma, Vishnu and Siva constitute the trinity (doctrines based on the Puranas as distinguished from the Vedas). Viewed in the light of their functions, they represent the creative, preservative and destructive aspects of the Divinity. Though they are represented as having different personalities in the Puranas, it is also emphasized always that they constitute the one Godhead. Brahma is to be distinguished from Brahman, the Impersonal Absolute, 76.

Brahmacharya: the state of a Brahmacharin.

Brahmacharin: a celibate student undergoing mental

and moral training under a preceptor in the old Hindu style; novice in a Hindu monastery, preparing for the life of a monk, 293.

Brahmakunda: a sacred region in the Ganges at Hardwar, 114.

Brahman, Saguna: the Absolute personalised and considered as the origin, support and end of the manifold universe, 39.

Brahmananda, Swami: a Sannyasin disciple of Sri Ramakrishna, also known by the pre-monastic name of Rakhal, 75, 117, 161, 225, 252.

Brahmani: the familiar name of Yogeswari, the ascetic Brahmin woman, who instructed Sri Ramakrishna in the mysteries of Mother-worship, 36.

Brihadaranyakopanishad: one of the ten principal Upanishads or philosophical treatises of the Vedas. It is one of the highest authorities on Vedanta philosophy, 83.

Brindavan: a place of pilgrimage, considered the holiest by the Vaishnavas of the Radha-Krishna cult, 108 et seq 215.

Brinde: a maidservant at Dakshineswar in the days of Sri Ramakrishna, 55.

Bull, Mrs. Ole: an American disciple of Swami Vivekananda, 257, 285.

CHADDAR: a garment used for covering the upper part of the body.

Chaitanya: at great medieval religious teacher of India, who taught the philosophy and practice of passionate love of God, centred in the cult of Radha and Krishna; it means also consciousness, 32.

Index and glossary

Chatterji: a Brahmanical family name, special to Bengal, 18, 19.

Chameli Puri: a celebrated Sannyasin of Banaras, 254–5.

Chandra Devi: Sri Ramakrishna's mother, 24, 93.

Chapati: Indian bread, made of wheat flour flattened into round disks and baked in fire, 66, 71, 78, 85.

Cossipore: a suburb of Calcutta, where Sri Ramakrishna stayed for treatment and attained Mahasamadhi, 102.

DAKSHINESWAR: the suburb of Calcutta wherein is situated the Kali temple of Rani Rasmani, in which Sri Ramakrishna stayed for the greater part of his life.

Dandi Sannyasin: a monk carrying always a sacred staff, as a part of his vow, symbolic of knowledge, 225.

Deoghar: a place of pilgrimage and health resort in Bihar, midway between Calcutta and Banaras, 108.

Devi: literally, feminine of Deva, meaning Goddess. It is also a common suffix to feminine names, as Sarada Devi, Chandra Devi, etc.

Dharma: morality: duty; religion. Dharma (morality), Artha (wealth), Kama (pleasure) and Moksha (liberation) are regarded as the four supreme values of life (Purusharthas), 226.

Durga Puja: the great autumnal worship of the Divine Mother, 12, 258, 263, 264.

ETERNAL FEMININE, The: 281 et seq.

GADADHAR: the name by which Sri Ramakrishna was known in his boyhood, 117, 127.

Gadai: Shortened form of Gadadhar, 122, 127.

Ganges, The: an important river of North India, having its source in the Himalayas. The Hindus consider it very sacred and look upon it as a goddess. Sprung from the feet of Vishnu (God), its waters spread like a natural sacrament, washing off the sins of all who bathe in it with faith. Sri Ramakrishna and the Holy Mother held it in great reverence, and while in Calcutta, they generally stayed close to its banks. Sanctity of, 147, 154.

Gaurdasi: same as Gauri-Ma, this being the term by which the Holy Mother addressed her. See 'Gauri-Ma'.

Gauri-Ma: a woman disciple of Sri Ramakrishna and companion of the Holy Mother, 70, 84, 118, 137, 309; an account of, 277, et seq. also known as Gaurimani.

Gaya: an important place of pilgrimage where Hindus from all parts of India go to perform the obsequies of their ancestors, the belief being that rites performed there release the souls of the dead from all obstructions to higher evolution, 245.

Gayatri: a sacred Vedic Mantra that has become the common prayer of the Hindus, especially of the higher castes, 248.

Gerua: ochre colour of the cloth worn by Sannyasins.

Ghosh: a family name of a certain caste in Bengal.

Girish Chandra Ghosh: the great Bengali dramatist and ardent householder disciple of Sri Ramakrishna, 185, 223, his mystic experience about the Holy Mother, 185–86, 195, Durga Puja at his house, 263.

Girls: education of, 21.

Gita, the Bhagavad: the great Hindu Scripture.

God as Mother: 209, 315 et seq.

Godavari: a river flowing right across the Deccan, 252.

Index and glossary

Golap-Ma: a woman disciple of Sri Ramakrishna and companion of the Holy Mother 69, 70, 72, 78, 84, 86, 87, 101, 107, 116, 121, 123, 145, 176, 198, 201, 230, 247, 250, 270, 280, 320; account of, 273 et seq.

Gopal Senior: a monastic disciple of Sri Ramakrishna, otherwise known as Swami Advaitananda, 66, 245.

Gopala: a name of Sri Krishna, especially in his aspect as a young boy.

Gopaler-Ma: an old woman disciple of Sri Ramakrishna, 67, 262, 286.

Gopi: milkmaid of Brindavan loving Sri Krishna as her sweetheart, 110.

Gupta: a family name in Bengal indicating a particular caste.

Guru: ideal of 159, 295, and mind as, his right to test a disciple 169.

HAMSA: a swan; figuratively a holy man, as in Paramahamsa, 221.

Hamsi: feminine of Hamsa, 221.

Hardwar: a holy place of great fame, situated in U.P. in North India. A large number of Sannyasins live there. It marks the place whence the Ganges begins to flow into the plains, 114.

Hari: a name of Vishnu.

Harish: a devotee, 119, 244.

Harivallabh Bose: a brother of Balaram Bose, 246.

Hatya: a form of penance, 92.

Holy Mother, her life: birth and childhood, 15; education, 16-18; marriage 19 et seq; first visit to Dakshineswar, 30 et seq; visions, 33–4, 37; uniqueness of her marriage life, 38 et seq; 45 et seq; 81 et seq;

initiation, 54; spiritual practices, 51; experience of deep meditation and Samadhi, 113, 124; life at Dakshineswar, 51, 60 et seq; attack of dysentery, 91; spleen enlargement, 93; complaint of her mother about her having no children, 41; daily routine of life at Dakshineswar, 64 et seq; about her wearing ornaments, 71–2; at Syampukur and Cossipur, 100 et seq; fasting at Tarakeswar, 104; pecuniary difficulties, 116, 119, 121; suffering at Kamarpukur, 116 et seq; Harish episode, 244; spiritual ministering, 155 et seq; performing Panchatapa, 127; Mohammedan dacoits, 206–7; police vigilance over her village home, 269, prayer for the welfare and strength of the monastic organization, 245, 255; examples of being worshipped, 175, 263–4; daily routine and habits in later days, 228; income and expenses, 266; way of making food offering to the Master, 213 et seq; cause of her physical suffering, 161 et seq; assuming the sins of devotees, 161 et seq; susceptibility to the touch of impure souls, 161 et seq; last illness and passing away, 301 et seq; message, 288 et seq.

— her pilgrimage: to

Brindavan, 108 et seq; Allahabad, 114; Gaya and Bodh Gaya, 245; Banaras, 108, 253, 254, et seq; Ramakrishna Mission Sevashram of Banaras, 253; Sarnath, 254; Puri, 246; Rameswaram, 248–50; Bangalore, 251–2; Belur Math, 257–8, 264.

— and

Bhaskarananda, 109; Chameli Puri 254; Girish Ghosh, 185–6, 195, 223, 263; Yogananda, 114–5, 259.

— her relatives: relation with brothers, 129 et seq;

attachment for Radhu, 135 et seq; snapping the attachment for Radhu, 310–12; examples of troubles from relatives, 129–34, 147, 260, relatives contrasted with devotees, meaning of her domestic entanglements, 141 et seq.

— Sri Ramakrishna: her stay with him, 38, 53 et seq; his love and respect for her, 39, 58, 64, 71 et seq; her training under him, 58 et seq; his worship of her, 46 et seq; his special instruction to her, 53, 58, 140; her service to him, 60, 101 et seq; her acceptance of his ideal of life, 40, 82; her post-mortem experiences of him, 109, 113–4, 117, 121, 214, her reminiscences of him, 26–7, 30, 34–5, 36, 53, 56, 62, 66, 68, 71, 73, 75, 78, 85, 86, 87, 132 et seq.

— her personality: physical features, 197–9; spirit of independence, 76 et seq; sympathy for even the erring, 69, 76, 205; example of courage, 95 et seq; 244 et seq; freedom from fault-finding nature, 112; Yogin-Ma's vision about her immaculate purity, 147; absence of egotism, 219; sense of her own divinity, 217, 321, intellectual qualities, 219–20; liberality as spiritual teacher, 167 et seq; insight into spiritual future of disciples, 179 et seq; manner of initiation, 177; extreme consideration for devotees, 167 et seq; devotees subjecting her to inconvenience 174, patience and forbearance, 174–5; catholicity as teacher, 177, 320; kindness and love, 203, 209; same-sightedness, 322–4; power of detachment, 149–50; ideal of womanhood, 293 et seq; Madonna ideal, 284; sense of motherhood, 75, 281; Motherly principle in her, 143 et seq; Mission in life being manifestation of motherhood, 75, 201,

209, 315 et seq; model life, 281–3.
— her teachings: on
charity, 233; cult side of , 288 et seq; cultural side, 292; et seq; fault of others, not finding the, 312, 317; financial dependence on others, dangers of, 128; Guru, 159, 160, 172; Guru, responsibility of, 167, 321; meditation and Samadhi, experiences of, 55, 57–8, 111, 113, 125; monasticism versus household life, 192 et seq; realization, 55; renunciation 194; Sannyasa and Sannyasins, 191 et seq; spiritual practice, 51–2, Sri Ramakrishna, 78–80, 177.

Hriday; a nephew of Sri Ramakrishna, who constantly attended on him during the period of his austerities, 41, 73, 75, 93 et seq.

ISHTA KAVACHA: amulet pertaining to one's Chosen Ideal, 109.

JAGADDHATRI PUJA: a special worship of the Divine Mother in one of Her aspects known as Jagaddhatri, 90, 98, 213.

Jagannath: literally, Lord of the Universe, but the word is specially used to denote the Deity of the great temple at Puri, 246.

Japa: silent repetition of Divine Name or an occult formula , keeping count either with a rosary or fingers. This kind of repetition occupies an important place in the Hindu system of spiritual practices. See 'Holy Mother, 'her teachings on Japa.'

Jayrambati: the Holy Mother's native village. Famine at, Mother's temple at, 11, 13.

Jnana: spiritual knowledge; spiritual illumination.

Jnani: a follower of the path of knowledge.

Index and glossary

KALIDASA: the greatest of Sanskrit poets and dramatists, well known for his drama, the Sakuntala, 19.

Kali Kumar: the second brother of Holy Mother, often referred to as Kali, 89, 129, 131, 133, 152.

Kalipada Ghosh: 74.

Kali Puja: a special worship of the Divine Mother as Kali 12, 257.

Kalpa: an age or cycle of vast duration according to the computation of Puranas.

Kamarpukur: the birth-place of Sri Ramakrishna, situated about 60 miles north-west of Calcutta 12, 129 et seq.

Kausalya: mother of Sri Rama who is regarded as an incarnation by the Hindus.

Kedarnath: a place of pilgrimage in the Himalayas, specially sacred to Siva, 254.

Khichuri; a preparation of rice, pulses, vegetables and spices, all boiled together, 13, 243.

Khoka: Swami Subodhananda, a disciple of Sri Ramakrishna. He was fondly called 'Khoka' (meaning 'child') for his childlike simplicity and innocence.

Koalpara: a village on the way to Jayrambati. Koalpara Ashrama, 150, 163, 201, 203, 210, 221, 267, 301.

Krishna, Sri: one of the greatest incarnations whose exploits are sung in the Bhagavata and the Mahabharata. The Bhagavad Gita it supposed to be the words of Sri Krishna, 112.

Kundalini: the spiritual power of man, lying dormant at the base of the spinal column. Rousing of, 299.

LAHA: a rich family of Kamarpukur, 28.

Lakshmi: a niece of Sri Ramakrishna; commonly known

as Lakshmi-Didi (sister Lakshmi), 16, 73, 79, 84, 85, 105, 107, 108.

Lakshmi: a name of the Divine Mother in Her aspect as the consort or female counterpart of God Vishnu or Narayana 210, 286.

Lakshminarayan: 80.

Latu: See 'Adbhutananda.'

MADONNA: ideal of, 284.

Madhavacharya: otherwise known as Vidyaranya. He was an epoch-making figure in the history of Indian philosophy after Sankaracharya. He is the author of several commentaries and treatises which reveal his encyclopaedic knowledge, 27.

Madhura Bhava: literally 'the attitude of sweetness'. In the devotional philosophy it means a form of Divine love in which the devotee looks upon the Deity as his sweetheart. The most noteworthy example of it is the love of Radha for Sri Krishna. The philosophy of this form of love has been expounded in great detail by Sri Chaitanya and his followers, 77.

Madurai: a great and ancient city of South India, forming the centre of Tamil culture. It is noted for its great and wealthy temple of the Divine Mother, known as Meenakshi, 249.

Mahabharata: a great Indian epic of encyclopaedic size and range. It has been one of the most dominant influences of Indian culture.

Mahamaya: one of the names of the Divine Mother, signifying Her function as the Cosmic Illusionist, 158, 188, 198.

Maharaj: a term of respect, especially applied to

members of Holy Orders.

Mahayana: a wide-spread form of Buddhism, also known as Northern Buddhism, noted for its theistic spirit and wonderful humanism, 289.

Mahesvara: literally means 'supreme Godhead'; specially applied to Siva, 76.

Mahendra Nath Gupta: See 'Master Mahashay'.

Maku: a niece of the Holy Mother, 132, 140, 261.

Mantra: a divine Name or occult formula used for continuous repetition by spiritual aspirants; also sacred texts chanted at the time of rites and worship, 248.

Manu: a great law-giver of ancient India, whose great work, the Manu Smriti, has been a dominating influence in Hindu law and code of morality, 21, 28.

Marriage: in girlhood, 20 et seq; in early Aryan Society, 27.

Master, The: an honorific name for Sri Ramakrishna.

Master Mahashay: the familiar name for 'M' or Mahendra Nath Gupta, the author of the *Kathamrita* in Bengali whose English translation is well known as *The Gospel of Sri Ramakrishna*. He was a prominent householder disciple of the Master, 123.

Mathur: a son-in- law of Rani Rasmani and her successor as the proprietor of the temple of Dakshineswar. He was a great devotee of Sri Ramakrishna and took upon himself the duty of looking after all the worldly needs of the Master, 37, 87.

Moon: as uncle of all children, 53.

Motherhood, The principle of: its manifestation in the Holy Mother, 280 et seq, 315 et seq.

Muslim: a follower of the Islamic faith, 206.

NAHABAT: the small building to the north of Dakshineswar Kali temple, where the temple orchestra used to play at stated hours. The Holy Mother was accommodated in this building while living at Dakshineswar, 35, 40, 47, 56, 84, 85.

Nalini: a niece of the Holy Mother, being the daughter of her brother, Prasanna Kumar, 132, 140, 141, 193, 292, 261, 323.

Nanak: a medieval Indian teacher of devotional philosophy. He is the founder of Sikhism, and his teachings are noted for their high monotheism and rejection of caste, 254.

Narayana: a name of Vishnu, the second of the Hindu trinity. See 'Brahma'.

Naren: the pre-monastic name of Swami Vivekananda. See 'Vivekananda'.

Nera: a child of Maku, one of the nieces of the Holy Mother, 150.

Nilmadhav: an uncle whom the Holy Mother nursed in his last days, 260.

Niranjan: the pre-monastic name of Swami Niranjanananda, a Sannyasin disciple of Sri Ramakrishna, 186.

Nirvikalpa Samadhi: the experience in which consciousness attains to subject-objectless state, 125.

Nivedita, Sister: the monastic name of Miss Margaret Noble, an Irish disciple of Swami Vivekananda, 235, 257, 280.

Nivedita Girls' School: 272.

Nyasa: a rite forming part of worship, its chief feature being the touching of various parts of the body, accompanied by the utterance of Mantras. It signifies the identification of the worshipper's limbs with those of the Deity, 46.

PANCHATAPA: a form of austerity, 123.

Panchavati: a group of five trees at Dakshineswar, 63, 73, 87.

Pandit: learned scholar in any branch of Hindu learning; a Brahmin.

Panihati: a place near Calcutta closely associated with Sri Chaitanya. A great religious festival is held every year at this place and the Master used to visit it on those occasions, 220.

Parasara Samhita: the code of law and socio-religious observances according to the sage Parasara, 27.

Parsi: a small religious and racial community in India, who follow Zoroastrianism. They are the descendants of old immigrants from Persia who were forced to leave their homeland owing to Muslim persecution. Now they are a small but very flourishing community in India, 28, 165.

Payasam: rice cooked in milk boiled down to the required consistency and sweetened.

Paisa: a quarter of an anna. Sixteen annas make one rupee, the former Indian Currency unit, 130.

Phalaharini Kalipuja, 45, 50

Pranayama: exercises for the control of the vital energies through the control of breath, 236.

Prasada: food or anything else that has been offered to the Deity. Devotees consider it sanctifying to partake of it, 229.

Prasanna kumar: the eldest brother of the Holy Mother,

89, 121, 129, 131.

Prasannamayi: a respectable elderly woman of Kamarpukur, who was a friend of Sri Ramakrishna in his boyhood days, 117, 119, 120, 121, 122.

Premananda, Swami: a Sannyasin disciple of Sri Ramakrishna, also known by the pre-monastic name of Baburam, 78, 117, 217, 225, 227, 247.

Puja: worship, ceremonial adoration, Durga Puja, Kali Puja, etc., and Pujas or worships of the Deity in those particular aspects.

Purana: a series of voluminous religious literature, consisting of 18 texts and dealing with a variety of subjects like devotional themes, philosophical disquisitions, histories of royal dynasties, legends regarding the exploits of God and heroes, cosmology, geography, and in fact, every form of knowledge that was known to the ancients. Their interest, however, is primarily devotional, and their very remarkable achievement consists in the way in which they have given a spiritual orientation to the whole field of human achievements and thought. They have been the most potent influence in Hindu life and thought, 28.

Purdah: a seclusion of women, 60.

Puri: a famous place of pilgrimage for the Hindus, where the temple of Jagannath is situated, 246, 252.

Purnabhisheka: the highest initiation according to Tantras, corresponding to sannyasa of the Vedic tradition, 277.

Purnananda: 54.

RADHA, RADHIKA: the great woman contemporary

and devotee of Sri Krishna, God incarnate, who loved Him as her sweetheart. Her love, being untainted by the least touch of worldliness, has been accepted in Hindu devotional literature as the highest expression of the longing of the human heart for the Divine, 110, 315.

Radharamana: a name of Sri Krishna, meaning the lover of Radha, 112.

Radhu: a niece of the Holy Mother. Her full name was Radharani; but she used to be called as either Radhu or Radhi. The posthumous daughter of the Holy Mother's fourth brother, she was her ward in a special sense, 134 et seq. Holy Mother snapping the attachment for, 234, 250, 302, 310.

Radhu's Mother: see 'Surabala.'

Rajahmundry: an ancient city on the banks of the Godavari between Madras and Calcutta, 252.

Rakhal: see 'Brahmananda.'

Rama, Sri: one of the great Incarnations, as popular and widely worshipped as Sri Krishna. The great Indian epic, the Ramayana, commemorates his exploits. 315.

Ramachandra: the Holy Mother's father, 12, 25, 36, 88.

Ramakrishnananda, Swami: a Sannyasin disciple of Sri Ramakrishna, known also by his pre-monastic name of Sasi, founder of the Math at Madras, 248.

Ramakrishna Punthi: a metrical work on Sri Ramakrishna by Akshay Kumar Sen, 204.

Ramayana: the great epic by Valmiki on the life and exploits of the divine incarnation, Sri Rama.

Ram Datta: a householder disciple of Sri Ramakrishna,

also referred to as Ram Babu and Ramchandra Datta, 50, 107.

Rameswar Chatterjee: elder brother of Sri Ramakrishna, 24.

Rameswaram: a great all-India centre of pilgrimage situated in South India and noted for its Siva Temple, 248 et seq.

Ramlal: a nephew of Sri Ramakrishna, 63, 76, 119, 120, 126.

Ramnad, Raja of: Ramnad used to be a principality in the southernmost region of India in pre-British days. Now the Rajas are there, but they have no ruling powers. The particular Raja referred to in the book was a devotee of Swami Vivekananda, 250.

Rasagolla: a Bengali sweetmeat made of the solid portion of coagulated milk and sugar, 164, 195.

Rasmani, Rani: the foundress of the Kali temple at Dakshineswar, Calcutta, 37.

Ravana: the ten-headed Monster King of Lanka who went to war with Sri Rama.

Rishi: one who has evolved enough to see or realize spiritual truths.

SACHCHIDANANDA: a formula indicating Brahman and meaning Existence-Knowledge-Bliss Absolute.

Sadhana: means of attainment; especially applied to practices for spiritual realization.

Sadhu: a holy man; a Sannyasin in general.

Saiva: a worshipper of Siva.

Sakta: a worshipper of Sakti.

Sakti: power; especially, Divine creative power, conceived as the Mother of the universe or Female

Divine Principle, 291, 317, 319.

Sakuntalam: a famous Sanskrit drama by Kalidasa, 19.

Salagrama: a small round stone emblem of Vishnu used for worship, 247.

Sambhu Mallik: a householder devotee of Sri Ramakrishna, 63, 91.

Sandesh: an Indian sweetmeat made with the casein of milk, 231.

Sankaracharya: the great Vedantic teacher of India who established the dominance of non-dualistic philosophy, 224, 318.

Sannyasa: monastic life. Holy Mother's attitude towards it, 192.

Sannyasin: a monk.

Saptasati: a text of 700 verses in Sanskrit in glorification of the Divine Mother, held in very great reverence among devotees, also known as Chandi, 226, 279.

Sarada: the maiden-name of the Holy Mother. See 'Holy Mother'.

Saradananda, Swami: a Sannyasin disciple of Sri Ramakrishna, also known by his pre-monastic name of Sarat. An account him, 39, 49, 123, 131, 140, 165, 190, 265, 270, 271, 285, 307.

Saradeswari Ashrama: an educational institution for girls started by Gauri-Ma, 278.

Sarala: a disciple of the Mother who tended her in her last illness, 307.

Sarat: see 'Saradananda'.

Sarasvati: an aspect of the Divine Mother, specially looked upon as the presiding deity of knowledge, 74, 87.

Sarnath: the site of an ancient Buddhist monastery and seat of learning, near Banaras, 254.

Savitri: a famous Vedic Mantra which has become the common prayer of the Hindus: also known as Gayatri, 27, 248.

Shivananda, Swami: one of the Sannyasin disciple of Sri Ramakrishna, fondly known as Mahapurushji, 202, 264.

Shodasi Puja: worship of the Divine Mother as Shodasi, 45 et seq, 50.

Siddhi: 317.

Simhavahini: the Mother Deity of a temple at Jayrambati; literally, the Mother with the lion as her vehicle, 92, 99, 173.

Sita: the wife of Rama and the heroine of the epic of Ramayana. She is considered the ideal of Indian womanhood, 72, 87, 250.

Siva: the third of the Indian Trinity, 321.

Smriti: codes compiled by great sages on tradition, morality, law, administration, etc. In general all scriptures other than the Vedas are also called Smritis, 20.

Sri Ramakrishna: crucial test, subjecting himself to, 39; predictions about his passing away 104-5; demise of 105; early history of 23, et seq; Holy Mother, his attitude towards her, 40; Ishta kavacha of, 109; relics of 107; his remarks on the Holy Mother, 39–42, 78, 79.

Sudhira, Sister: a disciple of the Holy Mother. She was in charge of the Nivedita Girls' School, 280.

Surabala: an insane sister-in-law of the Holy Mother, referred to also as 'Pagli', mad woman, crazy sister-in-law, etc. She was the wife of the Holy Mother's youngest brother, Abhay Charan, and the mother of her pet niece Radhu, 134 et seq.

Suren Mitra: a householder disciple of Sri Ramakrishna.

Swami: a title indicating a Sannyasin and meaning 'master'.

Swadeshi Movement: 269.

Syamasundari Devi: the mother of the Holy Mother, 14, 89, 118, 131, 261.

Syampukur: a suburb of Calcutta where Sri Ramakrishna stayed for treatment for some time during his last illness, 100, 101.

TANTRA: a vast body of literature in Sanskrit dealing with philosophy, rituals, observances, worship of Deities, magical rites, etc., all in relation to the rousing of man's psychic powers or expanding his consciousness into Divine Consciousness.

Tarak: the pre-monastic name of Swami Shivananda, 264.

Tarakeswar: a place on the way from Jayrambati to Calcutta, 94.

Tilbhandeswar: the image of Siva in a temple at Banaras 254.

Totapuri: the great Sannyasin who initiated Sri Ramakrishna into Sannyasa and the practice of the disciplines of non-dualistic philosophy, 39, 254.

Trailokya: the son of Mathur Babu and his successor as the proprietor of the Dakshineswar Kali temple, 94.

Trigunatitananda, Swami: a Sannyasin disciple of Sri Ramakrishna, also known by the pre-monastic name of Sarada prasanna (shortened to 'Sarada') 74, 115, 271, 286.

Trivarga: the three mundane values of life: virtue, wealth and pleasure; and the Dandi Sannyasin, 226.

UDBODHAN OFFICE: the Holy Mother's Calcutta residence, so called because the 'Udbodhan', the Bengali magazine of the Ramakrishna Order, is published from there, 137, 265.

Uncle Moon: 53.

'Uncles': 129.

Upanayana: investiture with the sacred thread, incumbent on Hindus of the three higher castes, 27.

Upanishads: the philosophical sections in Vedic literature, dealing with problems relating to soul, God, Nature, human destiny and the like. They are in a sense the basis of all Hindu philosophy, especially of the Vedanta system, 83.

VAIDYANATH: an image of Siva at Banaras. 253.

Vaishnava couplet: 87.

Vaishnava Tantra: the scriptures of the Hindu sect called Vaishnavas or Vaishnavites, meaning worshippers of Vishnu, 117.

Vamachara: worship of Sakti or Female Energy conceived as the wife of Siva, 317.

Vasuki: a legendary serpent of great prowess, 272.

Veda: the principal scripture of the Hindus in archaic Sanskrit, constituting the world's earliest literature, 277.

Vedanta: the most important and influential system of Indian philosophy, based on the Upanishads and Badarayana's Aphorisms, 271, 316.

Index and glossary

Viraja Homa: Sacrificial ceremony relating to passionless state. It is a simple Vedic rite preparatory to one's entering the life of Sannyasa, and consists in making oblations into the sacred fire with the chanting of certain inspiring Vedic texts indicative of renunciation, 277.

Vishnu: God as the preserver of the Universe, enumerated as the second person of the Hindu Trinity, Brahma, Vishnu and Siva, 247, 315.

Vishnupur: a place of pilgrimage which is also a district town in Bengal. It is about eighty miles from Calcutta and used to be the last railways station for one travelling from Calcutta to Jayrambati, 247, 267.

Viswanath: God of the universe, but specially denotes the Deity, Siva, of Banaras, 109.

Vivekananda, Swami: the foremost of Sri Ramakrishna's Sannyasin disciples, known also by the pre-monastic name of Narendranath Datta or by the still shorter term Naren, 75, 106, 117, 125, 126, 202, 225, 257, 258, 290.

WOMANHOOD: the essential principle of, 280 et seq.

YAJNAVALKYA: a great philosopher of the Upanishads; also a law-giver of later times, 28.

Yama: the name of a law-giver of olden days, 27.

Yantra: ritualistic diagrams of the Tantras, possessed of great occult significance.

Yatra: a traditional devotional dramatic performance of Bengal.

Yogananda, Swami: a Sannyasin disciple of Sri Ramakrishna, also known by his pre-monastic name of Yogen. His initiation by the Holy Mother, 59, 75, 98,

108, 113, 115, 123, 147, 247, 259, 260, 285.

Yogen: see 'Yogananda.'

Yogin-Ma: a woman disciple of Sri Ramakrishna and a lifelong companion of the Holy Mother. Her full name was Yogindra Mohini Biswas, but was called by the Holy Mother as Yogin. This name is to be distinguished from the identical name by which Swami Yogananda was familiarly known after his premonastic name of Yogindra. To distinguish it from that of Yogin Ma, we have spelt it as 'Yogen'. The Holy Mother distinguished him by adding the prefix 'son to the name. An account of, 275 et seq; her reminiscences of the Holy Mother, 56, 65, 72, 100, 111, 112, 124, 145, 210, 230.

Yogin: see 'Yogin-Ma'.

ZAMINDAR: a person holding land under a special tenure called Zamindari right; a landlord, 276.

For Furthur Reading

Holy Mother Sri Sarada Devi *(By Swami Gambhirananda)*

Sri Sarada Devi, the Holy Mother: Life and Teachings
(Subsidised Edition)

The Gospel of the Holy Mother

The Mother As I Saw Her

Sri Sarada Devi, the Holy Mother: Conversations

Teachings of Sri Sarada Devi, the Holy Mother

For Further Reading

Holy Mother Sri Sarada Devi (By Swami Gambhirananda)

Sri Sarada Devi, the Holy Mother: Life and Teachings (Subsidised Edition)

The Gospel of the Holy Mother

The Mother As I Saw Her

Sri Sarada Devi, the Holy Mother: Conversations

Teachings of Sri Sarada Devi, the Holy Mother